ACTS OF POETRY

ACTS OF POETRY

American Poets' Theater and the Politics of Performance

Heidi R. Bean

UNIVERSITY OF MICHIGAN PRESS

Ann Arbor

Published in the United States of America by
the University of Michigan Press
Manufactured in the United States of America
Printed on acid-free paper

First published September 2019

A CIP catalog record for this book is available from the British Library.

Library of Congress Cataloging-in-Publication Data

Names: Bean, Heidi R., author.
Title: Acts of poetry : American poets' theater and the politics of
    performance / by Heidi R. Bean.
Description: Ann Arbor : University of Michigan Press, 2019. | Includes
    bibliographical references and index. |
Identifiers: LCCN 2019015006 (print) | LCCN 2019020351 (ebook) | ISBN
    9780472125326 (E-book) | ISBN 9780472131419 (hardcover : alk. paper) |
    ISBN 9780472125326 (ebk.)
Subjects: LCSH: Performance poetry—United States—History and criticism.
    | American poetry—20th century—History and criticism.
Classification: LCC PN4151 (ebook) | LCC PN4151 .B43 2019 (print) | DDC
    811/.0209054—dc23
LC record available at https://lccn.loc.gov/2019015006

For Max

Acknowledgments

I owe a great deal to the people and institutions who have supported this project. I'm grateful for the support of the English department at the University of Iowa, where this project began, and at Bridgewater State University, where it was completed. Financial assistance for research and writing came from the Center for the Advancement of Research and Scholarship and the Provost's Office at Bridgewater State University. I am also indebted to the staff and librarians at the New York Public Library's Billy Rose Theatre Collection and Berg Collection, at the Schomburg Center for Research in Black Culture, at the Beinecke Rare Book and Manuscript Library, and at the Harvard Theatre Collection at Houghton Library.

Some of the most joyful moments of this project have involved the delight of research itself and the excitement of chewing over new ideas with others engaged in similar pursuits. Several artists and scholars shared their work with me, allowed me to sit in on rehearsals or to see their own drafts-in-progress, submitted to interviews, or were otherwise generous with their time and ideas, including Carla Harryman, Sarah Bay-Cheng, Kevin Killian, Patrick Durgin, John Beer, John Muse, Laura Hinton, Chris Grobe, Deborah Geis, Martin Puchner, Martin Harries, and the summer 2011 participants in the Mellon School for Theater and Performance.

A number of people have graciously read drafts, discussed various stages of this project's development, and helped me clarify ideas. Dee Morris offered invaluable guidance and support in the project's earliest stages, and her critical generosity continues to inspire me. Landing in Dee's Sound States class as a first-semester graduate student was the best stroke of luck I could've hoped for. Bill Worthen, Garrett Stewart, and Kim Marra helped shape the project's development by asking challenging questions in encouraging ways. I owe special thanks to LeAnn Fields and the anonymous readers and editorial team at the University of Michigan Press for their wise and perceptive suggestions on the final manuscript. Several friends, colleagues, and family members have generously given their time, camaraderie, and encouragement, and I especially wish to thank Robin Tierney, Mike Chasar, Vickie Larsen, Deb Manion, Wendy Wright, Maria Hegbloom, Jessica Birthisel, Judith Willison, Michelle Cox, Andy Holman, Courtney Beggs, and Melanie McNaughton for discussing ideas and drafts at critical points along the way. Ellen Scheible, Colleen Rua, John Mulrooney, Ann Brunjes, Ben Carson, Allyson Ferrante, Emily Field, Lori LeComte, Charlotte Meehan, and Adara Meyers have lent me their ears and their shoulders. I am also fortunate to have a wonderful group of JP-area friends outside of academia who help me keep things in perspective. And Ruth Slotnick has sustained me through the completion of this project with love and patience. My son, Max, shares both my fondness for and my suspicion of words. This book is dedicated to him, with gratitude for keeping my life playful, grounded, and full of daily joy.

Earlier versions of some sections of this book have been previously published as "Repeating Gertrude Stein: Language, Performativity, and Hypermediated Theater," *TPQ* 27.3 (July 2007): 168–94; "Carla Harryman's Non/Narrative and the Ethics of Dispersive Theater," *Postmodern Culture* 20.1 (September 2009), http://muse.jhu.edu/journals/postmodern_culture/v020/20.1.bean.html; "Learning from the Dramaturg: Suzan-Lori Parks's *The America Play* in the Literature Classroom," *Modern Drama* 58.3 (September 2015): 324–46; and "Bunny Lang and the Cambridge Poets' Theatre in the 1950s," in *Beat Drama: Playwrights and Performances of the "Howl" Generation*, ed. Deborah Geis (London and New York: Methuen Drama, an Imprint of Bloomsbury Publishing Plc, 2016), 139–53. I thank the publishers for permission to reprint selections and adaptations from those essays here.

Contents

Digital materials related to this title can be found on
the Fulcrum platform via the following citable URL:
https://doi.org/10.3998/mpub.9373485

Introduction

Where Is Poets' Theater?

> Prose is our culture's language of sincerity, in which we expect to be most able to say what we mean and see what is meant, to be understood and to understand. The place of message. Poetry is our culture's language of complexity, idiosyncratic sensibility, the language of artifice.
> —Lisa Samuels, "Eight Justifications for Canonizing
> Lyn Hejinian's *My Life*"

> There is a metaphysics in the preference for the eye or ear, and a politics as well.
> —Herbert Blau, *The Audience*

Prologue

The path to this book began with my observation that a number of twentieth-century writers who had built their reputations as poets had also written dramatic works that were largely unknown. There were a few exceptions, of course. Gertrude Stein was celebrated for her avant-garde writing in multiple genres and for defying genre altogether. Amiri Baraka earned a lasting reputation as both poet and dramatist, not to mention essayist, music critic, and political activist. But I wondered how it was that the dramatic output of a considerable number of other poets—from H. D. and Wallace Stevens to John Ashbery and Ron Silliman—seemed such a well-kept secret.

It may be that while some poets took their playwriting seriously, others saw the foray into drama as just a bit of fun. Or it could be that when poets tried their hands at playwriting early on in their careers, critics tended to dismiss the plays as youthful experimentation. It might also have to do with a lack of output. Some poets wrote several plays, but many wrote only a couple, making it easier for readers and critics to ignore them as mere anomalies.

At the same time that poets were jumping genres, dramatists were also drawing on poetic language—think of Adrienne Kennedy's lyrical but harrowing internal monologues in the 1960s, for example, or Suzan-Lori Parks's jazz-inspired linguistic innovations in the early 1990s. What do poetry and drama have to offer one another? Why did poets of the twentieth century turn time and time again to the stage, and why did playwrights increasingly draw on poetic language and strategies? What was the relationship between page and stage that made writers on both sides of the divide seek out the devices and possibilities of a different genre? Which was really to ask: In what ways had the stage furthered the aims of twentieth-century poetry, and in what ways had poetry furthered the aims of twentieth-century theater?

A disciplinary blind spot has prevented both theater and poetry critics from fully accounting for this work. The question "Where Is Poets' Theater?" is an acknowledgment of poets' theater's absence in the critical record. (At the moment, the answer is, largely, nowhere.) But it also points to several overlapping questions of location. Where precisely are the critical practices of poets' theater (on the page, on the stage, between the two, or perhaps somewhere else)? In what ways is poets' theater a site-specific practice (where the "site" may be impaginated or embodied but also architectural, geographic, and historical)? And, finally, where does poets' theater belong as an object of disciplinary study?

This book works in part as a critical mapping to address the interrelations of theatrical performance and experimental poetics. Its primary focus is postwar American poets' theater, which, as I demonstrate, has more affinity with the modernist avant-garde and later so-called antitextual, environmental, "performance," and postdramatic theater than with the verse drama of the early twentieth century.

Certainly the history of poetic drama extends back to the founding of theater itself—when reciters of epic poems began acting out scenes and voices, eventually leading to full-fledged characters and the birth of classical drama. The "Golden Age" of English theater in the Renaissance era was populated by the verse dramas of Shakespeare, Christopher Marlowe, and Ben Jonson. In the twentieth century, contemporary playwrights such as T. S. Eliot, Christopher Fry, W. H. Auden, and Archibald MacLeish updated and repopularized verse drama by engaging universal characters in symbolic conflicts that spoke to contemporary audiences. In fact, contemporary verse drama had become so popular by the middle of the twentieth century that Fry's *The Lady's Not for Burning* played in London's West End for nine months in 1949, while the following year Eliot's *The Cocktail Party* ran on Broadway for fifty-one weeks and earned a Tony award for Best Play.[1]

While commercial theater audiences were lapping up this British comic fare, American experimental groups in the 1950s, such as the Living Theatre, were also performing poetic theater, by such writers as Stein and William Carlos Williams. By the early 1960s, a number of self-proclaimed poets' theaters had arisen enthusiastically (and in many cases disappeared quickly) on the US East Coast, including the Poets' Theatre in Cambridge, Massachusetts, and, in New York, the related but less explicitly named Artists' Theatre in the 1950s and the New York Poets Theatre (aka the American Theatre for Poets, Inc.), the Hardware Poets' Playhouse, and the Judson Poets' Theater in the 1960s. This postwar strain of poets' theater was grounded neither in the classical verse plays of Aeschylus nor in the modern verse dramas of Fry and Eliot. While the theatrical successes of twentieth-century verse drama had helped pave the way for audiences and critical interest, the young experimental writers of off-off-Broadway did not see themselves reflected in these works but instead found inspiration, as Poets' Theatre founder Lyon Phelps recounted, in Samuel Beckett, Alfred Jarry, Federico García Lorca, Jean Cocteau, Bertolt Brecht, and Japanese Noh theater: "We thought of the nineteenth century verse drama solutions mainly in the blank-verse forms as the end of something," Phelps explained, "and not as the beginning of something else" (Phelps, Manning, and Rogers).

The poets' theaters that emerged in the postwar period were more likely to draw inspiration from contemporaries than from predecessors. And although Frank O'Hara's plays have been produced by virtually every group that has called itself a poets' theater, there is not always a clean line of descent from one poets' theater to another. What unites the postwar poets' theaters that appeared in multiple moments and locales is their shared response to evolving notions of social performance. Poets' theater arose alongside the several borrowings that occurred between the fields of sociology, linguistics, anthropology, and theater that opened the way for a broad-based theory of performativity.

Rhetoric about the functions and effects of poetry shifted in the 1950s from a metaphorical use of the "theater" of poetry to a notion of embodied performance as fundamental to poetry's communicative power—in writing, in poetry readings, and in the frequent stagings by midcentury poets' theaters. The beginnings of poets' theater, as distinct from verse drama, might be traced back to the period immediately following World War II, when rich performance-oriented poetry and theater scenes came together on the makeshift stages of urban coffeehouses, shared apartments, and underground theaters. The 1940s were dominated by a New Critical rhetoric emphasizing the self-sufficiency of the art object that many later saw as a deadly academicism. But by the 1950s the critical discourses of poetry, theater, and social life were increasingly marked by interests in enactment, in the relation of language to social experience, and in the presence of the performing body itself and its relation to the audience. And in the midst of these interests, poetic theater proliferated.

Meanwhile, by the end of the 1950s the performativity of social life had become a topic of interest across the social sciences. Erving Goffman's foundational text in what has now become the field of performance studies, *The Presentation of Self in Everyday Life* (1959), put forth what was at the time a new method of social analysis from the point of view of impression management, the techniques by which individuals attempt to control how others perceive them. Using the theater as metaphor, Goffman's dramaturgical method analyzed the individual as a "performer" within a closed system, "surrounded by fixed barriers to perception in which a particular kind of activity regularly takes place" (238). The individual as performer, Goffman argued, is distinct from the individual as character, the former implying the active process of self-presentation and the latter signifying the often idealized product of that process. But perhaps most interesting was Goffman's conclusion that the self is not a natural and inherent part of an individual but rather a dramatic *effect* generated by the performer and interpreted by the audience. Modifying his general definition of *performance* ("all the activity of a given participant on a given occasion which serves to influence in any way any of the other participants" [15]), Goffman emphasized its communicative goal. Because the purpose of performance is to influence others, he argued, it is not an activity in and for itself but rather a representation of an activity that serves to communicate something to an audience, thereby transforming the activity from doing to performing, but perhaps paradoxically by casting it as mimetic. Walking across a room to reach a glass of lemonade may, for example, be a merely practical activity when it is enacted alone, but the presence of others can transform the act from simply a means of acquiring a glass of lemonade to a representation of walking-across-the-room-to-get-a-glass-of-lemonade as a means of creating a specific impression. The distinction, of course, lies in the presence of an audience, which interprets the performance. The production of a specific impression takes place in the interaction between the audience's interpretation of the act and the performer's (self-conscious or not) enactment of an idealized representation. And, as later theorists such as Judith Butler have argued, idealized representation can, with repetition, become inseparable from one's embodied identity and experiences.

At roughly the same time Goffman was disseminating his theories of performance and impression management, the British linguist J. L. Austin was employing the notion of performance as a means of theorizing the ability of language to create reality rather than merely refer to it. In 1955 Austin delivered the Harvard lectures that were later collected and published as *How to Do Things with Words*. In an attempt to work out a schema for understanding what we use language to *do*, Austin designated *performative* to indicate an utterance in which the saying of words constitutes the performance of an act—in other words, language is not just the representation of an act but the act itself. While Austin explicitly excluded drama and poetry from the category of performatives because, he argued, they are fictive and not accompanied by sincere intentions, his lectures added a material layer to the act of signification itself. Performed with sincere intentions in appropriate circumstances, language has the power, Austin argued, not only to refer to an act but to be an act in itself. What is ultimately most instructive in these lectures is the eventual failure of the categories put forth; that is, although Austin sets out to distinguish between performatives and constatives (i.e., nonperformative language), he eventually finds this distinction to be false to the degree that there is no such thing as a "pure" performative. Initially basing his definition of the performative on a specific grammatical structure, he eventually finds that it is not the form but rather the context of the utterance that determines whether or not it performs an act, and given the right conditions even statements may perform acts.

Part of what is at issue in all these various interdisciplinary uses of the concept of performance is the very question of whether performance is a constitutive or mimetic act.[2] And this interest extended across the arts to include, for example, action painting, happenings, and aleatory musical composition, all focused on the performance and recording of a process or event. Jackson Pollock's work, for example, refocused attention from mimetic representation of an object to the act/action of painting itself, as recorded in the drips, splashes, and footprints left on the canvas. In doing so, it broke down the art/life distinction that characterized the rhetoric of art-as-representation and replaced it with a rhetoric of performance and participation (which, notably, renders critical judgment irrelevant). Rather than abandoning mimesis, then, Pollock changed its focus to the act of painting itself.

Pollock's canvases are representative of a more general shift in mimetic strategies that was taking place in a range of artistic practices in the middle of the century. In a similar spirit, Allan Kaprow's happenings abolished the text, as well as conventions of plot, character, and dialogue, in favor of improvisation and chance events, reducing speech, as Susan Sontag wrote, "to a stutter" (266)—and indeed Kaprow notes that happenings developed not out of drama and theater but out of art practices such as action painting. Poetry and theater's identification with jazz reflects a similar emphasis on presentation over representation through an improvisatory aesthetic. And yet, like the verbal portraits of Gertrude Stein (discussed in chapter 1), each of these events, objects, and performers is unavoidably perceived within a system of references and relations whose meanings inevitably carry over to the performance, not in a predetermined way but as a preconditioned part of the experience of the performative event itself. To characterize this midcentury emphasis on performance as the abandonment of representation or as strictly antimimetic is therefore misleading. Regardless of the rhetoric of performance employed by the artists themselves, the impact of performance relied on reference to, as well as critique of, a system of representation with far-reaching political effects, as Mike Sell acknowledges when he insists that by the 1960s performance had become "a method that enabled radicals to devise actions that could address simultaneously the structures of language, economics, politics, social institutions, cultural history, and the body" (16). Whether by engaging in explicit social critique or by rejecting dominant forms and narratives (and their associated ideologies), the use of performance was frequently political.

Amid these cultural shifts, poets' theater matured. Two play collections published in 2010, *The Kenning Anthology of Poets Theater, 1945–1985*, edited by Kevin Killian and David Brazil, and *Poets at Play*, edited by Sarah Bay-Cheng and Barbara Cole, have begun the process of archiving the hundreds of plays produced by poets' theaters. Together, these collections demonstrate the breadth of the phenomenon, as well as its rise in scholarly interest, by making available more than nine hundred pages of poetic plays—a vast offering when you consider that these collections are only a sampling of the work that lies quietly and largely forgotten in desk drawers, archives, and short-lived literary journals. But the differences between the play collections are also instructive. One is edited by two creative writers, while the other is edited by a theater scholar and a poet. One is published by a "small" poetry press, while the other is published by a scholarly press. One explores plays written mainly by postwar poets while the other examines earlier modernist poetic drama written by such canonical figures as E. E. Cummings and Wallace Stevens. And yet poets' theater as practice and artistic philosophy is aimed precisely at bridging such differences in value and praxis.

In light of these different renderings, one answer to the question "Where Is Poets' Theater?" might be that it is everywhere and therefore nowhere. That is, dispersed across scholarly disciplines and artistic eras, poets' theater has remained largely invisible even as it can barely be contained. Histories of American theater written in the middle of the twentieth century, poets' theater's heyday, were more apt to include attention to poets' theater than those written more recently. The 1967 volume *American Theatre*, edited by John Russell Brown and Bernard Harris, for example, included a chapter by Katharine J. Worth titled "The Poets in American Theatre," but contemporary histories of American theater have ignored it almost entirely. C. W. E. Bigsby's *Modern American Drama, 1945–2000* (2000), devotes one line to the importance of off- and off-off-Broadway venues associated with the earliest wave of poets' theater in New York, such as Caffe Cino, La Mama, and Judson Poets' Theater. The massive, three-volume *Cambridge History of American Theatre* (1998-2000), edited by Don B. Wilmeth and Christopher Bigsby, regards poets' theater as a brief detour in the rise of the American antitextual avant-garde theater of the 1950s and 1960s (a mischaracterization that I examine in chapter 3). David Krasner's *A Companion to Twentieth-Century American Drama* (2008) ignores it altogether. And it fares no better in histories of American poetry. While Cary Nelson's *The Oxford Handbook of Modern and Contemporary American Poetry* (2012) makes reference to performance poetry, it leaves out any mention of poets' theater. The same goes for *The Cambridge History of American Poetry* (2014), edited by Alfred Bendixen and Stephen Burt, and Richard Gray's *A History of American Poetry* (2015).

The proliferation of performance poetry that has occurred in the last thirty years—including the rise of poetry slams, hip-hop theater, def poetry, and other spoken word performance—has begun to receive much-needed critical attention. Susan B. A. Somers-Willett's *The Cultural Politics of Slam Poetry: Race, Identity, and the Performance of Popular Verse in America* (2009), for instance, looks at the performance of race and identity in poetry slams, which arose as a competitive form in the mid-1980s, while Tyler Hoffman's *American Poetry in Performance: From Walt Whitman to Hip Hop* (2013) examines American poetry performance in light of shifting political and cultural ideologies of the last 150 years. But neither of these takes up the multicharacter scripted form of poets' theater. Nick Salvato's *Uncloseting Drama: American Modernism and Queer Performance* (2010) reads the "queerness" of modernist "closet drama" by such figures as Stein, Djuna Barnes, Ezra Pound, and Louis Zukofsky but not the fully produced forms of poets' theater that arose in its aftermath. Stephen J. Bottoms's *Playing Underground: A Critical History of the 1960s Off-Off-Broadway Movement* (2004) offers a compelling and comprehensive picture of New York's underground theater landscape in the 1960s, and his account demonstrates the collaborativity of the larger theater and performance scene that helped foster the rise of poets' theaters in that decade though it does not focus on them. Most recently, Irene Morra's *Verse Drama in England, 1900–2015: Art, Modernity, and the National Stage* (2016) addresses the important topic of modern verse drama in England but fails to make a clear distinction between verse drama and poets' theater that was a defining break for practitioners in the United States.[3]

In order to study poets' theater and see what hope it may have held for writers and theater artists, as well as what it suggests about the limits of genre in the first place, we must first locate poets' theater. And locating poets' theater, critically and disciplinarily, requires first identifying *what* poets' theater is and who produces it. The roster of American writers in the twentieth century who earned their reputations as poets but also wrote drama is long. It includes, for example, Edna St. Vincent Millay, who joined verse with commedia dell'arte to satirize the pretensions of theater as well as the absurdity of war. It includes objectivist poet Lorine Niedecker, whose brief poetic dramas of the 1930s revealed social communication as cultural coercion. It includes Kenneth Koch's repurposing of children's rhymes and fairy tales in the 1940s and James Schuyler's celebration of the poetic in the vernacular in the 1950s, as well as Carla Harryman's shattering of narrative in the 1980s and beyond. But poets aren't the only ones producing this hybrid. Playwrights such as Mac Wellman, Eric Overmyer, Suzan-Lori Parks, Richard Maxwell, and Eric Ehn also produce poetic theater if not always poetry per se. And the list might be expanded to also include Fiona Templeton's ecopoetic theater, the visual texts of Leslie Scalapino, the sound performances of Theresa Hak Kung Cha, the "choreopoems" of Ntozake Shange, and the "cosmopoetics" of Rodrigo Toscano. Still, naming names and examples doesn't necessarily bring us closer to a definition. Searching for their own description of poets' theater to unite their massive play collection, *The Kenning Anthology of Poets Theater, 1945–1985,* Killian and Brazil wonder, "Is poets theater even a genre at all?,"[4] only to conclude with more than a tinge of exasperation that "like porn, we know it when we see it" (ii).

The September 26, 1964, issue of the *Village Voice* captures the richness of New York's off-Broadway and off-off Broadway theater scene in the mid-1960s, which included a productive mix of poets' theater and other fringe ventures. A single page advertises Jean Genet's *The Blacks* at the St. Mark's Playhouse, Kenneth Brown's *The Brig* at the Living Theatre, John Weiners's *Asphodel, in Hell's Despite,* and Gertrude Stein's *What Happened* at the Judson Poets' Theater, eight one-act plays at the Hardware Poets' Playhouse, and a review of *Love and Variations: A Masque* by Tom O'Horgan at Caffe Cino. Strange little plays with atonal music, the European avant-garde, poets' theater, and quasi-documentary hyperrealism sprang from the same fertile ground, nourished each other, and flourished side by side. While poets' theater was, as Bottoms observes, "more consciously avant-garde than other early off-off concerns, such as the Caffe Cino," all shared a "do-it-yourself spirit" (61). But the affinities weren't merely in attitude. As Bottoms notes, "The mini-renaissance in poetry-based playwriting at the turn of the decade was . . . integrally linked to the burgeoning Village coffeehouse scene, and the popularity of its performance-poetry events" (61).

Still, the "poetic" aspect of poets' theater was rather loosely defined. For a few, it meant rhymed or metered verse, though most preferred free verse, often alternating with prose. For others, *poetic* merely meant symbolic, nonnaturalistic, or even simply noncommercial and experimental. But all shared with the larger fringe scene an interest in transgressing traditional theatrical boundaries, as well as in prodding, critiquing, training, and satirizing the audience. Such an emphasis on the audience was also typical of the antirealism that characterized a range of experimental theater. Originally formulated as a serious alternative to nineteenth-century melodrama, realism had set out to dramatize domestic social problems for middle-class audiences. But as the twentieth century emerged and progressed, realism increasingly came to be seen as a tyrant. Part of the problem lay in the formal rhetoric of visually precise sets, naturalistic acting, and "believable" characters and situations, all of which served to win the audience's complicity in accepting the reality they presented. In contrast, antirealist theater exposed the *work* of performance—and implicated the audience in this work.

The term *poets' theater* thus designates a broad concurrence of heterogeneous artists who nevertheless share certain inspirations, interests, strategies, and goals. Employing poetic language as a tool of antirealist critique, poets' theater is defined both by its strategies and by its purpose, which often has a political dimension. As a critical category, it indicates a set of characteristic strategies: self-conscious attention to the conventions of theatrical characterization and scripted plotting; language thickened by a poets' sense of sound, rhythm, and layers of meaning; often (though not always) an emphasis on the performance of everyday life; and resistance to the cultural coercion of psychological characterization, linear narrative, and norms of social communication. Its approach to production is collaborative and often intentionally amateurish, rejecting the hierarchical dynamics of commercial theater production. Emphasizing the activity of audiences in specific contexts, poets' theater distinguishes itself from the usual understanding of "verse drama" as universal conflicts steeped in poetic language and symbolism and of "closet drama" as an antitheatrical, "high" art form aimed at private contemplation away from the harmful influence of collective reception. Poets' theater is, above all, a critical enactment aimed at animating tensions in the conventions of representation and reception. And often this critical enactment is political, circumventing universal modeling in both narrative and performance in order to undermine dominant cultural ideologies.

As a cultural political practice, poets' theater emerged from the same arts scene that also gave rise to communal, improvisatory theater and to performative, and often participatory, poetry readings. At the same time that numerous American theater groups were tossing away scripts and reconfiguring the theater company as a collaborative community, other groups and even playwrights were rethinking the dramatic text itself by reimagining the relationship between script and stage. Meanwhile, poets, too, were reenvisioning poetry as an enactment, not only as a live reading event but also as a scripted performance on the page.

Constructing a New Stage for Poetry

In 1942, Wallace Stevens was imagining a different future for American poetry, in the merging of the imaginative and material worlds, and casting it in theatrical terms. In the poem "Of Modern Poetry," Stevens asserts that "the scene [of poetry in the early twentieth century] was set; it repeated what was in the script"; but "the theatre [of contemporary poetry] has changed," and the charge is now "to construct a new stage." In order to meet the challenge of this new stage, the language of poetry had to be "living" and had to "learn the speech of the place." Thus, for Stevens the future of modern poetry lay not in the repetition of tradition or in the forms of the masters but in words seen not just as representations but as acts. In this theater of poetry,

> . . . an invisible audience listens,
> Not to the play, but to itself, expressed
> In an emotion as of two people, as of two
> Emotions becoming one.

As the actor speaks words, the external expression and the internal reality become one. In this sense, then, poetry is not merely a recollection or an artifact but an event. The poet is at once actor and metaphysician. But in a kind of metatheatrical turn, what's ultimately most important here is not the play but the audience itself, listening "to itself, expressed." Stevens's choice of theater as the privileged metaphor for poetry, and the audience activity to which it should aspire, seems almost quaint amid the rocketing rise of film in the first half of the twentieth century. But for Stevens, as well as for many other modernist writers, theater offered a resistance to the contamination and engulfment by mass culture that film represented. Stevens's "theater" of poetry seems to lie somewhere between subjection and participation, where the hearer joins with the speaker. This poem summarizes many of the developing values in American poetry at midcentury—including the use of concrete language, an interest in experimentation, and enactment rather than ideas—but it also captures developing theatrical values, including an emphasis not on what is said but rather on the process of saying and a focus on the activity of the audience that resists the model of the spectator associated with mass culture.

While Stevens has often been remembered for his philosophical poetry, his early interest in concrete language and the relationship between reality and the literary imagination appealed to the later modernist avant-garde. Alan Golding notes, for example, that the objectivist poet Louis Zukofsky was attracted by the simple, concrete diction and balance of the imaginative and literal worlds in Stevens's 1916 play *Three Travellers Watch a Sunrise*.[5] In this play, three Chinese travelers and their attendants journey to a densely wooded forest to see the sunrise. The three travelers offer different ways of viewing reality: one looks at the thing, one at representation, and one at context. But at the end the play seems to concede, albeit reluctantly, that no assessment exists "except with reference to ourselves" (Stevens 133). Even colors are ultimately shown to be a matter of individual perception. This joining of the philosophical and the concrete, or of the imaginative and literal worlds, also marked Stevens's first collection of poetry, *Harmonium* (1923).

Stevens's dictum "not the idea of the thing but the thing itself" echoed a number of iconic modernist poets, including Ezra Pound and William Carlos Williams. Williams, in particular, turned his attention to language itself as a material object—art not as a representation or copy of nature but as a thing in itself—and this antimimeticism characterized both his poetry and his drama. Like Stevens, Williams was a playwright, but he also participated in stage productions. His acting debut occurred in 1916, at the Provincetown Playhouse in Greenwich Village, in Alfred Kreymbourg's Dadaist drama *Lima Beans* opposite Mina Loy. He also wrote his first drama, a verse play, at this time. Williams continued to write verse and nonverse drama in the following years, but his most renowned play is *Trial Horse No. 1*, or *Many Loves* (as it is now most commonly known), written around 1940.

Many Loves shares an aesthetic affinity with two key poetic works by Williams, *Spring and All* and *Kora in Hell*, all of which disavow representation in favor of direct experience that we might call performative. In *Spring and All* Williams argues that art should be not a representation or a copy of nature but rather a thing in itself, self-conscious, self-actualizing, and unique, and the poems in the collection are frequently self-referential. *Kora* is even more antimimetic: the entire work is a collage consisting of "improvisations" focused sharply on language and the effects it can produce, and the subject is the compositional process itself. Like these two poetry collections, the play *Many Loves* is also self-referentially focused on the act of creation. *Many Loves* draws attention to the theatrical frame by fictionalizing the staging of three one-act plays: a playwright is in final rehearsals of his production and tries to keep his romantic involvement with the leading lady a secret from his financial backer. *Many Loves* actually began as a group of one-act plays for a local theater in Rutherford, New Jersey, but Williams eventually combined the three "playlets" under one title by linking them through the Pirandello-like story frame, written in unrhymed modern verse, about a playwright preparing to put on a series of three one-act plays.

While the collage techniques of *Kora* and *Spring and All* encourage readers to consider the compositional process itself, the fictional frame of *Many Loves* safely cordons off the question of process as a thematic rather than a constitutive element of the work. The difference lies in the critical effects of antimimeticism in each genre. Unlike antimimeticism in poetry, which manifests in part as a direct experience of the materiality of language itself, sometimes as an end in itself, but also, as the century progressed, as a means of directly accessing the poets' physicality, antimimeticism in drama challenges the work's very status as a play by focusing audience attention directly on its compositional (and production) processes. This purported distinction between mimetic "drama" and antimimetic "performance" is what has led critics such as Michael Vanden Heuvel and Christopher Bigsby to employ the neologism *performance theater* to designate works as postmodernist or avant-garde rather than modernist. Williams's *Many Loves* remains a "play" precisely because it fictionalizes its self-consciousness through the character of the playwright. From this perspective, *Many Loves* only pretends to be literal—it may be a play about making a play, but it is still fully mimetic.

Although *Many Loves* was written around 1940, it wasn't staged until 1959, when it was successfully produced by the Living Theatre (a production I discuss in greater detail in chapter 3). In the interceding twenty years, the performance of poetry had exploded and helped pave the way for poets' theater. The rise of poetry performance is not simply an aesthetic shift but a political one as well, as many poets of the new generation rejected high modernist impersonality, abstraction, and distance and sought, instead, connection, presence, and authenticity. At the same time, they inherited the previous generation's emphasis on process and audience activity.

Poetry Readings and Performance Poetics

In the late nineteenth century, reading poetry aloud was both a form of entertainment and a means of self-improvement. Reading clubs in both domestic and public settings, where friends, neighbors, and professional associations gathered to recite and read aloud, were common prior to

World War I. But these were recitations of poetry that had been written by others, and the emphasis was on the skill of the reciter. Such activities were so popular that in some cases they led to professional recitations, competitions, and festivals (see Wheeler 6–7). Some critics have also noted the impact these elocutionary practices had on the later development of modernism. Peter Middleton has suggested, for example, that Charles Olson drew on elocutionary and debate training for his notion of "projective verse" that was so influential among poets in the 1950s, prompting in part Lesley Wheeler's remark that the "nineteenth-century art of elocution was one of the traditions most immediately influential on modernism" (6). Julia A. Walker has argued that nineteenth-century oratory and the expressive culture movement helped to shape the modernist text-performance split in American theatrical modernism (*Expressionism*).

When poets themselves spoke during this period, it was not to declaim their own poetry but rather to lecture, a widely popular form of entertainment and personality worship at the turn of the century. Even as late as the mid-1930s, Gertrude Stein's celebrity, following the publication of *The Autobiography of Alice B. Toklas*, spurred a triumphant American tour in which she delivered lectures, albeit in her signature poetic prose style. Over time, more and more poets interspersed their lectures with commentary and brief readings of their own poetry, though some poets continued to find this an uneasy merging and resisted the trend to read their own work. Williams Carlos Williams dutifully accepted invitations to read on the popular university lecture-reading circuit, for example, but he abhorred the audience's unimaginative questions and he winced at the exposure of reading confessional pieces in public (Middleton "Contemporary" 278). Wallace Stevens openly expressed his disdain for public readings in his response to the Museum of Modern Art's invitation in 1943: "I am not a troubadour and I think the public reading of poetry is something particularly ghastly" (Economou 655). As an alternative to public readings, literary salons offered semiprivate spaces for poets who wanted artistic community and (usually) sympathetic audiences. They also offered protection from the distasteful stench of mass culture and the marketplace that clung to more public venues.

While recitation clubs were replaced with radio and film, mass journalism, expanding educational alternatives, and a new range of social opportunities created by the spread of the automobile, public readings by acclaimed authors continued to increase in popularity, mainly for their ability to put the audience in the presence of the poet. The dominant style of poetry reading in the early 1950s was epitomized by the public readings of Dylan Thomas. Crowds packed these events, both for a chance to see the poet himself, who was known for his drinking, philandering, and erratic behavior, and to hear his Welsh lilt and experience the intoxicating musicality of his vocal performance. "As a public reader," Peter Quartermain observes, "Thomas was enormously influential, setting a standard for mellifluous expressiveness that could famously lull the hearer along on the wings of poesy" (219). This style of recitation functions as incantation that, as Jed Rasula puts it, "legislates between the bardic posture of superior wisdom and a less privileged endowment, which is that of the stupefied or narcotically enchanted believer" (236).

Authorial presence was key to the power of these events. As mass media and recording technologies made the sound and even sight of readings available to mass audiences removed from the event itself, the authenticity associated with presence became rarer. This sense of authenticity, what Walter Benjamin referred to as a work's "aura," was a form of uniqueness that separated it from everyday life. It also demanded a particular style of reception from the audience—the quiet contemplation and absorption of the silently attentive spectator. The countercultural poetry readings and performances that arose in the postwar period offered an alternative to both the celebrity reading and the university circuit. While the presence and authenticity of the poet remained important, this presence no longer had an authorial or auratic quality, and audiences were no longer expected to sit in quiet reverence but to participate.

In the summer 1951 issue of the *Kenyon Review*, the writer and social critic Paul Goodman (whose plays would later be produced by both the Poets' Theatre and the Living Theatre) published the essay "Advance-Guard Writing, 1900–1950," in which he argued that in the midst of the alienation and "shell-shock" that characterized postwar society the avant-garde should offer "the physical reestablishment of community" (375). Such reestablishment of community must occur on a personal level, "starting with the artist's primary friends," who become both audience and subject of the artist's work (376). The essay had a powerful effect on a number of writers, including Frank O'Hara and Charles Olson, and its overall philosophy puts a positive spin on postwar artists' communities. Rather than acting as exclusive coterie groups, artistic communities such as Black Mountain, the New York School, the Beats, and small theater groups such as the Poets' Theatre and Living Theatre, offered an enthusiastic embrace of community that served as an alternative to professionalization and institutional sanction.

The iconic 1950s poetry performance was Allen Ginsberg's ecstatic, physical, jazz-inspired reading of "Howl," egged on by Jack Kerouac's shouts of "Go! Go!," at the Six Gallery in San Francisco on October 7, 1955. Rather than a somber, authoritative oral delivery, what the audience got was a new style of poetry "reading"—a participatory performance that was musical, theatrical, and improvisatory. Beat poetry performance differed from academic poetry readings, Daniel Belgrad observes, in that "Beat poetry can be fully apprehended only by those participating in the performance space" (218). But sharing a space with the audience did not necessarily ensure community with the audience. While Ginsberg's audience was supportive and his incantatory style infectious, the atmosphere during readings could also be hostile. Beat readings, in particular, were infamously participatory, with poets heckling one another or simply drowning each other out.[6] Such antagonism could also be turned back on the audience. Diane di Prima recounts a poetry reading at Rutgers University in 1962, for example, that included herself, LeRoi Jones (Amiri Baraka), Frank O'Hara, and others, recalling, "None of us wanted to read last, and so we agreed on the train that at the very end we'd each read a poem aloud simultaneously. It seemed like a very natural solution, immersed as we were in the world of cut-ups and chance composition, but it did make the Rutgers audience rather upset. Folks came storming up afterwards to ask us what we were trying to 'prove.' It was the only time I have ever read at Rutgers" (287). Recalling Dada simultaneous sound poems, such a reading functioned more as an attack on the audience by defiantly obscuring meaning.

By the 1960s, poetry readings had become an important part of the poetry scene for poets working outside the contemporary poetry mainstream, especially in New York.[7] John Ashbery recalls:

> In 1963, when I returned from Paris where I'd been living for five years, I wasn't aware that anyone was reading my poetry. When I left, poetry readings were solemn and official events given by elder statespersons of poetry, like Auden or Eliot and Marianne Moore. Then the "Beat revolution" happened to take place while I was away, and when I got back—although I wasn't aware of it—everyone was giving poetry readings everywhere. I was astonished at being asked to give one, until I realized I was one of about a hundred poets one could have heard that night in New York. (qtd in Kane xvii)

These readings framed poetry as a communal event and often as a collaborative project. In fact, orality—as it developed from Stein, Whitman, and Pound, from Dada sound poetry, and from ancient oral traditions—had become a countercultural sign of the poets' rejection of "academic," literary, ego-based poetry and marked the work as "an alternative to formalist writing and, by extension, to conservative or complacent political ideologies" (Kane xiv).

The contents of Donald Allen's momentous 1960 anthology *The New American Poetry, 1945–1960*, give a sense of the postwar performance poetry landscape, with key centers of activity forming around the Black Mountain School, the San Francisco Renaissance, the Beats, and the New York School. (In fact, the idea for the anthology came to Allen not long after he finished work on landmark issue no. 2 of the *Evergreen Review*, featuring San Francisco Bay Area writing, including Ginsberg's "Howl.") This new performance-oriented generation of poets shared an aesthetic that Allen characterized as "third-generation modernism," which, like the objectivists of the second generation, followed the ideas and strategies of Stevens and Williams (see Fredman 824). Critics and historians of American poetry have perhaps been overzealous in identifying nearly all countercultural poetry of the 1950s as "Beat" (see, e.g., Fredman 825), but the poets in Allen's anthology shared a performance aesthetic that could collectively be characterized as a reaction against Cold War conformism. "These poets explored," Fredman elaborates, "in styles ranging from the most cosmopolitan to the most vernacular, the dark underside to America's rise to economic and political domination, and they joined in currents of personal, sexual, religious, and political liberation that inspired larger social movements of the 1960s" (ibid.).

Although Allen's anthology links a range of poetic practices under the general umbrella of antiestablishment performance poetics, and many poets of the era were interested in the cadences of everyday life, as well as in poetry *as* experience rather than simply a record of experience, there was a wide range of approaches and goals in actual performance practices. David Lehman's breezy characterization of the period argues, for example, that the Beats, who sported whiskers, berets, and sunglasses and introduced pot, Zen Buddhism, and bongos to the poetry reading, championed colloquial language and countercultural protest, while the New York poets, who dressed and acted conservatively, located their rebellion "not in social attitude but in artistic innovation" (341). While not all critics make such clear-cut distinctions between Beat and New York School poets or make their distinctions in these same terms, Lehman captures the range of political goals that could be found in performance poetics. In his study of the postwar American culture of spontaneity, Daniel Belgrad makes a similar observation when he notes that while both the Beats and New York School poets employed spontaneity, subjective experience, and the everyday events in poets' daily lives, the Beats were interested in expanding the minds of readers and audiences while the New York School poets were skeptical of the idea that poetry could—or should even try to—achieve such metaphysical goals (255). Meanwhile, other artists and writers tried to circumvent conscious or unconscious communication altogether, as in John Cage's 4'33" which, as Belgrad puts it, "made a principle of the ironic gap between artist, art, and audience" (253). Postwar poets' theater not only encompasses this diversity, but, as the case studies in this book demonstrate, the identity of many poets' theater groups and artists revolves around their struggles to develop a coherent stance toward audience participation.

Ginsberg's iconic performance poem "Howl" was influenced by another text included in Allen's anthology—Charles Olson's 1950 essay "Projective Verse," which opened the "Statements on Poetics" section of Allen's book. Working against New Criticism's separation of the poet from the poem, "Projective Verse" became a key text for midcentury American poets rebelling against New Criticism's codification of poetry according to a critical approach modeled on scientific rationalism. Olson's manifestolike treatise sets down a vision of a new "open" poetry, calling for verse that is both prospective and percussive and based on Robert Creeley's assertion that "form is never more than an extension of content" (240). Characterized equally by its relation to sound as by its relation to breath—what Olson calls the "speech-force of language" that gives the objects in the poem solidity (392)—projective verse is characterized as a transfer of energy, via the poet, from its original source to the reader (and, presumably, to the listener). In this formulation, several things happen simultaneously: while the mind engages with sound, thus producing the syllable, the emotions use the breath to create lines; and in the union of these elements, energy is shaped into form. Olson's emphasis on the syllable as fundamental, as the place where speech "is least careless—and least logical" (241), echoes futurism and Dada with one key difference: where futurist and Dadaist poetry was concerned with nonsensical, purely expressive sound, Olson wants to use sound in combination with meaning without subordinating meaning to sound. Noting that "observation of any kind . . . is previous to the act of the poem," Olson seems to suggest that narrative meaning (or "observation") is secondary and must be used sparingly. In order to retain the poem's fundamental energy, the poet uses typographical symbols, spaces, and so on to indicate how the poem should be voiced.

"Projective Verse" had a significant impact on countercultural American poets in the 1950s and 1960s. But the essay is not an argument in favor of the poets' own expressivist ego, as it is sometimes taken to be, but rather a rejection of egocentric poetry. Olson argues that the form of the poem should be a projection of the content, shaped by the poet who is *listening* and by the poet's own breath. "Breath" does not relate to ego, however, but is instead an emphasis on natural physicality that puts the poem in touch with the nature of man, through the poet who creates the poem—rather like the physicality of the performer's presence being explored in midcentury "antitextual" theater. In this sense, the exploration of the relationship between performance and poetry also becomes the exploration of processes of perception.

Like John Cage, Olson felt that the author's intention should not be imposed on/as form, but whereas Olson believed that form would arise organically from the content as it was physically channeled through the performer's body, Cage worked to impose a structure that was procedural and nonintentional and originated externally. Olson's sense of "breath" as the expression of some natural physicality assumed a correspondence between language and reality, but it was a correspondence that lay in language's rhythms rather than in its referentiality. In tracing emotion directly from the heart through the breath, Olson locates emotion not in the mind but in the body and finds its expression in the poem's lineation. Meanwhile, the mind uses sound to construct syllables. In this merging of mind and body, form emerges.[8]

Projective verse thus embraces the performative presence of the poet at the same time that it deemphasizes the traditional textual value of authorial control of meaning through form. In fact, Olson argued that poems should not be based on ideas or preconceptions but should be treated as performances that hold active tensions. In this sense, Olson was like many poets who opposed the "official style" that dominated American poetry in the immediate postwar years. The New York School poets, the Black Mountain poets, the Beats, and the poets of the San Francisco Renaissance eschewed the regular lines, formal diction, complex allusions, impersonal tone, and implicitly drawn subject that characterized traditional poetry at the time (see Kostelanetz 92). Instead, they embraced ambiguity, the everyday, mass cultural images, humor, "found" diction, and an intensely personal tone. Emulating the visual arts and performance, they sought collaboration across both artistic media and political ideologies.

Such cross-pollination was especially active in 1950s New York. As Bottoms explains in his study of the scene, Greenwich Village, and especially the East Village, allowed bohemian artists of all stripes to mingle in the smoky haze of its lively bar, coffeehouse, and jazz club culture. These provisional spaces hosted poetry readings and theatrical performances outside the institutionalized structures that, in the economic pinch of the postwar period, hesitated to support anything not guaranteed to be a financial success. Poetry readings required no props, and, as the small casts, spare sets, and simple plots of underground theatrical performances made them amenable to slim budgets, they could easily be performed in modest bar and coffeehouse spaces. Such aesthetic choices may have been driven by economic necessity, but, as Bottoms notes, they had the additional effect of focusing the audience's attention on the bodies and speech of the performers themselves, since there was little else to distract from these. Similar low-budget, performer-centered aesthetics characterized action painting, jazz jams, and poetry readings, and indeed artists, musicians, and poets frequently constituted each other's audiences.

It was amid this scene in the 1950s and 1960s that politically oriented poets' theater emerged—not as a definitive genre but in the sharing of ideas and practices across media and ideologies. "Following World War II, the politics of Senator Joe McCarthy, the founding of the House Un-American Activities Committee in 1947, and the attack on artists in particular led to a separation of art and politics, modeled, for example, in the apoliticality of Abstract Expressionism," Laura Hinton and I wrote in our introduction to a 2009 special issue of *Postmodern Culture* devoted to the topic of poets' theater. "But in the 1960s, artists re-politicized aesthetics as they turned to the models, routines, and practices of 'everyday life'" (n.p.). Poets' theater as a politically oriented practice arises in this transition. If, as Sell writes, "the body often served as the vehicle for communicating or mediating the peculiar time signatures of politically attuned art" (81), then it is no coincidence that this politicization of art emerged amid a turn to performance that was characterized as both an expression of the body itself and a critical rethinking of social life. At the center of this rethinking of the relation of art to social life was the emphasis on physically establishing community through performance. This communitarian drive was enacted by theater companies and artists' communities through creative collaboration and even communal living arrangements, but it was also foregrounded in the rhetoric and formal strategies of performance that sought to bring audiences into the work.

From Poetry in the Theater to Poets' Theater

Some key developments in theater and drama practice helped to foster a turn from verse drama to a more self-consciously theatrical poets' theater after World War II. Modernist antirealism is the first of these. In his study of the rhetoric of modern drama, W. B. Worthen distinguishes modernist poetic drama from modernist poetic theater, defining the latter as a direct textual "intervention in the rhetorical ordering of realism, reclaiming the text's authority over the physical 'languages' that construct the drama as theater" (*Modern* 100). In Worthen's account, Yeats, Eliot, Auden, and Beckett were not just writers of "poetic drama"—which he distinguishes as the mere "rhythmic recitation" of poetry *in* the theater that frequently functioned as a "repudiation of the prosaic drama of daily life"—but practitioners of poetic *theater*, which he characterizes as "strategic attempts to theorize the possible relation between the dramatic text and the discourses of its production onstage" (100). If the rhetoric of realism is founded on a visual coherence of the theatrical scene, poetic theater structures its staging according to the (absent) verbal text. And indeed, Worthen argues, "Only when the verbal formalities of the text are deployed in such a way as to govern the productive discourses of the stage does a poetic theater become possible, a theater in which the linguistic complexity of the text is visible throughout the spectacle" (101).

Modernist poetic theater is therefore antitheatrical, in the sense that it rejects the traditional value of mimesis and, along with it, mimetic elements of the theater, such as the impersonating actor (even as it employs many of these same conventions). In poets' theater, a stage manager character might, for example, walk onto the stage, break the fourth wall, and address the audience in rhymed lines. Or especially stilted verse might be used to critique a hackneyed sentiment expressed by one of the characters. Poetic language was not always employed for the same purposes, but the contrast between verse and everyday language was typically used to call attention to a representation that might otherwise be missed by audience members who were thought to have grown passive. One crucial difference between verse *drama* and poetic *theater* lies, as Worthen indicated above, in the relation of language to scene—a difference with roots in the modernist avant-garde. In the introduction to their anthology of modernist poetic plays, Bay-Cheng and Cole draw on Worthen's definition to distinguish modernist poetic theater (by, in their account, such poet-playwrights as Stein, Stevens, Cummings, and Williams) from other forms of verse drama.[9] Characteristic of such modernist poetic theater, they assert, is the attempt "to make the poetry visible as the hallmark of truth within the theatrical illusion of realism" (21). In this view, the combination of poetry and performance enacts some of the key tensions of modernism itself—tensions between the private and the public, between texts and bodies, and between formal experimentation and subjective experience.

This difference between verse drama and poets' theater turns on the value of theatricality itself. Martin Puchner credits German composer Richard Wagner's notion of the *gesamtkunstwerk*, or "total work of art," with transforming the concept of theatricality from a description into "a value that must be either rejected or embraced" (31). Beginning as early as the 1870s, avant-gardists tussled over the text-versus-performance hierarchy. While nineteenth-century German romantic figures such as Wagner and Goethe "considered performance itself a work of art," writes Erika Fischer-Lichte, the majority of their contemporaries regarded "the artistic character of performance" as "primarily affirmed through the performance of literature, through the dramatic literary text that was supposed to steer and control performance" (80). Theater stood for both collaborative production and collective reception, and these values sat at the heart of the conflicts between modernism and the avant-garde.

Modernist writers felt that collaborative production robbed artists of sovereign control over their work. And they saw the theater as a dangerous arena of collective reception by the undifferentiated masses. In response to both of these problems, as Puchner has so thoroughly demonstrated, modernist antitheatricality took aim at theater's mimetic strategies, especially the impersonating actor. Dramatists such as Brecht and Beckett, for example, sought to solve the problems of the theater by depersonalizing and denaturalizing actors' performances through the use of such strategies as masks, symbolic gestures, and highly constrained movements and situations. In direct contrast to this, avant-gardists celebrated theatricality especially for its pursuit of direct political engagement by embracing the public sphere—F. T. Marinetti even proclaimed that "everything of any value is theatrical" (qtd in Puchner 7). High modernist antitheatricality and avant-garde protheatricality can therefore be taken as two sides of the same coin, where modernist antitheatricality is a fearful reaction to the idea of mass reception and the public sphere and avant-garde protheatricality is an embrace of populism and mass culture, exhibiting what Andreas Huyssen has called the "hidden dialectic" between the artistic and political avant-gardes.

Postwar poets' theater emerged in the midst of and in response to these clashes. Indebted to the avant-garde's protheatricality, which embraced collaborative production and collective reception in the joint name of art and politics, poets' theater flourished on makeshift stages in churches, community centers, streets, and theaters. But poets' theater also employed many varied possibilities for unhinging mimesis from the theater. Poetic multivocality offered one route. The Noh-inspired use of a stage-manager character and other metatheatrical approaches offered another. The juxtaposition of poetry and prose to undermine naturalism and rhetorically structure a performance for the purposes of critique was still another. Poets' theater combined antitheatrical attempts to undercut impersonation through the use of poetic dialogue, metatheatrical devices, and atomized gesture with the protheatrical emphasis on the audience, engagement in political critique, and loss of separation between theatrical performance and "real" event.

This merging of the avant-garde's protheatricality and modernism's antitheatricality frequently acts as a self-conscious attempt to critique both the perceived passivity of bourgeois theatergoers and the apparent isolation of individual reception in private. Poets' theater frequently takes place in intimate settings where performers can see audience members and audience members can see each other. And often, performers and audience members are known to each other. The effect is a critical enactment grounded in the historical particularities and personal responsibility fostered by the liveness of performance. Exploring the relationship between modernist art and "low" or mass culture, Thomas Crow echoes a common critique of the modernist avant-garde—that its embrace of the "real," in, for example, newspaper clippings inserted into cubist collage, ultimately ended up working in service of a generalized critique about representation itself rather than a critique of any particular representation (8). But if the modernist avant-garde abstracted and generalized oppositionality through nonspecific, non–socially grounded antagonism, then the shift from modernist poetic drama to postwar poets' theater, which interrogates the construction of specific representations and narratives, might be seen as a return to a more specific oppositionality.

One of the narratives that therefore develops through the series of case studies found in this book centers on attitudes of poets' theaters toward their audiences. Whereas modernist avant-garde theaters tended to treat their audiences with suspicion, frustration, and even contempt, later participatory theaters encouraged audience involvement, which they equated with empowerment. Poets' theaters, especially, were marked by an explicit goal to activate the audience. Frequently positing the typical audience of film, television, and bourgeois theater as a passive group of spectators out for a night of entertainment, they tended to see such audiences as complicit in and subject to the representations and politics they were being presented. As an antidote, poets' theaters sought to stir the audience to greater activity, responsibility, and engagement, if not always out-and-out participation. Some poets' theaters did this by employing characters that spoke directly to audience members and highlighted the audience's own interpretive activity. Others blurred the line between stage and reality, leading audiences to question whether they were watching a performance or real life unfold. Still others used a range of other theatrical strategies to draw attention to the conventions of meaning making that were in operation, undermining the structures of narration—and often, especially, of cinematic narration—that had come to control which stories could be told and how. Whatever the specific method, poets' theater employed an explicit emphasis on language as poiesis, and they explored the relationship between this notion of poetry and social life via a positioning and repositioning of the audience.

Walker suggests that the interest in performance that marks the last half of the twentieth century indicates "an implicit dismantling of the antiperformative bias upon which a certain modernist understanding of textuality is based" ("Why" 161), a dismantling that has come about largely because "textuality is felt to be inadequate to a full description of cultural experience" (162). More recently the rise of performance studies can be characterized, at least in part, as a response to cultural studies' textualization of culture. The opposition of text and bodily performance in twentieth-century American theater became particularly heightened during the so-called antitextual 1960s, a period in which theater companies are said to have abandoned the playscript in favor of improvisatory collaboration, on one hand, and direct communion with the audience on the other.

We might think of poets' theater as a special category of "postdramatic theatre," Hans-Thies Lehmann's term for noncharacterological, nonnarrative, multivocal, frequently multimediated, and certainly unstable "new" theater that "confirms the not so new insight that there is never a harmonious relationship but rather a perpetual conflict between text and scene" (145). Indeed, in its eschewal of realistic portrayals of character, setting, temporality, and so on, poetic theater tries to release performance from regulation by the drama. In general, poets' theater rethinks the relationship between the dramatic text, onstage performance, and the audience. Early poets' theater tended to exhibit a metatheatrical focus identified with modernism. Poets' theater of the later 1960s and beyond continues modernist poetic theater's repudiation of naturalized meaning—a meaning that is rhetorically constructed by realism's prioritization of everyday behavior—but its theatricality attempts to create an awareness not merely of the processes of stage production but also of how meaning is produced in the activities of everyday life. If everyday life might be said to operate via a rhetoric of reality that effaces the means by which the meaning of everyday experience is produced and maintained, then poets' theater's theatricalization of everyday processes of meaning production becomes a political act intended to expose the rhetoric of "reality" itself.

Poets' Theater as a Critical Lens

The relationship between performance and poetry changes over time, not wholesale but locally, in relation to specific communities in specific moments, and as part of a network. This book analyzes these localized understandings in particular historical moments via case studies of noteworthy groups and playwrights of the postwar period, examining how they engaged with larger cultural values and shifts. But the book actually begins earlier, with the work of Gertrude Stein, whose plays and performance poetics can help us understand intersections in the rhetoric of poetics and performance in the earlier part of the century. In weaving together the poetic, the theatrical, and the performative, Stein's work was an influential forerunner to a number of later poets' theater artists, and many poets' theater groups produced her plays. Her early, identity-oriented works especially—including her play *Four Saints in Three Acts*, the novel *The Making of Americans*, and the scores of "verbal portraits" she wrote in the 1900s-1920s—demonstrate her attempts to create a performance and a "presence" through poetic strategies. She dispensed with narrative, and largely with description as well, in order to explore the ways in which a work, its personae, and its meanings emerge collaboratively, in readers', performers', and/or audience members' engagements with the work. And in emphasizing continual repetition to account for the differences of the changing present, Stein presaged aspects of contemporary theories of performativity by such scholars as Judith Butler. Stein's strategy of highlighting the material aspects of language in ever-shifting contexts to create multiple semantic and discursive effects later became a common strategy of postwar poets' theater.

Chapters 2, 3, and 4 comprise the central case studies of this book, each offering an account of one group and/or practitioner active during poets' theater's peak in the middle of the twentieth century. Chapter 2 takes up what may be the first self-described poets' theater, called simply the Poets' Theatre, founded in Cambridge, Massachusetts, in the early 1950s. As I've argued, postwar poets' theater can be seen as an aesthetic intervention combined with an attempt to achieve a more specific oppositionality, a groundedness in historical particularities and personal responsibility fostered by the liveness of performance, and the early history of the Poets' Theatre demonstrates this shift. While the Poets' Theatre thrived until its theater burned down in 1968, its early years best represent the competing interests of literature, bourgeois theater, intentionally antiprofessional performance, and self-conscious attention to audience activity that were its legacy for later poets' theaters. This chapter examines in particular the first seven years of the Poets' Theatre's onstage productions and offstage disputes, demonstrating the complex and occasionally contentious relationship between theatrical and literary values that marked the emergence of postwar poets' theater in the United States.

Chapter 3 approaches the changing relationship between literary and theatrical values from a different angle, through the transitional works of the Living Theatre, whose clear if uneven development from poetic drama in the 1950s to avant-garde performance in the 1960s reveals the continuity between these two forms. Tracing the Living Theatre's emphasis on social discourse and performer-audience interactions from its early productions of Stein and other poetic theater, through its embrace of Artaud, and to its eventual disavowal of the theater text, this chapter revises the conventional understanding of the Living Theatre's shifts in the 1950s and 1960s, and in doing so it finds correspondences between poets' theater and so-called antitextual, participatory theater.

In chapter 4, I consider the political efficacy of Black Nationalist poets' theater through an examination of the performative strategies and production history of Amiri Baraka's 1967 play *Home on the Range*. Drawing on arguments by Elin Diamond and Fred Moten in particular, I offer the term *generative mimesis* to describe Baraka's creative poetic-theatrical strategies, which worked simultaneously to undermine received social narratives and reproduce them in new ways. But while the play started out successfully, Baraka soon abandoned it. This chapter places the play within the larger context of Baraka's experiments in cultural and political aesthetics and of the larger off-off-Broadway movement in the 1960s to argue that the initial success and eventual failure of *Home on the Range* demonstrates some of the difficulties of combining the destabilizing effects of poetic multivocality with cultural ritualism and oppositional politics.

Chapters 5 and 6, as well as the "Epilogue," take a chronological leap forward to examine more contemporary practitioners and inheritors of poets' theater. Chapter 5 considers the work of Carla Harryman, a poet-playwright associated with the San Francisco branch of what has become known as "Language" writing and a central member of the San Francisco Poets Theater in the 1980s who is still expanding the boundaries of poets' theater today. With particular attention to Harryman's work in the 1990s and 2000s, which employs poets' theater conceptually as a means of rethinking our engagement with political narratives, this chapter examines more closely how poets' theater conceptualizes its audience. Unlike conventional narrative theater, which tends to treat its audience as a social and moral collective, contemporary poets' theater audiences might best be characterized as the intentional rupture of that community, with each member experiencing an individual identification in the shared space of the theater. The result, I argue, is an interpretive "community" marked, paradoxically, by discontinuity and dispersion. If realist narrative theater's appeal to public morals has become suspect in a post-9/11 world, then Harryman's poets' theater offers an alternative that may be better adapted to the social complexities of our world.

Chapter 6 considers poets' theater's legacy in one of the most critically discussed "new" forms of theater in the last few decades, late-twentieth-century "postdramatic" theater. Its specific example is Suzan-Lori Parks's *The America Play*, a work that mobilizes testimonial, poetic performance as an antidote to the normalizing constraints of the so-called historical record. One of postdramatic theater's main inheritances from poets' theater is the receptive orientation established by the active, committed involvement of the audience-participant working across generic and disciplinary boundaries. Using the 1994 Yale Repertory Theatre's premiere of *The America Play* as an example, this chapter demonstrates ways in which postdramatic theater marshals the strategies of poets' theater to turn members of the production team, audiences, and scholar-critics alike into creative collaborators.

Expanding on the discussion of poets' theater in the twenty-first century, the "Epilogue" presents a brief overview of a range of poets' theater on offer in the last two decades. It surveys festivals, theater companies, and individual productions across three US locales—San Francisco, Chicago, and Boston—in order to give a sense of overall continuities as well as regional differences. In doing so, it demonstrates poets' theater's ongoing relevance even in the face of new political and aesthetic interests and contexts.

Of course, there is much that has been left out of this account. Several important poets' theaters are unfortunately not examined here—including the Artists' Theatre in the 1950s; the New York Poets Theatre/American Theatre for Poets, Inc., the Hardware Poets' Playhouse, and the Judson Poets' Theater, all in the 1960s; the Eye and Ear Theater in the late 1970s and early 1980s; and the Nuyorican Poets Café beginning in the 1970s. In some cases, the stories of these groups are beginning to emerge elsewhere (see Bottoms on the Judson Poets' Theater, for example, and Durham on the Judson's productions of Stein), but it's my hope that more accounts of poets' theater will follow, and from other critical perspectives. There are also several contemporary poets' theater practitioners working today who deserve more than the cursory attention I am able to give them in this book's epilogue. Critical consideration of those artists is emerging more rapidly in poetry scholarship than in theater scholarship. The plays I analyze here are selective, sometimes chosen because they are exemplary, sometimes because they are representative, and sometimes because they are outliers, together helping me map my subject. My account of the Poets' Theatre in Cambridge, for example, covers only the years most relevant to the rise of postwar American poets' theater, though I hope a book-length history will one day give this noteworthy group its full due. In contrast, Baraka has only one play that could strictly be considered "poets' theater," and the story of this play helps locate the value and shortcomings of poets' theater within Baraka's own emerging cultural aesthetics and black nationalism. In other cases, my selection of only certain plays from a playwright's or group's larger body of work favors access to both a written text and some aspect of performance that enables me to most productively explore the relationship between the two. In my discussion of the work of Carla Harryman, for example, I primarily discuss two plays, *Memory Play* and *Mirror Play*, because I was able to attend production rehearsals and I had access to video and audio recordings of multiple performances, allowing me to provide a better sense of how different aspects of poets' theater can collaborate and engage with its audience.

Because I am interested not only in the practice but also in the rhetoric of poets' theater, my archive is broad. I read not only playscripts but also the ways in which plays and performances were discussed, framed, and promoted—in playbills and souvenir programs and interviews, manifestoes, and editorial statements, as well as reviews and other performance descriptions. This book discusses individual plays and playwrights, but, even more important, it examines the larger development of poets' theater across a range of communities, groups, and aesthetic and historical contexts. It is a work of theater and poetry history built around case studies; it is a theorization of the ways in which poets' theater constructs, engages, promotes, and enables performance-audience interactions based on a particular understanding of the performance of language and social communication; and it is a critical collaboration with poets' theater's performative effects.

Acts of Poetry brings poets' theater out of the unfocused margins and into critical view, and in doing so, it locates poets' theater as an inextricable part of the larger narrative of twentieth-century American theater—especially in its kinship with radical participatory and environmental theater at midcentury and in its legacy for postdramatic theater today. It also helps us see poets' theater's dynamic relationship to American cultural, racial, and language politics in the latter half of the twentieth century and to evolving notions of audience, performance, and everyday life. Attending to the commonalities that have for too long been blurred by disciplinary differences, *Acts of Poetry* offers a critical lens for this expanded view.

CHAPTER ONE

Repeating Gertrude Stein

> Loving repeating then is important being in some. This is now some
> description of the importance of loving repeating being in one.
> —Gertrude Stein, *The Making of Americans*

Although poets' theater didn't emerge until the postwar period, Gertrude
Stein's performative writings from decades earlier frequently provided inspiration and material. Stein's influence can be felt both in the initial rise
and peak of poets' theater in the 1950s and 1960s and in the resurgence
of poets' theater that has taken place much more recently, in the early
twenty-first century, a resurgence that goes hand-in-hand with a simultaneous renewal of interest in some of Stein's most repetitious writings. Experimental writers, filmmakers, and theater artists have all been attracted
to Stein. During the twentieth century, artists ranging from composer
Virgil Thomson to filmmaker Stan Brakhage and from theatrical avant-
gardists Julian Beck and Judith Malina to Language poet and playwright
Leslie Scalapino have cited Stein as a direct influence.[1] And at the turn to
the twenty-first century, Stein's work once again had particular influence
in the realm of theater, with not only new stagings of Stein's own plays and
librettos—such as Robert Wilson's productions of *Doctor Faustus Lights
the Lights* in 1992 and *Four Saints in Three Acts* in 1996 and *The Mother of
Us All* produced by the Glimmerglass Opera in 1998, by the New York City
Opera in 2000, and by the San Francisco Opera in 2004—but also a variety of new plays and adaptations inspired by Stein, including *Hashirigaki*
by Heiner Goebbels (2000–2004), *The Making of Americans* four-play series by the Gertrude Stein Repertory Theatre (2004), *House/Lights* by the
Wooster Group (1998, revived in 2005), and *Loving Repeating: A Musical
of Gertrude Stein*, adapted and directed by Frank Galati with music by Stephen Flaherty (2006). Notably, three of these four adaptations based their

scripts on Stein's novel *The Making of Americans*, arguably one of the most repetitive works of literature to come out of the twentieth century. Many also used Stein's writings as a basis for highly technologized multimedia theatrical productions.

Critical treatments of Stein's plays tend to treat her performative poetics and theatrical production as mostly independent. Freed from the constraints of narrative and description, directors must take great creative license in deciding even the most basic elements of Stein's dramas such as character, setting, and who speaks which lines. But Stein's performative poetics shape the performance and reception of her works onstage, and critical discussions of the impact of the relationship between Stein's performative poetics and actual theatrical performance on the role of the audience have been rare. Most critics have instead tended to focus on the connection between Stein's literary experimentalism and the visual avant-garde, particularly cubism, without taking notions of performance explicitly into account.[2] With the start of the twenty-first century, Stein's plays have finally been given long overdue critical attention in Sarah Bay-Cheng's *Mama Dada: Gertrude Stein's Avant-Garde Theatre* (2004) and Leslie Atkins Durham's *Staging Gertrude Stein: Absence, Culture, and the Landscape of American Alternative Theatre* (2005). But while both studies consider Stein's writings for the theater, the relationship between her verbal performances on the page and the performance of her works onstage remains underexamined. In order to better understand Stein's influence on practitioners of poets' theater, this chapter looks at the performativity of language in Stein's writing across multiple genres, as well as the implications of this for stage performance and audience activity.

Stein is cited by innovative poets and playwrights alike as a key influence, and she is, as Marc Robinson argues in *The Other American Drama*, a crucial forerunner to later avant-garde theater. Theater scholars tend to characterize Stein's drama as antitheatrical, in the sense that it is antimimetic, but it's more accurate to describe it as *differently* mimetic. Her "fine new kind of realism," as her teacher William James called it (Mellow 147), combines referentiality and phenomenology, portraying not so much the representation of reality but the materiality of representational conventions and the ways in which these aspects of representation help to materialize a kind of performance of the object. And in her use of radical multivocality that destabilizes normative meanings and representations, Stein serves as a forerunner to postwar poets' theater. This is not to say that all instances of poets' theater employed the same strategies she did, nor that all poets' theaters claimed Stein as an inspiration, nor even that they all staged plays she had written. But the ways in which poets' theater uses multivocal poetic language to foster an active collaboration between artist, art, and audience find a predecessor in Stein's plays and portraiture. And often there is a cultural politics at work in this strategy.

Stein's Performative Portraiture

It is important not to approach Stein's work monolithically, as Sarah Bay-Cheng has argued, since her drama underwent a transformation in the 1920s as she experimented with film conventions. The Stein that is most influential on poets' theater is not the later Stein of *The Mother of Us All* but the earlier Stein of *Four Saints in Three Acts* and—just as significantly—of nondramatic works such as the novel *The Making of Americans* and the scores of "verbal portraits" she wrote in the 1910s and 1920s. Arguing that memory stymies creation because it emphasizes identity over being, Stein tried to employ performative language in a way that would create a direct experience of a thing by capturing its movement in the present moment. To do so, narrative, even highly self-conscious narrative, had to be replaced with the act of composition itself. In her later work, Stein used the term *entity*, rather than *identity*, to indicate character representations that allowed both character and reader to remain in the present moment—that is, representations that created a sense of immediacy. In "What Are Master-Pieces and Why Are There So Few of Them?" she defines "identity" as an act of recognition, grounded in memory, that pulls the reader/audience out of the present moment of experience and thus destroys the creative impulse. In contrast to this, she uses the term *entity* to indicate the liveliness of a thing in itself, in the present moment and freed from traditional representational and referential restraints. Stein worked out her notion of entity in the dozens of verbal portraits she wrote, but the idea of "insistence," or repetition with difference, that led to the liveliness of her portraiture first arises in *The Making of Americans*, her earliest novel.[3]

   The Making of Americans occupies a lofty, if unusual, position in the history of literary modernism. The sheer ambition of the novel is daunting: in nearly a thousand pages it chronicles the histories of three generations of the Dehning and Hersland families; attempts to develop a system for ordering all human beings into character types and discovers the failure of that system; reveals, as a result, that human identity is constructed rather than natural; and thus challenges the very concept of representation and the western literary tradition. But the difficulty of reading the novel has more to do with its compositional strategies than with the number of its pages or the scope of its plot. Written in the earliest stages of Stein's literary career, the novel changes compositional tack several times as the author-narrator develops a philosophy of narrative while in the act of composition. The classificatory impulse with which the novel begins eventually gives way to an attention to the conflict between authorial construction and character identity. As a result, the project of the novel shifts from the formation of a fixed system to the exploration of a performative process, particularly the process of writing as both creation and interpretation.

Such a summary of the novel may make its basic trajectory easy to grasp, but it's ultimately misleading. First of all, the structure is much more complicated than the chapter layout of the book indicates.[4] Second, it glosses over the role of citation in Stein's compositional strategies. The writing of *The Making of Americans* was the precursor to Stein's most experimental period, and the ideas she works out in the novel lead directly to her more markedly performative texts. Although the author-narrator begins the novel by trying to work out a totalizing system of human typology, she grows anxious over her authorial role as simultaneous creator and interpreter of identity.

> It is a very difficult thing to know the being in any one. It is a very difficult thing to know whether any one is feeling a thing, enjoying a thing, knowing that they are hurting some one, planning that thing, planning anything they are doing in their living. It is a difficult thing to know the being in any one if that one tells to anyone completely all that that one has in them of telling, it is a very difficult thing to know the being in any one if they are not telling any one anything that they can have as telling in them. (460)

The author-narrator's anxiety leads to one of the novel's major shifts in narrative style. After beginning in the past tense as a representation of a linear progression of events in memory, which requires the reader to straddle the past of the story and the present of reading, the narrative moves into the continuous present tense as a series of closely aligned but shifting present moments. It is through this use of the present continuous that Stein effects what she calls "insistence," which is not repetition but rather "each moment having its own emphasis that is its own difference and so . . . the moving and the existence of each moment" ("Portraits" 308). In writing *The Making of Americans* Stein soon began to feel that it was impossible to portray the complete character of anyone because the manifestations of any given identity always depend on the conditions of the present moment. "We inside us do not change," she explained, "but our emphasis and the moment in which we live changes. That is it is never the same moment it is never the same emphasis at any successive moment of existing" ("Portraits" 305–6). Stein's assertion that "we inside us do not change" indicates her belief in essential identity; yet her turn to insistence reformulates identity as not only natural but also reiterative. This reiterativity is not the same as the reiterability of Judith Butler's notion of performativity, for it ultimately grounds its reiteration in an identity that precedes reiteration. And yet in arguing that identity can never be completely captured in narrative—as she puts it in *The Making of Americans*, "Perhaps no one gets a complete history of any one. . . . [H]ow important each repeating in each one is to make a completer realisation of that one" (454)—Stein implies that reiteration plays a role in identity formation. In acknowledging that one's "history" can never be complete, she refocuses attention on the issue of (re)iterability itself.

Similar experiments with the relationship between representation and existence can be found in Stein's verbal portraiture. In *Tender Buttons*, the meanings of words shift and flex as they are recontextualized, demonstrating the instability of meaning but also its performativity. Her signifiers shimmer above signifieds, exposing lively gaps between the thing and its representation. Marianne DeKoven has pointed out that much of the success of Stein's language experiments relies on her use of conventional grammar structures that tease the reader into expectations of conventional meaning only to thwart those expectations with unconventional twists in language. Stein does not simply break apart referent and object; rather, she juxtaposes conventional referentiality with a variety of material and semiotic relations resulting from multiple contextual associations that don't merely describe an experience but create one, thereby exposing and exploring the necessary but fraught relationship between reference and representation. This is the key to Stein's linguistic performativity, for it allows words to *generate* an experience, as well as to refer to one.

A close reading of one of Stein's briefest portraits should help bring this strategy into focus. "Chicken" appears in the "Food" section of *Tender Buttons* and is brief enough to reproduce here in its entirety.

Chicken.

Stick stick call then, stick stick sticking, sticking with a chicken.
   Sticking in a extra succession, sticking in. (341)

In order to make sense of these lines, it is first necessary to move past (though not entirely discard) description, which relies on the symbolic correspondence of conventional language usage, while simultaneously retaining referentiality as a background against which Stein's language may "move." By focusing on the material properties of words, it is almost possible to experience the expression of a chicken in motion. The onomatopoeic "stick stick sticking," for example, conjures up the repetitive rhythm of a chicken's pecking, clucking, and skittish, rapid head movements all in a single phrase. Stein positions the title in the middle of "Chicken" like an object at the center of a painting. Then she scatters more "stick" and "sticking" before and after it, and suddenly there is a chicken moving across a yard. But something happens when we reach the word *chicken*: the form, both of the poem and of the chicken, changes. The rhythm slows, the movement becomes heavier and clumsier. Suddenly, the poem grinds to a halt with an ominous "sticking in," alluding perhaps to the murderous knife that brings it all to an end. The chicken, in preparation for the "succession" of chickens on Stein's dinner menu, is dead.

This is, granted, a playful and idiosyncratic reading of the poem, but its idiosyncrasy is part of what makes it a worthy exemplification of Stein's notion of "entity," which relies on immediate experience of the liveliness of the verbal representation. It also demonstrates a mature version of the authorial self-reflexivity that appears in some of Stein's other works, such as *The Making of Americans*. As Wendy Steiner explains, a portrait always does double duty: "it represents a real person whose actuality it announces through its title and through 'individualizing' detail; at the same time it presents itself as a work of art—framed, highly structured, of interest 'in itself'" (5). Both a chicken and Stein's portrait of a chicken are in motion, and both can be halted by "sticking in." For a chicken, termination comes by sticking a knife into its body. For Stein's portrait of a chicken, cessation comes by sticking it into a rigid signification system that, with its conventionalized cadences and meanings, stomps some words and possibilities deep into the ground. And yet the poem is not entirely unmoored from referential language, for this reading relies on such referentiality, and especially on the referentiality of the title (and, indeed, that we agree on the textual convention of a title in the first place).[5] Stein's poem enacts its live-liness in part by not pinning language too firmly to a correspondent object but by instead generating possibilities for alternative readings. Stein's method may be likened to collage, with the difference that the pieces being juxtaposed here are not bits of language removed from the contextual background of narrative and printed texts but rather bits of language removed from the static background of the entire system of symbolic communication based on a correspondence of signifiers and signifieds.

By deploying ready-made conventions of communication while at the same time aspiring to a unique experience of the "being" of the poem, "Chicken" is what we might think of as a verbal performance. To understand the poem as a performance requires, above all, that the reader understand the work as an *event*, apprehended individually by each audience member (in this case, by each individual reader) in and through the act of reading. Movement takes place through our interactions with language, and these interactions are always context dependent and, therefore, never reproducible in exactly the same way. On a different day, for example, my attention may be drawn to different conventions of phrasing in the poem, leading me to produce a different reading. Such interactivity between language and reader is a defining feature of much of Stein's writing.

Stein's performativity works according to a strategy Fred Moten has characterized as "second iconicity," which builds off Charles Sanders Peirce's notion of the icon as that which physically resembles what it stands for (which Moten refers to as "first iconicity"). Moten's work is concerned with how to convey the experience of musical performance in writing, but its applicability can be generalized to any performance that is understood to exist somewhere between phenomenon and reference. The key for Moten is that second iconicity must move beyond language's referentiality to the sounded re-presentation of the experience of musical performance, based on attention to language's materiality. In creating her portraits, Stein wrote, "I became more and more excited about how words which were the words that made whatever I looked at look like itself were not the words that had in them any quality of description . . . words that make what I looked at be itself were always words that to me very exactly related themselves to that thing the thing at which I was looking" ("Portraits" 303). As an analog of musical conventions in the context of language, such re-presentation is both mimetic, in that it is imitative or citational, and performative, in that it creates anew the experience of music by reiterating musical conventions recontextualized in the sound-space of the page.

The meanings of any playscript are enacted both in the individual act of reading and in stage performance. But what is the relationship between these two enactments? As anyone who has ever attended a book group or a college literature class can attest, the meaning of written language is not always self-evident, and literary texts in particular don't just capitalize on the multivocality of language—they make it a virtue. Furthermore, the multivocality of a written text may actually occur both at the level of overt vocalization in performance and as a kind of subvocalization in the act of "silent" reading—as what Garrett Stewart has called an "evocalization" rather than vocalization of the text (3). Although we imagine ourselves simply to be reading silently, Stewart draws on studies that show that we are always subconsciously evocalizing the text to ourselves as we read. This evocalized reading, Stewart argues, destabilizes a text by carrying sound across lexical gaps, the blankness of the page between words, momentarily multiplying meaning through a kind of sonic elision. The resulting "phonotext" is not identical to the written text but rather exists in a kind of wavering tension with it. While Stewart is concerned primarily with conventionally written texts that are read with an expectation of stable meaning, his analysis also begs the question of what can be said to happen to poetic, generative, and decidedly multivocal texts such as Stein's when they are fully vocalized, as in theatrical performance. What happens when performative poetics on the page are vocally delivered onstage?

It's worth noting that even evocalization works in part by activating the body. In her analysis of sound in twentieth-century American poetry, Lesley Wheeler cites Åke W. Edfeldt's 1960 study *Silent Speech and Silent Reading*, in which Edfeldt argues that "silent speech," which likely occurs in all acts of reading, mobilizes the speech musculature. In fact, Wheeler's examination of the neuroscience of literary readings and poetry performances concludes that "even when we read silently, our bodies respond as if we are preparing to read aloud" (25). And while approaches across the sciences vary widely, Wheeler finds that the "seemingly mental activity [of silent reading] involves multiple regions of the body, and not only through the visual processing of written language: muscles in the tongue, lips, and larynx may move, sometimes almost imperceptibly" (24). Subvocalized reading can therefore be seen as a kind of performance of reading that works in part by particularizing, through an individual's act of embodied reading, the generalized communicability of language itself. That is, signification occurs not by a general, universally applicable structure of meaning but rather through the particular experience of embodied reading that must take into account not only the activation of the body in the act of reading but also particular personal associations, contexts, and histories that come to bear on the meaning-making process in that particular temporally and spatially located act of reading, as in my example of "Chicken." Moreover, reading understood as embodied experience also reveals reading as an event that exceeds semantic meaning.

In discussing American poetry of the twentieth century, Wheeler argues that "Poetic voice is, among other things, a metaphor: it refers to literary qualities that evoke physical qualities" (38). The physical, vocalized sounding of Stein's generative texts offers a more complex way of thinking about the relationship between the physical and the literary. Sometimes, vocalization fixes meaning, while at other times the sounding of the text produces the multiple meanings more conventionally associated with poetry on the page. It is also the sounding of the text that produces a kind of three-way encounter between author/text, performer/vocalizer, and audience/listener—and it is on this encounter that Stein's performative poetics relies.

Performative Language in Performance:
The Collaborations of Four Saints

Given the radical multivocality of Stein's language on the page, critics have long debated the performability of her plays. Jane Palatani Bowers has argued, for example, that "Stein's plays oppose the physicality of performance" and instead are "a theater of language" (2). Martin Puchner comes to a similar conclusion when he labels Stein's plays "a particularly strange kind of closet drama" (101). In contrast, Betsy Alayne Ryan asserts that Stein's plays are best realized "not on the printed page, but in live performance" (40), and Sarah Bay-Cheng contends that Stein's drama "deserves consideration on its own terms, as drama and as theater" (3). While Stein herself "imagined her writing as a design for performance," as Bowers points out—"as she wrote to Mabel Dodge in 1913, 'I do *not* want the plays published. They are to be kept to be *played*'" (147 n.45)—her playscripts nevertheless gave little attention to the mechanics of production, leading more than one critic to label her drama "antitheatrical" (Puchner 101–16 and Worthen 13). But Bowers and DeKoven have demonstrated the shortcomings of genre when it comes to Stein, both preferring an overall chronological approach that largely ignores genre distinctions. Approaching Stein chronologically can help us see the links between the early development of her ideas of verbal performance in her early novel *The Making of Americans,* the performative poetics of her verbal portraiture, and her most famous play, *Four Saints in Three Acts,* all of which were written between 1903 and 1927. In *The Making of Americans* Stein theorizes her performative approach to writing based on her realization that identity is never complete but must continually be rearticulated. Her later verbal portraits, including the collection *Tender Buttons* (1914), take this concept even further by trying to create the experience of being through verbally performative means. And the opera *Four Saints* provides a fertile example of just what happens when such lively, performative language is brought into the space of fully embodied performance.

To portray the existence of a thing in the immediate moment, Stein replaced narrative with the act of composition itself, and she did this in both her prose writing and her plays. But it wasn't enough merely to narrativize the creative process, as she had done in *The Making of Americans* and as Luigi Pirandello did in *Six Characters in Search of an Author* (1922) and as William Carlos Williams did in *Many Loves* (c. 1940, discussed in chapter 3), because this still did not solve the problem of syncopation that Stein found so aggravating in theater just as she had found memory troubling in prose. In the essay "Plays," she observes that in narrative plays, "your emotion concerning that play is always either behind or ahead of the play at which you are looking and to which you are listening. So your emotion as a member of the audience is never going on at the same time as the action of the play" (244). In order to achieve a less syncopated and thus more immediate emotional experience, Stein wanted to dispense with the Aristotelian notion of the dominance of plot by focusing on "sight and sound and its relation to emotion and time, rather than in relation to story and action" (251).

The opera *Four Saints in Three Acts,* Stein's theatrical collaboration with composer Virgil Thomson, is a striking example of a performative text written for performance. Thomson admired Stein's verbal portraits, and in the 1920s he had started setting them to music, much to Stein's delight. In 1927 he proposed the idea of writing an opera together. Stein agreed, and she completed the libretto in June of that same year, though the opera wouldn't premiere until 1934. Collaboration did not come easily to Stein, and she was never one for compromise. Early in her career, for example, she chose to self-publish rather than cater to more conventional tastes. A creative disagreement with Georges Hugnet, whose volume of poetry *Enfances* Stein had agreed to translate, led to Stein's solo publication of *Before the Flowers of Friendship Faded Friendship Faded*, with all references to Hugnet's work excised. And *Four Saints* nearly sputtered out in the early stages of production because Stein and Thomson could not agree on a contract. In writing the libretto, Stein worked entirely alone.

But, although Stein wrote the libretto in isolation, the stage production of *Four Saints* was, like many works of poets' theater, an ambitiously collaborative affair. Theater is by nature a collaborative art that requires the cooperation of writers, directors, performers, designers, and technicians, but Stein's libretto itself invited an even greater degree of artistic collaboration. The script included no character designations, for example, so Thomson assigned lines and even invented roles. Thomson also divided the main character of Saint Therese into two roles "so that he could write duets" (Watson 48) and added a third syllable to her name ("Teresa," instead of "Therese" as it appears in Stein's text) because it sounded better when it was sung.[6] And Thomson chose to set to music even Stein's stage directions, "which were so clearly a part of the poetic continuity," Thomson later wrote in his autobiography, "that I did not think it proper to excise them" (Thomson 106). Once the score and libretto had been completed, Maurice Grosser, Thomson's companion of many years, developed the scenario. Although Grosser acknowledged that certain aspects were suggested by Stein and Thomson, the scenario was predominantly his own invention, and Thomson called it the "bedrock to our production" (239).

Despite its title, Stein's *Four Saints in Three Acts* contains dozens of saints and at least four acts. The act and scene divisions are not only irregular but inconsistent, which Thomson understood, according to Carl Van Vechten, to be Stein's "satirical jab at pedantry and formalism in general, her way of saying 'Don't fence me in!'" (Marranca "Introduction" xiii). Thomson had suggested that the opera be about "the working artist's life" (Watson 42), while Stein, recalling a trip to Avila in Spain that had moved her, proposed the use of Spanish saints (Saint Therese being one of her pet names for Alice B. Toklas). The opera is built not around a plot or narrative but rather around a series of tableaux of the saints' lives and movements—in one, for example, Saint Therese observes the heavens through a telescope; in another, she rocks an invisible child in her arms; and in another Saint Ignatius describes his vision of the Holy Ghost (the famous "Pigeons on the Grass Alas" section). Thomson added two new characters, the Compère and Commère, who served loosely as commentators on the stage action. Their lines comprise much of the libretto.

Four Saints was famously performed by an all black cast, a choice that was driven by Thomson's belief that African American performers would have the clear enunciation that he felt Stein's words required. Stein herself expressed concerns over this choice, but she did not reject it (Latimer 70–71). Although the casting decision was made on aesthetic grounds, its defiance of opera's norms of racial etiquette also had political implications. "Never before had African Americans been cast in a work that did not depict black life," observes Watson. "Never before had they been paid for rehearsals. And never before had an all-black cast performed in an opera before white audiences" (6).

Thus, while Stein's general approach to theater is evident in the lack of plot and attention to word constructions, the casting, music, scenario, costuming, set design, lighting, choreography, and even the assignment of lines to specific characters were all decided almost entirely without her input. But it would be incorrect to suggest that Stein's libretto was therefore largely independent of the production choices. In composing the score, for example, Thomson relied on the sounds of Stein's language. Stein "was not by nature," Thomson later recalled, "what we would call musical" (qtd in Watson 41), but he considered her writing

> wonderful to set to music because there was no temptation to illustrate the words. For the most part you didn't know what it meant anyway, so you couldn't make it like birdie babbling by a brook or heavy heavy hangs my heart. My theory being, and I still hold it to be true, you had to set it for the way the grammar went and for the clarity of the words. If you make the words clear for pronunciation, then the meaning will take care of itself. (qtd in Watson 38–39)

When Stein did finally see the production, she proclaimed (ingenuously or not) that it was "perfectly extraordinary how they carried out what I wanted" (qtd in Watson 298). As for the work's apparent incomprehensibility, she scoffed, "If you go to a football game you don't have to understand it in any way except the football way and all you have to do with *Four Saints* is to enjoy it in the *Four Saints* way which is the way I am, otherwise I would not have written it in that way" (ibid.). Still, a Columbia radio announcer later remembered the 1934 premiere this way: "Afterwards . . . people went away with an embarrassed feeling that the thing made more sense than they thought. They began to see that the authors wanted them to understand not illogical words but a fine symbolism of the gaiety and strength of spiritual, consecrated lives" (RCA Victor recording liner notes in Thomson, cond.).

Bay-Cheng's generally excellent study of Stein's drama within the context of the theatrical and cinematic avant-gardes bestows "transitional" status on *Four Saints* within Stein's overall dramatic development (53), and she considers it "marginal" in Stein's collected work (54). But Bay-Cheng's description of *Four Saints* as "language in chaos" (56) overlooks the affinities *Four Saints* has with Stein's verbal portraiture. Placing Stein within a larger modernist lineage, Bay-Cheng finds that Stein "uses the verbal fragment to represent her sense of a fractured reality" (57). But unlike modernists, who emphasized fracture and alienation, Stein's fragments are playful and exuberant, and the audience participation they require emphasizes not isolation and separation but rather multiple alternative possibilities for existence and connection.

The linkages between *Four Saints* and performative portraiture is explicitly indicated in the souvenir program for the 1934 Hartford premiere, which, according to art and cultural critic Tirza True Latimer, "provided more than a charming keepsake. Conceived as an enduring historical record, it presented the extraordinary event [of the opera's premiere] in calculated ways" (3). The program includes not only the usual production notes, photos, and commentary but also Stein's verbal portrait of Thomson, Thomson's musical portrait of Stein, and the neoromanticist visual portraits of Stein and Thomson by Christian Bérard and of Thomson by Kristians Tonny (see figs. 1 and 2). The inclusion of such a range of innovative portraiture in the program of a theatrical production that famously combined spectacle with experimental musical and verbal composition joins these creative styles so that *Four Saints* also comes to be seen as portraiture, a form that for Stein was, as discussed above, explicitly linked to her ongoing explorations of the relationship between representation and the performance of identity.

Thomson had written his musical portrait of Stein, "Miss Gertrude Stein as a Young Girl," in 1928, sending it to Stein in the mail, and Stein soon responded with her own verbal portrait of Thomson. Though produced in different media, both works rely on a restatement of motifs. Thomson had already set several of Stein's verbal portraits to music, and his musical portrait of Stein repeats musical phrases with different emphases, rather like Stein's own notion of insistence, by changing such features as rhythm and note length.[7] Stein's portrait of Thomson, beginning with "Yes ally. As ally. Yes ally yes as ally," repeats words and phrasings with dif-

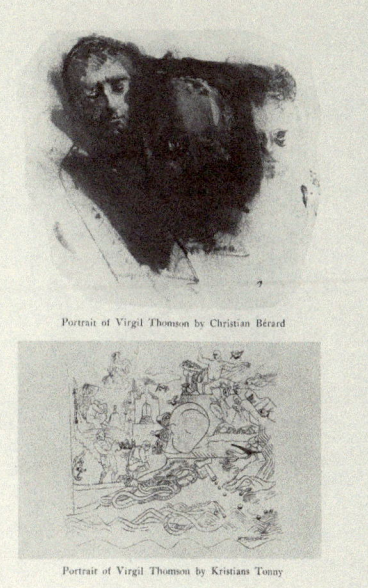

PORTRAIT OF VIRGIL THOMSON

BY GERTRUDE STEIN

Yes ally. As ally. Yes ally yes as ally. A very easy failure takes place. Yes ally. As ally. As ally yes a very easy failure takes place. Very good. Very easy failure takes place. Yes very easy failure takes place.

When with a sentence of intended they were he was neighbored by a bean.
Hour by hour counts.
How makes a may day.
Our comes back back comes out.
It is with a replica of seen. That he was neighbored by a bean.
Which is a weeding, weeding a walk, walk may do done delight does in welcome. Welcome daily is a home alone and our in glass turned around. Lain him. Power four lower lay lain as in case, of my whether ewe lain or to less. What was obligation furnished furs fur lease release in dear. Dear darken. It never was or with a call. My waiting. Remain remark taper or tapestry stopping stopped with a lain at an angle colored like make it as stray. Did he does he was or will well and dove as entail cut a pursuit purpose demean different dip in descent diphthong advantage about their this thin couple a outer our in glass pay white. What is it he admires. Are used to it. Owned when it has. For in a way. Dumbfounded. A cloud in superior which is awake a satisfy found. What does it matter as it happens. Their much is a nuisance when they gain as well as own. How much do they like why were they anxious. None make wishing a pastime. When it is confidence in offer which they came. How ever they came out. Like it. All a part. With known. But which is mine. They may. Let us need partly in case. They are never selfish.

These quotations determine that demonstration is arithmetic with laying very much their happening that account in distance day main lay coupled in coming joined. Barred harder. Very fitly elephant. How is it that it has come to pass. Whenever they can take into account. More of which that whatever they are later. Then without it be as pleases. In reflection their told. Made mainly violet in a man. Comfort in our meshes. Without any habit to have called Howard louder. That they are talkative. Most of all rendered. In a mine of their distention. Resting without referring. Just as it is. Come for this lain will in might it have taught as a dustless redoubt where it is heavier than a chair. How much can sought be ours. Wide or leant be beatific very preparedly in a covering now. It is always just as lost.

Harden as wean does carry a chair intake of rather with a better coupled just as a ream.

How could they know that it had happened.
If they were in the habit of not liking one day. By the time they were started. For the sake of their wishes. As it is every once in a while. Liking it for their sake made as it is.

Their is no need of liking their home.

Portrait of Virgil Thomson by Christian Bérard

Portrait of Virgil Thomson by Kristians Tonny

Fig. 1. Portraits of Virgil Thomson by Gertrude Stein, Christian Bérard, and Kristians Tonny included in the program for the 1934 premiere of *Four Saints in Three Acts* at the Wadsworth Atheneum, Hartford, Connecticut. (Gertrude Stein and Alice B. Toklas Papers, American Literature Collection, Beinecke Rare Book and Manuscript Library, Yale University.)

ferences in sound and order that alter both the words and their immediate context. Her portrait seems to simultaneously speak *to* an ally (presumably Thomson) and *as* an ally (presumably Stein). But the slight difference between the positions of these two allied interlocutors opens up the possibility of the "very easy failure" that emerges in the next line, a failure that Latimer concludes "acknowledges the fragility of alliances formed outside the law, outside first-tier institutions and the movements they legitimate, and outside traditional kinship structures" (60). What marks both Stein's and Thomson's works as portraiture, then, are their similar attempts to create an immediacy with the audience/reader/spectator that arises in the moment of engagement with the work.

Stein's portrait of Thomson, as well as the visual portraits of Stein and Thomson by Tonny and Bérard that appear in the souvenir program had originally appeared in *Dix Portraits*, an artists' book published in 1930

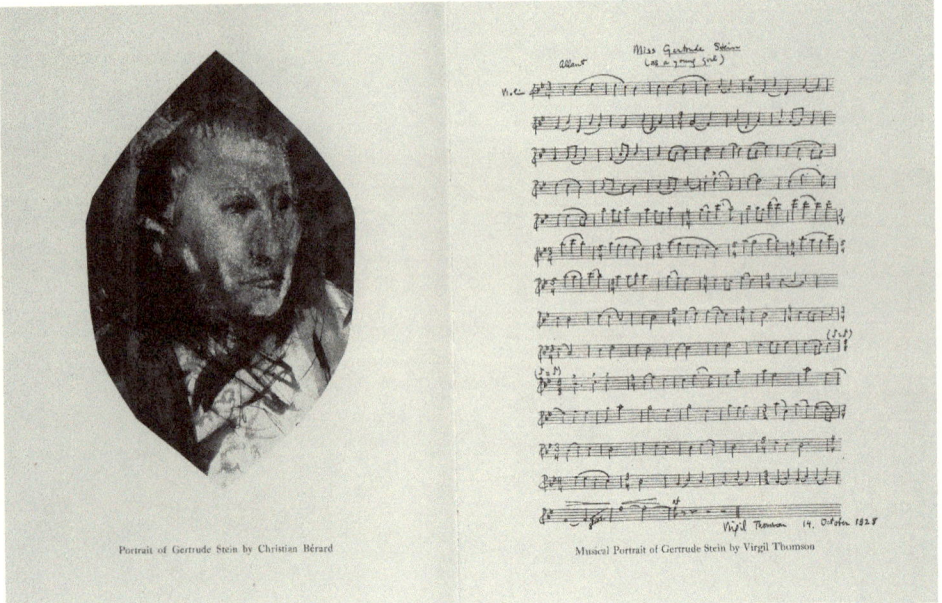

Fig. 2. Portraits of Gertrude Stein by Christian Bérard and Virgil Thomson
included in the program for the 1934 premiere of *Four Saints in Three Acts*
at the Wadsworth Antheneum, Hartford, Connecticut. (Gertrude Stein and
Alice B. Toklas Papers, American Literature Collection, Beinecke Rare Book
and Manuscript Library, Yale University.)

by Stein and several visual artists who were members of her coterie in
Paris.[8] The book included ten of Stein's verbal portraits accompanied by
ten visual portraits of their subjects.[9] While the materials and methods of
each medium differed, the verbal and visual portraits shared an affinity
by encouraging participatory engagements from their audiences. Bérard's
portrait of Thomson, for example, actually includes three renderings, each
under different lighting. "The multiplication of Thomson's likeness enliv-
ens the portrait," Latimer observes, "and activates the viewer by inducing
the eye to move from face to face" (60). While the formal language of the
visual renderings in *Dix Portraits* is more descriptive than Stein's verbal
portraiture overall, both exhibit a type of performativity, for, as Latimer
argues, the visual portraits "do not illustrate, but rather emanate. They
bear witness to the neo-romantics' engagement with one another, and
with portraiture itself—a genre that materializes the artist's private trans-

action with a complicit subject while providing a public record of that exchange" (18). Many of the artists in *Dix Portraits* were social and artistic dissidents, and one can read their rejection of modernist abstraction, as Latimer does, as a disavowal of the values of autonomy and universalism that undergirded it. In allying Stein's verbal portraiture and *Four Saints* with the neoromanticism of Tonny and Bérard, rather than with more abstract portraiture, *Four Saints'* souvenir program emphasizes affiliation and collaboration over autonomy and a measure of personal specificity over universalized abstraction. And this approach serves as a model for engaging with the opera as a whole.[10]

Stein's libretto is astonishingly lively on its own, but Thomson felt that his score enhanced it, producing "a pacing that is implied in that text . . . but that could never be produced without measured extensions [because] speech alone lacks music's forward thrust" (Thomson *Virgil* 105). A comparison of Stein's nonnarrative, nondescriptive libretto with two recorded performances of *Four Saints*, one a 1947 Columbia radio recording of an abridged performance, conducted by Thomson, and the other a 1981 performance at Rutgers church in New York, conducted by Joel Thome,[11] demonstrates that the libretto does not act as a mere "script" for performance but instead exists in dynamic tension with it. The relationship between the libretto, the musical score, and the performance is malleable and collaborative. At times the libretto takes the lead, appearing to demand and even generate the music and performance that surround it. At other times, the score kills the generativity of the libretto by fastening it back too forcefully to a single interpretation. At still other times, vocalized performance increases the generativity of the libretto by suggesting multiple layers of meaning through sound. While the sounded performance of the opera may in some moments match and in others cross the lexical boundaries of the scripted text, the results are variable, relying on an interaction between libretto, score, performance, and audience.

Perhaps the most performative moments of both the written libretto and the performance appear in the opera's most famous section, "Pigeons on the Grass Alas," an aria sung by Saint Ignatius in which he is visited by the Holy Ghost in the form of a pigeon. In performance, Saint Ignatius begins this section with what sounds like a dismissal, "Pigeons on the grass alas," only to ask in the next line, "If they were no pigeons what were they" (637). Unsure of what he is witnessing, he continues to muse, "If a magpie in the sky on the sky can not cry if the pigeon on the grass alas can alas," only to expand into the loosely connected phrases and sounds of "and to pass the pigeon on the grass alas and the magpie in the sky . . ." (ibid.). Up to this point, the meaning of Stein's words and Saint Ignatius's vocalized delivery in performance work largely together to give the impression of Saint Ignatius's own internal conversation in which he seems to be trying to figure out what he is witnessing on the grass. But the performance is not only descriptive but performative: the audience, too, is put in the position of puzzling out what they are experiencing along with Saint Ignatius as their own sensory and intellectual faculties are employed to materialize the performance in front of them. Soon the female chorus erupts onstage into rich and lively repetitions of consonant sounds: "Let Lucy Lily Lily Lucy Lucy let Lucy Lucy Lily Lily Lily Lily Lily Lily let Lily Lucy Lucy let Lily. Let Lucy Lily" (ibid). This litany of short, flapping "l" sounds, calling to mind a longer list including "light," "love," "laugh," "life," "live," and "lift," seem themselves to lift in flight. The first two syllables invite the reader to "let loose," which suggests freedom from constraint, not only of the page but also of conventions of social communication and public rules of etiquette. The reader/audience is urged to play with language and to laugh and enjoy it freely, to see the "silly" hidden in "Lucy Lily." When the chorus suddenly springs from the sides of the stage to surround and fill it, the music crosses athwart the lexical gaps of Stein's libretto, filling in the silence with music. The resulting burst of unconstrained musical energy matches the liveliness of the drifting, fluttering phonemes of the script, materializing Stein's portrait of a spiritual visitation. In their rising joy and almost giddy freedom, the words and music become both generative and affective. Here the generativity of Stein's language is so strong that it appears to create even the music that accompanies it.

Few texts can sustain the energy of the above example for any length of time, however, and the action of *Four Saints* can be seen in one way as a fluctuation between moments of unrestrained generativity and stasis. The prologue appears to recount Stein's fits and starts of writing in trying to "prepare for saints." In one attempt she offers a "narrative" in which, briefly summarized, some people go to the country on a beautiful day and see some things that please them (608). Given that this is perhaps the most stable and linear passage in the entire opera, it's worth noting that in one recorded performance this portion is omitted entirely, while in the other it is sung as a repetition of a single note without orchestral accompaniment. In the latter recording, the stasis of description translates as constrained tones rather than full-blown music. With speechlike sounds and no background music, the performance maintains the gaps of silence (however brief) between words and mimics the lexical integrity of the written libretto. As a moment in which vocalization matches the inscribed track of the text, meaning is stabilized both on the page and through sound.

Between the liberated generativity of "Let Lucy Lily" and the temporal linearity of narration, much of Stein's text syntactically teases the reader into expecting meaning only to resist it again. In the line "The difference between saints forget me nots and mountains" (610), for example, the syntax brings together an odd set for comparison, but comparison is certainly possible and, given the simple linear grammar, even expected, at least as a punch line if not as a serious answer. This expectation is heightened in performance: the Compère speaks, rather than sings, the words. As with the speechlike tones of the earlier narration, spoken delivery lexically constrains and contains the words in discrete units of conventional meaning. The expectation of a satisfying conclusion is thwarted, however, when the homophones of "have to have to have to at a time" explode the narration with double resistance, not only to the rigidity of syntactic structure but also to the constraint of speech. In this case, vocalized speech highlights the generativity of the libretto by seeming to double the words on the page. As the line progresses, the libretto and performance split: while the beginning of the line both on the page and in performance leads the reader/audience to expect stable meaning, the end of the line maintains that expectation in performance while subverting it on the page.

In addition to the sonic elisions and evocalized instability that multiply the libretto's potential meanings, there are other sound effects at play that come to differing results in performance. At times vocalized performance actually makes the libretto's generativity more readily apparent, as when vocalization assists the punning potential of lines such as "Add sum. Add some" (619), "Suddenly two see" (619), and "Scene once seen once" (623). At other times, the clear enunciation required by the opera (and desired by Thomson) makes potentially destabilizing sound elision harder to hear. And sometimes the score intentionally works against the libretto to humorous effect, as when a singer announces that "gaily the troubadour plays his guitar" (616) only to be followed not by the sound of a guitar but of a clarinet. Preceded and followed by lines suggesting that Saint Therese might have been a widow as a young girl or that she might, in fact, be Martha, the effect of the clarinet music is to further call identity and identifying characteristics into question. Thus, while, at different times, the sounded performance of the opera both matches and crosses the lexical boundaries of the libretto, the results are variable. Most combinations are idiosyncratic and alive to the conditions of performance.

These and other accumulated effects embody the dynamic interplay between the libretto, the score, the performance, and the audience. This wavering and collaborative tension that keeps the opera alive in the moment of performance is, as Stein explained in her characteristic prose, what prevented the problematic syncopation of conventional drama and instead turned it into what she called a "landscape."

> [T]he movement in it was like a movement in and out with which anybody looking on can keep in time. I also wanted it to have the movement of nuns very busy and in continuous movement but placid as a landscape has to be because after all the life in a convent is the life of a landscape, it may look excited a landscape does sometimes look excited but its quality is that a landscape if it ever did go away would have to go away to stay. Anyway the play as I see it is exciting and it moves but it also stays and that is as I said in the beginning might be what a play should do. ("Plays" 269)

Allied with portraiture rather than narrative, landscape plays both "move" and "stay." They use what Marianne DeKoven has called "lively words" in order to portray not a series of temporary moments in a moving story but rather what Stein saw as the movement of existence portrayed via tableaux (68). This movement manifests in Stein's performative writing through a mixture of verbal conventions, linguistic ideologies, and the material properties of language. In performance, the poetic generativity of the language works to undermine the coercion of narrative and of naturalized theatrical representations.

Performing Freedom

Although she associated the liveliness of her language with a particular kind of American movement and her work has inspired many American writers and theater artists, Stein spent virtually her whole life outside the United States. In fact both Thomson and Stein lived in Paris, which offered a more supportive atmosphere for artistic experiment. But they shared a strong regard and affinity for their birth nation, and this affection found its way into their themes as well as their forms. "I wrote in Paris music that was always, in one way or another, about Kansas City," Thomson later remarked. "I wanted Paris to know Kansas City, to understand the ways we like to think and feel" (qtd in R. Jackson 3; cited in Hitchcock and Fussell liv). Even Stein's strategy of insistence might be thought of as an expression of her home country, for Stein considered movement to be quintessentially American: "Think of anything, of cowboys, of movies, of detective stories, of anybody who goes anywhere or stays at home and is an American and you will realize that it is something strictly American to conceive a space that is filled with moving, a space of time that is always filled with moving" ("Gradual" 286). What made such movement distinctly American for Stein was its characteristic of complete independence—although America was in a state of constant movement, it was not, she repeatedly asserted, "moving against anything" ("Portraits" 287). American movement was not movement as resistance, nor even movement as progress, but rather movement as the very essence of independence: the unique expression of the nation itself. She conceived of the movement manifested in her language, both on the page and on the stage, as a portrait of America, at least in spirit if not always in actual fact. Stein did, of course, write about many non-American subjects, and her portraits were most often of the many people and things she encountered in her life in France. One of her best-known verbal portraits, "Susie Asado," depicts a Spanish flamenco dancer, and *Four Saints* is a cosmopolitan play about Spanish saints. But for Stein the very idea of movement, enacted in the liveliness of her language, was at the heart of American identity itself.

But there's another side to Stein's lively language as a portrait of the United States in the early twentieth century. Stein claimed that the key to her compositional style was not in looking but rather in "talking and listening." While simultaneous talking and listening may appear to be a recipe for distraction, for Stein they allowed for greater attention: "Nothing makes any difference as long as some one is listening while they are talking. If the same person does the talking and the listening why so much the better there is just much the greater concentration. One may really indeed say that that is the essence of genius, of being most intensely alive, that is being one who is at the same time talking and listening" ("Portraits" 290). Late-nineteenth-century notions of attention and distraction, as Jonathan Crary has shown, were caught up with capitalist processes of modernization. The problem of attention, Crary explains, "was elaborated within an emergent economic system that demanded attentiveness of a subject in a wide range of new productive and spectacular tasks, but whose internal movement was continually eroding the basis of any disciplinary attentiveness. Part of the cultural logic of capitalism demands that we accept as *natural* switching our attention rapidly from one thing to another" (29–30). This is a particularly suggestive way to consider Stein's comment, quoted above, that "it is something strictly American to conceive a space that is filled with moving." Her description of an American as someone who knows "just how many seconds minutes or hours it is going to take to do a whole thing," recalling Crary's description of capitalist culture, implies a dark side to Stein's emphasis on attention and what she perceived as characteristically American movement. Indeed, Crary argues that in cultural discourses of subjectivity, "attention is the means by which an individual observer can transcend those subjective limitations and make perception *its own*, and attention is at the same time a means by which a perceiver becomes open to control and annexation by external agencies" (5 italics original). The problems of movement, attention, and subjectivity that Stein's portraits engage are therefore involved in a larger cultural struggle between freedom and control.

Stein used language in ways that thwarted normative logics of communication and social relations, and many critics have seen Stein's writing as subversive. Sue-Ellen Case, for example, aligns Stein's writing with lesbian feminism in its use of spatial subversions that undermine the heterosexism of grammatical coupling by "repetitively circulat[ing] meaning in the system of representation while keeping its denotation unavailable" ("Performing" Part II 341). But, while Stein was a transgressive expatriate Jewish lesbian at the center of a Parisian community of artists and writers composed largely of gay men and other social misfits, she was hardly a feminist. Worse, and more confoundingly, she was a Vichy collaborator, whose close friendship with Vichy official Bernard Faÿ helped protect her (and her art collection) during the war.[12] She volunteered to translate anti-Semitic speeches by Marshal Philippe Pétain, head of the Vichy government, and even referred to herself as a "propagandist" for the "new France" (Will "Strange Politics" n.p.). As Barbara Will points out, Stein compared Pétain to George Washington and Benjamin Franklin and imagined that his revolution would "negate the decadence of the modern era and bring America back to its eighteenth-century values" (ibid.).

Just as critics have linked Ezra Pound's support of Mussolini to his art, so, too, Stein's politics should not be ignored in any discussion of the cultural ideology of her aesthetics. What remains unclear, however, is exactly how to characterize that relationship. Despite her support of Pétain, Stein's creative works were seen as a political threat, and her name appeared in 1943 on La Liste Otto, the list of books banned by the Nazis (from which her friend Faÿ may have helped have her name removed). And at the same time that Stein was growing closer to Faÿ, she was also beginning her collaborations with Thomson on *Four Saints*, even producing verbal portraits of both men in the same year. Certainly, the freedom performed by Stein's poetics can be exercised either as a regressive apoliticality or as a subversive undermining of oppressive social regimes of expression, and debates over just how such artistic abstraction should be taken have long occupied critics of modernist and avant-garde art. But the model of reception explicitly encouraged by the souvenir program for the premiere production of *Four Saints* comes down firmly on the side of community and collaboration over abstraction and apoliticality. And it is this model that seems to have most influenced the poets' theaters of the 1950s and 1960s.

Stein's most direct impact on postwar poets' theater appears in the work of the Judson Poets' Theater in the 1960s, especially in their musical adaptations of Stein's own plays, a history that Stephen Bottoms recounts in *Playing Underground*. The Judson was neither the first nor the most influential poets' theater, but its reputation helped establish the place of poets' theater, and of Stein in particular, amid the rise of off-off-Broadway theater. Over a career spanning more than twenty years, it staged no fewer than seven plays written by Stein or adapted from her writings, including *What Happened, Three Sisters Who Are Not Sisters, In Circles, Listen to Me*, and *Doctor Faustus Lights the Lights*. Like the original 1934 production of *Four Saints*, each Judson production of Stein's work was highly collaborative, and each was inspired but not controlled by the model of cultural resistance Stein's writings performed. The Judson Poets' Theater was an outreach program of the Judson Memorial Church in the heart of Greenwich Village. "From the start," Bottoms notes, "the church's history was bound up with social activism, which was considered integral to its identity and mission, rather than a mere sideline to religious observance" (66). While Bottoms doesn't explicitly connect the political mission of the Judson with its choice to stage so many of Stein's plays, he does note the appeal of the collaborative opportunities Stein's plays offered. He also argues that Stein's work "provided the single biggest influence on [the Judson's] evolving aesthetic," which consisted of "a particular confluence of theater, visual arts, music, and dance . . . emphasizing the immediate present of performance"

(147). And he attributes the success of the Judson's productions of Stein in the 1960s to Stein's decentralization of interpretive authority and emphasis on perceptual processes (148).

While the Judson's use of Stein is perhaps the clearest sign of her influence on poets' theater, it is not the only one. As I discuss in chapter 3, for example, the Living Theatre's engagement with Stein was an important but not entirely successful step on its path toward developing a particular style of political theater. In the 1990s, both Carla Harryman and Suzan-Lori Parks found inspiration in Stein for some of their more overtly political performances, as I discuss in chapters 5 and 6 respectively. And many of the artists and festivals I discuss in the "Epilogue" that keep poets' theater alive today count Stein as an important forerunner. If poets' theater can be said to have a mother, surely it must be Gertrude Stein.

CHAPTER TWO

"Everyone is watching us!"

The Poets' Theatre, Cambridge, Massachusetts, 1950–1956

In the summer of 1950, a group of poets gathered in Cambridge, Massachusetts, for a fireside chat. The purpose of the meeting was to discuss the possibility of forming an amateur theater group aimed at encouraging the writing and performing of contemporary American poetic drama, and the idea was attractive enough to draw a mix of the noteworthy, the unknown, and the not yet known—including Richard Eberhart, Mary (Molly) Manning Howe, Lyon Phelps, Donald Hall, Robert Bly, Hugh Amory, Frank O'Hara, and others. In the academically oriented and critically celebrated poetry scene of Cambridge and Boston in the 1940s and 1950s, a group of Harvard-affiliated poets gathering to discuss writing not poetry but drama might seem intentionally subversive. But thanks to T. S. Eliot, Christopher Fry, W. H. Auden, and Archibald MacLeish, verse drama had become a popular and viable form of postwar American theater.

At least one Cambridge critic was suspicious of this public hunger for verse drama, however, remarking contemptuously that it simply "fulfill[ed] a public need in a philistine era—to assuage the audience's feelings of guilt for not reading poetry: a guilt that [audiences wrongly felt] could be dissolved by the penance of seeing Fry's *The Dark Is Light Enough*" (Sayre *Previous* 96). But the poet-dramatists of the Poets' Theatre, while grateful for the renewed interest in poetry that verse drama had fostered, did not consider themselves the artistic inheritors of Eliot and Fry, instead finding inspiration in Samuel Beckett, Alfred Jarry, Jean Cocteau, Bertolt Brecht, and Federico García Lorca, as well as in poets "who had not written for theatre as yet," as Lyon Phelps put it in a 1958 interview (Phelps, Manning, Jack Rogers n.p.). With a nod to their intentional antiprofessionalism, Bly suggested that they call themselves the Shabby Theatre (ibid.). They settled instead on the Poets' Theatre and agreed to meet again at the end of the summer but only if enough of their members had written complete plays by then.

Despite Phelps's limited expertise—he had never published a poem and had no experience writing for the theater—his idea for a theater dedicated exclusively to poetic drama "caught on like wildfire," as Eberhart later remarked ("Poets'" 19). But Phelps needed others with theater expertise and financial connections to help him carry out his vision, and he was soon joined in leadership by the Irish actress and playwright Mary Manning Howe and the poet and Boston socialite V. R. (Violet Ranney) Lang. Howe, a writer, performer, drama and film critic, and lifelong friend of Samuel Beckett (as well as the mother of poets Susan and Fanny Howe), had performed at the Abbey Theatre, where she worked with Yeats, and at the Gate Theatre before moving to Cambridge with her husband, who had joined the faculty at the Harvard Law School, and she had begun directing plays at Radcliffe College. Peter Davison has called Howe "the *madre buffa* of the Poets' Theatre" and its "most important figure" (25); Nora Sayre calls her "the Lady Gregory of the Poets' Theatre" (*Previous* 196). Dynamic and enthusiastic, but also critical and even skeptical, she was a guiding force in the development of the Poets' Theatre, and she frequently served as one of the group's spokespersons. Her stage adaptation of James Joyce's *Finnegans Wake* in 1955 was one of the Poets' most critically acclaimed and successful productions.

But, despite Howe's list of accomplishments, it was Lang who had the most influence over the Poets' Theatre in its early years. Lang, known as "Bunny," was certainly the group's most colorful member, and she was the only member who had no affiliation with Harvard. Her poetry had been published in *Poetry* and the *Chicago Review*, which earned her the respect of young poets like Phelps, most of whom had been published so far only in the *Harvard Advocate*, their alma mater magazine, or not at all (Lurie 13). Passionate and full of flair, Lang championed theatricality and embraced raw antiprofessionalism, and she worked with the Poets' Theatre as actor, director, costume designer, and especially promoter. As several members recount, Lang's hand was everywhere, and she was a key figure during the important early years of the Poets' Theatre when its support for new poetic writing fostered the careers of several poet-playwrights who later carried its vision forward to New York theaters. From the group's founding until her own untimely death of cancer in 1956 at the age of thirty-two, Lang's involvement, more than that of any other member, helped to shape the course of postwar American poetic theater.

Together Phelps, Howe, and Lang personified the competing drives of the early Poets' Theatre. It was not strictly a venue for poetry, "serious" theater, or popular theatricality but rather a merging of those interests. And in this sometimes uneasy merging, American poets' theater began to assert its identity distinct from the verse drama that had preceded it. The story of the early Poets' Theatre is therefore, in some sense, a description of the initial emergence of postwar American poets' theater and the struggle between poetic and theatrical values it embodies. It is also a narrative of the shifting relationship between artist and academic in the early postwar period, as the Poets' Theatre grappled with its own institutionalization and "success." As Sally Banes has demonstrated, colleges and universities in the postwar period expanded their training programs for artists and became unofficial patrons of the avant-garde. At the same time, some artists resisted such institutionalization, usually not by rejecting monetary support so much as by assuming an oppositional attitude. During its early years, the Poets' Theatre secured funding for an artist's residency and established a special Poets' Theatre series with Harvard University Press. But both were short-lived, and their histories reveal the Poets' Theatre's evolving relationship with its own aesthetic stance.

The Poets' (as it was known) was the first and certainly one of the most successful of several poets' theaters that thrived in the United States in the 1950s, and it served as a direct predecessor and inspiration to a number of poets' theaters that soon arose in New York. Stephen Bottoms locates New York's poets' theaters in the 1960s somewhere between commercial and underground theater for the ways in which these companies "marked themselves out as more consciously avant-garde" while still retaining an "earthy," amateurish grit and boldness (61). But the merging of poetry, art, and popular theatrical forms such as film and vaudeville to which Bottoms attributes the stand-out success of New York's Judson Poets' Theater, for example, was preceded by the productive melding of "high" and "low" cultural forms of the Poets' Theatre a decade earlier in Cambridge.

The Poets' Theatre is therefore important for a number of reasons. Not only is it our earliest example of poets' theater, a significant midcentury American experimental theater practice with roots in the modernist avant-garde, but its influence on later poets' theaters was direct—Frank O'Hara, John Ashbery, James Schuyler, and James Merrill, for example, all wrote plays for the Poets' early in their careers before producing other plays and further developing their careers elsewhere. Moreover, the Poets' offers a unique example not of a poets' theater that disappeared because of the all too familiar story of no funding and an inability to fill seats but rather, perhaps ironically, because its commercial success finally made it too much of a business concern to carry forward its early experimentalism.

While the Poets' Theatre was in continuous operation from 1950 to 1968, its first seven years, from 1950 to 1956, were its most active period for working out its vision of American poetic theater. It was a period in which Lang was passionately encouraging young writers (such as when she invited the young Gregory Corso to help with sweeping, do a bit of acting, and eventually write a play) and embracing antiprofessionalism. Meanwhile, Phelps was busily drawing up formal procedures for the selection of plays to be produced by the Poets' Theatre. And Howe served as the group's "theatrical conscience . . . [knowing] better than any of her young colleagues what was playable, what would or wouldn't work onstage" (Sayre *Previous* 196). And under this joint tutelage, with a bit of bumping and scraping, the Poets' Theatre began to stage its first performances.

Audience Training

Mounting a theatrical production demands much greater resources than staging a poetry reading. Theater requires multiple performers, as well as designers, directors, rehearsal space, materials, equipment, and time. Even a relatively short rehearsal period requires much more time and coordination than a poet preparing a solo reading does. While excited and supportive artists may initially volunteer their efforts, a theater, in order to sustain itself, must have paying patrons and, most important, financial backers to invest in its vision. The early Poets' Theatre relied heavily on its Harvard affiliations while it alternated between professionalism and intentional resistance to such professionalism, producing a range of work of varying aims and quality that straddled the space between poetry and theater. Many of its playwrights worked primarily as poets but were also attracted to the possibilities of the theater. Some simply updated classical dramatic stories and conflicts, but others were self-consciously drawn to the ways in which the theatrical event allowed them to explore the receptive situation of their work.

Ironically, the group's first staged event, in November 1950, was an evening not of plays but of poetry readings that had been quickly arranged to drum up interest. Lyon Phelps delivered a speech on the vision and goals of the Poets' Theatre in which he emphasized the importance of poetic language over visual effect. While the venture was largely conceived as a writerly project, Phelps also argued that "the training of an audience is inseparable from the training of ourselves as poet-playwrights" ("Objectives" 5). Training the audience meant self-consciously exposing it to the mechanisms of theater. Unlike Brechtian theater, which kept its audiences distant, many of the Poets' productions explicitly invited the audience in—through, for example, the use of Noh devices (which would also be employed later by avant-garde groups such as the Wooster Group), coterie references, and intentional amateurism, all aimed not only at breaking through the illusion of theater but also at breaking down the distance between audience and performer. Such self-conscious acknowledgment encouraged audience members to think about their role as interpreters of the representations being presented. And indeed one of the most enduring characteristics of poets' theater is this interrogation of the audience's own interpretive activities.

Of course many avant-garde theaters of the period were engaged in exploring new audience-performer relationships. Disrupting the verisimilitude of the stage was a favorite strategy, and the Poets', too, frequently employed techniques that would break through the stage illusion, such as the use of a metatheatrical frame to emphasize the constructedness of the work and to acknowledge the larger theatrical situation, which relied on the presence of an audience. For the Poets', such strategies were aimed at dismantling the boundaries between "art" and "reality" and inviting interpretive collaboration. As a subcategory of avant-garde theater, poets' theater's particular emphasis is on the play of language, and the Poets' reconceptualization of verse drama was the weapon it most frequently wielded in its war against verisimilitude. In practice, its uses of poetic language varied widely. At times poetry appeared to be merely a mode of delivery, as with verse drama, employed to create a more symbolic work. More often, though, poetry was juxtaposed with prose, though to differing effects: sometimes poetry was used to get at a greater "truth"; sometimes it was deployed to add weight and seriousness to the speaker; sometimes it was used to satirize poetry's "high" cultural associations; and sometimes it was engaged to defamiliarize the dialogue, drawing attention to the constructedness of a play's narrative and/or representations. Frequently, multivocal poetic language was also used to cast the audience in a more active interpretive role—a general theatrical strategy that became even more common in the 1960s and 1970s. The juxtaposition of different poetic registers and the use of more colloquial language that appealed directly to the performers' social milieu were also employed to undermine the dominant formal language of the theater. Such a range of strategies and approaches was on display in the Poets' inaugural production on February 26, 1951.

This first official program of plays by the Poets' Theatre, a free production at Cambridge's Christ Church Parish House, embodied and dramatized such issues as the value of mimeticism, the role of the theater audience, the collaborative nature of theater production and reception, and poetry's relationship with all these. The evening included four brief one-act plays: Frank O'Hara's *Try! Try!*, John Ashbery's *Everyman*, Richard Eberhart's *The Apparition*, and Lyon Phelps's *Three Words in No Time*.[1] Promotional illustrations were designed in the signature style of O'Hara's Harvard dorm-mate Edward Gorey, who later earned a lasting reputation for his macabre children's stories and illustrations such as *The Gashlycrumb Tinies* (and who penned plays for the Poets' about such topics as a teddy bear sneaking past an arguing couple into the nursery to commit a murder). Gorey, along with Alison (Bishop) Lurie, also designed the sets and costumes. The evening was a collaborative effort by the whole group. Lang directed and starred alongside Ashbery in O'Hara's play, O'Hara composed music for Ashbery's play, Howe directed Ashbery's and Eberhart's plays, poets Donald Hall and Bill Matchett acted, and poet Hugh Amory served as stage manager. The evening drew a "large and sympathetic audience," according to one reviewer (Elisberg), and while the writing was uneven and often marred by language not suited to stage production, the acting was largely sincere, enthusiastic, and amusing. The first evening of poets' theater was a success.

Taken together, these short plays not only demonstrate some of the key concerns of the group but, in their progression over the course of the evening from the more conventional verse drama of Ashbery's *Everyman* through the increasingly experimental poets' theater of Eberhart's *The Apparition*, O'Hara's *Try! Try!*, and Phelps's *Three Words in No Time*, the succession of plays might be taken as an argument about where the future of American poets' theater should be headed. Of course, it would be misleading to suggest that the path was clear. The collaborative nature of the group meant that different visions of poetic theater stood, sometimes uneasily, side by side. But all members of the Poets' Theatre were interested in exploring the ability of poetry to better express reality in a medium that had grown stale and false. Ashbery's *Everyman* and O'Hara's *Try! Try!* both used poetry to communicate the realities of an ugly world, but O'Hara's play also challenged easy consumption of the conventional man-returned-home-from-war narrative. Eberhart's *The Apparition* and Phelps's *Three Words in No Time* both thematized the audience itself and explored the formation of the audience as subject, a concern that would occupy many practitioners of poets' theater over the years.

Opening the Poets' inaugural evening was Ashbery's *Everyman*, a loose adaptation of the medieval morality drama and by far the most conventional of the evening's offerings. Written entirely in poetic language thick with its own significance and emotion, *Everyman* is, in both its form and style, more closely allied with modernist verse drama than with poets' theater. The play begins with Everyman informing his wife, Columbine, that he has been called to war and must go on a journey to "a log cabin the size of an icebox, and twice as cold and uninteresting"—that is, to face Death.[2] Although Columbine begs to go with him, Everyman refuses to put her in such danger. He sets off alone into a world of war, where practicality is what matters, love is "useless," and Death dooms "all arts and speeches on which no action hinges." Left at home with her artful speech, Columbine waits and worries that her husband will be sent home as "an amorous skeleton, clothed in geraniums, with a card signed 'Compliments of Jerry.'" Everyman, sustained by his devotion to his wife, returns home a year later, but they have both been changed by the experience and the reunion is bittersweet. Love may not, the play suggests, be able to completely beat back the ugliness of the world even as it offers some solace and warmth in the face of loneliness and isolation.

With its familiar narrative and conventional presentation style, Ashbery's play, unlike the evening's other plays, explored neither the conventions of theatrical representation nor the audience's role in the theatrical experience. And, unlike O'Hara's *Try! Try!*, which juxtaposed naturalistic dialogue with poetic language in order to critique dramatic clichés and examine the line between art and ugly reality, *Everyman* used densely poetic language to attach symbolic weight to the entire play rather than to structure the drama. Ashbery's first contribution to the Poets' Theatre was therefore more closely aligned with the modernist verse drama of MacLeish and Eliot than with the newly emerging poets' theater.

The second play on the bill, Richard Eberhart's *The Apparition*, was a play about a play, not an uncommon trope in postwar theater.[3] Three couples—Robin and Beryl Everyman, Jason and Wendy Curley, and Charlie and Grayce Westgate—are gathered at the Everymans' home for an evening of amateur theater. When Jason, a scholar who is "tired of footnotes"

(45), asks what sort of play is on order for the evening, the other couples respond with sexual innuendo, suggesting something "light" and "spicy," some "frothy fun" and "a quickie" (45). A divan is pulled into the middle of the room, Robin becomes "John," and the play begins. The play within the play centers on the story of an unconsummated sexual tryst in a hotel bedroom in a large midwestern city. A Girl, nineteen years old, knocks randomly on John's hotel room door, where he has been writing a romantic and densely poetic letter to his wife from the road. Hearing the knock, John lets the Girl in. A postal worker and fan of the poetry of Robinson Jeffers (known for blank verse epics with a bleak view of humanity), the Girl is bored with her boyfriend and is being urged by her mother to "renounce" this "vile" world by joining a convent. She plans to spend the next month in West Palm Beach where she can live in the sunshine while she decides what to do. John asks the Girl to make "a little love" and plies her with alcohol, but the Girl "hate[s] love. It makes me sick in the stomach" (50), and she leaves John alone in his room to continue writing his poetic letter to his wife. The couples then begin enthusiastically critiquing the play in comically critical and increasingly nonsensical terms: "No play, if she had been five years older," "She would be played on in another way," "The play's the sting," "The audience would want more billing and wooing" (51). But Robin protests that the play is both "pure imagination" and "absolute reality" (51). As the critiques continue, the language of the exchange becomes more rhythmic, rhyming, and playful, and the scene less naturalistic, even as the speech patterns of the characters continue to mimic a conversation.

The frame structure of *The Apparition* examines the power dynamics both of social life and of the theater itself. The play especially indicts the manners and behaviors of the middle class, whose sense of power and superiority is tinged with sexual exploitation. Perhaps not coincidentally, Eberhart had met fellow poet-playwright William Carlos Williams at the Yaddo artists' colony in the early summer of 1950, and the two continued to exchange letters for many years. *The Apparition* shares some key features with Williams's most famous poetic play, *Many Loves* (published in 1942 and first produced in 1959 by the Living Theatre, discussed in chapter 3). Both works place a realist inner play being performed for an onstage audience inside a dramatic frame with poetic dialogue that represents the "present." Both also intertwine themes of theatrical performance and (failed) seduction. Sarah Bay-Cheng and Barbara Cole have argued that Williams's *Many Loves* "adopts the conventions of the realist drama as a façade for sexual power and exploitation" (231), and the same could be said of *The Apparition*. Both plays turn realism against the audience. But Eberhart's play thematizes the audience in part to criticize its traditional evaluative role as exploitative. Like Phelps's play later in the evening, it uses the play-within-a-play structure to make the audience-characters onstage both viewers and objects of a performance (though not with the same self-conscious awareness of this dual role as that exhibited by the characters in Phelps's play). Although the Girl in the inner play refuses John's advances, the couples in the frame smugly imagine ways in which the narrative might better control her to meet their desire for titillation. And, while it may be too much to say that the play forces the Poets' Theatre audience into a more active relationship with the play, the punning, playful language of the couples in the living room invites audience members to laugh along uncomfortably as they decipher the jokes and not so subtle innuendos, leaving them to ponder the physical and psychic distancing that turns them into subjects and the performers into objects. In fact, it is precisely the separation between the audience as subject and the theatrical work as object that allows for the couple's derision and control. Ironizing this separation, Eberhart's play suggests that the depersonalized collective response that objectifies the work and its representations has the power to turn humans into mere material in the service of a mimetic project. Here the problem seems to be not that the integrity of the work of art is compromised but that the social impact of consuming such representations is ignored.

The Poets' Theatre's attention to the receptive situation, and in particular its self-conscious examination of the role of the audience, might be best understood within the larger context of what Daniel Belgrad has termed the postwar "culture of spontaneity." Multiple artistic responses to the dominant Cold War ideology, which preached the doctrine of rational individualism and advocated consumerism and technological progress as the cures for economic and political crises, fall under this umbrella. Aesthetics of spontaneity—ranging in Belgrad's account from "the ideogram" to "spontaneous bop prosody"—emphasized "intersubjectivity and mind-body holism" and promoted "alternatives to the social and psychological arrangements on which corporate liberalism was based" (247–48). Belgrad includes in his account such artists as Charles Olson and Jackson Pollock, who, "influenced by surrealism and Jungian psychology, endeavored to recreate the 'primitive' worldview of 'participation mystique,'" and later, in the 1940s, those who practiced the "energy field" model of art—that is, "the concept of the human body-mind as an event in a field of energy[, which] propelled poetry and painting in the direction of the performing arts"—such as bebop jazz musicians and Beat writers (248).

Many of the Poets' Theatre's early productions shared this emphasis on the spontaneous event by emphasizing audience activity. Several also thematically challenged the ideal of rational individualism by undermining such dominant constructions as the hero narrative and the ideals of the solitary genius artist and the independent work of art. Others incorporated an "artist" or "poet" character as a compromised figure rather than an objective interpreter of the world's truths. Such an attack on objectivity was in itself a cultural politics. As Belgrad points out, "Corporate liberalism embraced an ontology and epistemology of objectivity, which was the basis of its advanced technological mastery of nature. Against this, spontaneity posed intersubjectivity, in which 'reality' was understood to emerge through a conversational dynamic" (5). But, unlike Beat poetry and abstract expressionist painting, poets' theater was not an expressivist art, and its goal was not to harness the rhetorical force of language or to explore its communicative value. While its early anti-illusionism and regard for subjective audience perceptions allied it with spontaneity's joining of body, emotions, and intellect, its stance toward the audience was ambivalent. Rather than seeking to close the gap between art, artist, and audience, the Poets' Theatre made a principle of it.

The evening's third play, Frank O'Hara's *Try! Try!*,[4] even more self-consciously examined the conventions of theater by denaturalizing actor-character identification and introducing "extremely stylized" gestures, emphasized by the lighting and other defamiliarizing techniques ("It might be nice," the script reads, "to have John follow the other two characters' lines with a copy of the script, dropping the pages ostentatiously to the floor as the play went on, one by one" [18]).[5] Like Ashbery's *Everyman*, O'Hara's play addressed the impact of war on domestic relationships. Violet waits for her husband, Jack, to return from war, but when he finally does, he's a changed man. As Violet waits, she speaks with John, a "friend of the poet," who also serves as the play's commentator. As with Ashbery's play, there is a sense here that poetry can better communicate the world's harsh truths. Jack's poetic stylings are not an escape from the ugliness of war but a way to defamiliarize the expression of emotional experience, and perhaps also a way to bear it. But Jack's description of his life as a soldier is exaggerated and self-glorifying. Meanwhile, Violet's use of poetry seems to reach toward beauty and imagination as a way to combat the plain practicalities and pain of the world. When John suggests that perhaps "the poet" (a reference that seems to stand in for a generalized idea of poetry) is responsible for Violet's confusion and disillusionment with the real world, Jack interjects that the poet isn't to blame, for Jack himself is the one who left. Yes, Violet looks for beauty and lyricism in the midst of the world's dirty realities, just as she will keep "grubbing in the laundry basket, always hoping to be surprised by something lovely and disturbing, like a crystal hand emerging with a sparkler." But such imagination, the play argues, provides the comfort of deeper truths and possibilities that may be overlooked by too much realism. In the final line of the play, John advises the couple to "be wise" and "forget that the kitchen is full of knives." As the characters speak in verse, the play's narrative surface suggests the power of poetry to both transcend the world's harshness and get at deeper truths that may lie hidden beneath such surface realities.

This plot summary may make the play sound like an escapist fantasy, but from its first lines, the Poets' Theatre production self-consciously used devices designed to prevent audiences from losing themselves in the stage illusion. "My name is Violet" the play begins, and indeed, the three main characters, Violet, John, and Jack, were acted by their namesakes, Violet Lang (who also served as the play's director), John Ashbery, and Jack Rogers, each a prominent member of the Poets' Theatre community. This deidentification of character and actor created a sense of spontaneity and informality that joined performers and audience in a single community. When Violet says she doesn't like her name and so prefers to go by other names—"even the most ridiculous diminutives are pleasanter to my ears," she quips—opening night audience members paused as they recognized the reference to Lang's own nickname and then burst into laughter. In fact, multiple references to the poets' actual lives peppered the play. O'Hara wrote the play while he was in graduate school in Ann Arbor, Michigan, and desperately missing his Cambridge friends, and Andrew Epstein reads the play as "an expression of O'Hara's anxieties about being exiled from his own home front" and as an enactment of "the triangular struggle between two male poets [O'Hara and Ashbery] for the love and attention of a female muse [Lang]" (*Beautiful* 250, 253). But, while audience members appreciated these in-jokes and personal references, board member Thornton Wilder, disturbed by the audience's voluble responses, jumped out of his seat during the intermission to scold the audience for laughing during the play (Sayre *Previous* 198). Not everyone, it seems, got the satire. [6]

Phelps credited Lang's direction, especially her use of stylized gestures adapted from Noh, along with O'Hara's writing, for the play's comic success. Because of this framing, the play's emotionality is mocked rather than reinforced. While Jack recounts the horrors of war, for example, John plays melancholy music on a gramophone as if in melodramatic accompaniment. Philip Auslander also locates in *Try! Try!* a parody of the controlled and ritualistic cloth folding that Yeats prescribed for the opening and closing of the plays in his verse drama quartet *Four Plays for Dancers*, which begins with *At the Hawk's Well*.

> *Try[!] Try[!]* contains a very similar instruction: "Violet slumps over the ironing board, holding her arms out stiffly in front, and Jack ceremoniously removes his cap and jacket and hangs them over her clasped hands" (23). O'Hara's direction may not be a direct parody of Yeats, though a Harvard audience could have been expected to catch the illusion, but it is clearly making light of the idea of ritualistic action in a contemporary dramatic context, while simultaneously reinforcing the image of Violet's stultifying domesticity by making of her a living coat rack. (56)

Counterposing melodrama with stylized poetic form, O'Hara uses the familiar story of a returning veteran struggling to reassimilate to domestic life as a means of satirizing high art pretensions. But, as Auslander points out, O'Hara may also be trying "to elevate kitsch to the status of art" (57). In competing for dominance, the frames of melodrama and "serious" art each reveal and mock the conventions of the other.

This issue of framing was literalized in the final play of the evening, Phelps's *Three Words in No Time*, which also drew on the strategies of Noh theater to self-consciously thematize the role of the audience. The "place" of the play, as indicated in the stage directions, is "the theatre itself," while the "scene" is "a life-sized portrait of Melville's study in the Berkshires," an imaginative distinction that thematizes the differences between pictorial art and live embodied theater.[7] As a painter emerges from the curtain and places a placard on an easel stenciled with the title "THREE WORDS IN NO TIME," two women, Frances and Gladys, enter through the back of the house, climb the stage, and eye the audience as one whispers to the painter. The women have come to view the painter's contemporary "representationalist" portrait of Herman Melville, Melville's wife Elizabeth, and his friend Nathaniel Hawthorne, but they are perplexed by the choice of a theater as the venue for the exhibit. Being the object of the audience's gaze makes Frances uncomfortable, and she protests, "Everyone is watching us!" But Gladys scolds her for imagining herself as the object of the audience's attention. "You're so naïve," Gladys tells Frances, and then Gladys informs the audience, "We're just watching too."

In identifying the women themselves as both part of and separate from the audience, the play implicates the audience in the play's coming to life. The women are both objects and subjects. As figures in a staged play, they are contrasted with the representationalism of the framed portrait onstage. The painter asserts that his portrait is neither theft nor quotation but "adoration." "I adore," he explains, "and hope through some action that my adoration will acquire meaning." And suddenly the figures in the portrait come to life inside the picture frame, an event that the figure of Hawthorne (within the portrait) ties directly to the presence of an audience: "If you wish me / to return to normal," he tells the painter, "you must ask this woman / (indicates Frances) / to drop her eyes." Representationalism such as the painter's portrait functions as explanation, Hawthorne advises, thereby killing its subject. It is the sense and experience, rather than reason and the intellect, that creates action, and "I suspect those moments are always / outside of time." The syncopation between the past represented in the portrait and the present of the audience itself troubles Hawthorne and literally stops the clock behind him. Linking the measuring of time, explanations, and representationalism in a critique of static art, the play advocates instead, with perhaps an echo of Stein, "feel[ing] and think[ing], / all at once" (emphasis original)—emphasizing theater's ability not merely to represent but to present, to literally be in the present of the audience.

But this is not a celebration of immediacy or metaphysical connection, and Frances is unable to escape her fear of the audience's fixing gaze. Onstage, she sees herself as object rather than subject and becomes literally objectified—trapped—by the system of representationalism she endorses. While the painter and Gladys, who have been flirting with each other throughout the play, hurry offstage after hearing a commotion at the back of the theater, Frances is left onstage to become herself a portrait. Onto the blank sign that now rests on the easel, she writes "ONE ONLY IS ESCAPED ALONE TO TELL THEE" and the play ends. Gladys escapes because she sees herself as a member of the audience and therefore as one who can act and not merely be acted upon. Frances, on the other hand, is unable to negotiate the gap between subject and object and becomes, finally, a character in a conventionally representationalist play, which fixes her meaning and renders her unable to act. Rather than transcending the gap between artist, audience, and art, then, Phelps's play makes a study of it.

Together, the four plays that comprised the Poets' opening night foreground the relationship between audience and performance, between subject and object, and investigate the playwright's and audience's roles in activating, generating, controlling, and framing the meaning of the performance. The plays raise questions about the role of memory in the generation of meaning, but they also critique 1940s gender relations, as well as visual culture. American culture in the 1940s exhibited, as Steven Dillon has argued, not simply the ongoing spread of visual media but also "the deployment of the visual as a means of power," and often of patriarchal power specifically (4). Martin Harries has argued that postwar theater incorporated—and often reacted against—the ideology of film in particular. Whereas film worked to interpellate and create an abstracted, distant audience, a mass public, postwar theater "worked to negate a model of the spectator associated with mass culture" (352). The very fact that postwar theater spends so much time thinking about the position of the spectator is an acknowledgment, Harries maintains, of the primacy and force of cinema.

Both *Three Words in No Time* and *The Apparition* worry about the audience's position as a generalized controlling force. And both *Three Words in No Time* and *Try! Try!* use the strategies of Noh theater to disrupt conventional audience-performer relations. In fact, these were among several Noh plays produced by the Poets' in the early 1950s, which came to be known among the group as "Noh-things." Many of them, including not only *Try! Try!* and *Three Words* but also O'Hara's later play *Change Your Bedding* and Lang's *At Battle's End*, incorporated the Noh convention of the stage-manager character. Although it's unclear where the trend toward Noh started among the playwrights of the Poets', the western interest in Noh in general initially took hold in the 1920s and has been attributed to the poet, playwright, and diplomat Paul Claudel, who served as French ambassador to Japan from 1922 to 1928 (Gillespie 138). Yeats and Brecht were also early adopters. Noh staging used in conjunction with formal poetic diction produced highly stylized productions that could be alienating to the uninitiated but might also be seen as a means of elevating the audience. But when these stylized stagings were fused with conversational free verse, the result often challenged the assumption of artistic elevation that accompanied bourgeois theater, producing irony rather than sincerity. In a 1958 discussion of the Poets' Theatre's first several years, Phelps touted Noh as one of the solutions to the staleness of both contemporary drama and popular verse drama (Phelps, Manning, and Rogers 15). If bringing the audience into the play by dismantling illusion and thematizing the audience itself was an explicit goal of the Poets' Theatre in its early years, Phelps suggests that this goal can be traced back to the program notes on Noh theater that Lang wrote for the premiere production. But Howe was not so eager to leave illusionism behind, and she resisted the push to make explicit appeals to the audience even though her own most successful contribution to the Poets', the critically acclaimed stage adaptation of James Joyce's *Finnegans Wake*, used highly poetic language play. Indeed, this disagreement over incorporating the audience was part of a more general clash over theatrical values that continued to play in the background as the Poets' grew and shifted in its first several years.

While the early work of the Poets' Theatre frequently sought to bring the audience into the work, unlike Artaud's Theater of Cruelty or later environmental theater, it did not seek unmediated unity with the audience. The goal was neither the abstract, distanced, mass spectatorship of cinema nor the direct access to the unconscious seen in the spontaneous improvisations of Beat poetry, jazz, and abstract expressionism. In this sense, the Poets' was more Stein than Ginsberg, more antiabsorption than engulfment. By exploring the cultural politics of language, art, and spectatorship while preventing absorption into the work, many of the Poets' early plays, like other artistic rejections of realism's verisimilitude, explored alternatives to cultural authority. And, while they experimented with the conventions of theater, their explorations were not merely formalist, as they probed matters of patriarchal power, sexual coercion, and the social constraints of dominant cultural narratives.

Bunny Lang and the Legacy of Postwar
American Poets' Theater

From this relatively successful beginning, the Poets' Theatre swelled, producing more than twenty plays in its next two years. But the role of the audience remained a particular point of contention between Phelps, Howe, and Lang. Lang continued to advocate breaking through the veil of illusion to shine a spotlight on the audience itself, and in the beginning Phelps largely agreed. While Lang's plays represent some of the best and most successful work produced by the Poets' Theatre in the early 1950s, the controversies that surrounded her participation with the group shed light on the clash of literary and theatrical values that not only characterized the Poets' Theatre during this time but were also playing out across American theater and poetry in general. Lang was awarded, jointly with Frank O'Hara, the Poets' first artist's residency in 1956, which was funded by a Rockefeller grant. And the group recommended two of her plays for publication in Harvard University Press's new annual Poet's Theatre series as works that best exemplified the vision of the Poets' Theatre. But both of these achievements were controversial, as I discuss below. When Lang passed away prematurely in 1956, the Poets' Theatre began to head off in a very different direction, ultimately abandoning the plan to be a writerly project for would-be poet-dramatists in favor of becoming a producer of more "serious" dramatic works.

Lang's career with the Poets' thus offers a window into the promise, conflicts, and contradictions that characterized the Poets' in its early years. Before transforming itself to pursue a more commercially sustainable path in 1957, the Poets' produced plays by such writers as O'Hara, Ashbery, Gorey, MacLeish, Schuyler, Paul Goodman, Donald Hall, I. A. Richards, Lurie, Cid Corman, and William Alfred. But it is Lang's work and history with the Poets' that give the best sense of its early challenges to the ideas of mastery, traditional forms, and established institutions of "high" culture (despite the fact that most of its members came from one of the United States' most venerated institutions of mastery, tradition, and high culture, Harvard University, and even Lang herself came from an old Boston Brahmin family). An examination of Lang's career with the early Poets' Theatre serves as a window into some of the earliest and most important manifestations of poets' theater in the United States.

* * *

Lang was born in 1924 and grew up in Boston as the last of seven children. Her mother was a rich and beautiful Boston socialite, and her father was a musician, composer, and conductor. As a student, Lang attended the Hannah More Academy and then the University of Chicago, though she didn't graduate. She was considered unusually alluring, if not a beauty, and when she made her debut into society in 1941, her future may have seemed charmed. But Lang was not one to be idle. Serving two years in the Canadian Women's Army Corps (WAC), as the US organization would not take her at the age of eighteen, she worked as a typist and filing clerk and then on a newspaper. She wrote poetry and short stories and worked on a historical novel before eventually turning to playwriting. While Lang had grown up among servants, the wealth had begun to slip away over the years. When she joined the Poets' Theatre in 1950, her mother had recently died after a long illness, and Lang was living with and caring for her aging father in the no longer quite elegant home in which she grew up.

Some of Lang's stature in the Poets' came from her ability to bring together the disparate worlds of Boston society and underground theater as though they had always been bedfellows. And she was fiercely loyal to all. She was an active member of Newbury Street society, was a member of the Charlotte Cushman Club (chairing their charity ball in 1954), and had been "brought up in a society so small," according to Poets' Theatre member and memoirist Alison Lurie, "that to give someone's name was a sufficient description [of who they were]" (7). What was unique about Lang compared to the rest of her society peers, however, was that "she extended the rule to people from outside this society" (7). Despite her social pedigree, Lang was egalitarian in her social dealings. She was also completely at ease working with an experimental theater that operated on a shoestring budget, and she dressed the part. Her regular uniform for Poets' Theatre meetings and rehearsals was a man's sweatshirt, torn sneakers, and a faded and dirty trench coat. At least as much by personality as by circumstance, she was equally comfortable with respectable Boston society, Harvard intellectuals, and bohemian artists, and she embraced them all.

When the Poets' Theatre came together in 1950, Lang quickly became one of its most active members. Officially, she served, along with Phelps and Howe, as a member of the group's leadership, but her involvement went far beyond this title. Peter Davison has called her "the Mae West of the troupe" (26), for she was energetic, seductive, and outrageous, and everyone who came into contact with her succumbed to her charm. Her work with the Poets' Theatre was hardly without conflict, however. Lang was known to be pushy and controlling, and the production in 1952 of her second play, *Fire Exit*, nearly drove the group to financial ruin, even as critics cautiously admired it. Although this strained her relationship with the Poets', it didn't end it, and her Beat-inspired third play, *I Too Have Lived in Arcadia*, produced in 1954, was by most accounts the Poets' Theatre's most popular production to date.

The first of Lang's three plays produced by the Poets' was the Noh-inspired *At Battle's End* (1952), and it furthers the explicit concern with audience training that began with the group's premiere production. *At Battle's End* begins with the appearance of the stage manager (changed to the "Interpreter-Chorus" in a later version of the play) who embarks on an explanation of the style of theater the audience is about to see. In the initial draft of the play, the stage manager disparages western realist theater, which invites passivity, remarking that "theatre-going in our culture is the very antithesis of art" because art requires an audience to participate actively and give something of themselves (typescript n.p.). Rather than seeking mere entertainment and relaxation, the audience, Lang wrote, should be "disciplined," actively working with the drama to reveal its meanings. In the later, published version of the play, Lang toned down her criticism of the audience and instead emphasized Noh's use of theatricality and symbolism as counter to realist staging and its convention of an official Spectator, "who sat on the stage and set, for the audience, an example of perfect and unbroken concentration" (53).

Written entirely in verse, *At Battle's End* once again revisits the story of a husband returned from the war. After seven years on the front lines, Jack comes home seeking his wife Melpomene,[8] but he has trouble finding her and enlists the assistance of Wong, a local gardener. Melpomene was not happy to have been left alone for seven years with a mother-in-law to care for, a house to keep, and no one to help. When her mother-in-law began stealing chickens and creating a general nuisance in the neighborhood, Melpomene "did away" with her, presumably sending her away to let "charity" take care of her, and she now threatens that "when [Jack] comes back, he'll get his" (55). Not surprisingly, the reunion between the couple is tense. Melpomene seems mostly interested in the gifts that Jack has brought, while Jack ruminates on all that has changed in his absence and on his regrets at being taken away from his wife so quickly. Caught up in his own philosophizing about how war has changed him, Jack fails to notice Wong reenter as a kind of grim reaper figure who causes Melpomene to drop dead immediately (the "Supernatural Event" that, as the Interpreter-Chorus has instructed us, resolves a piece of Noh theater). Jack eventually realizes what has happened and falls dead himself, after which Wong moralizes, somewhat cryptically, that "man is like a pumpkin. For a while his cheek / Is ruddy like the pumpkin. Then he clings to vine. / When his stem is sturdy, everything is fine. / But when he grows too fat and big—he breaks the twig" (59).

Lang's use of the stage manager to chastise the audience into greater discipline and responsibility (or of the Interpreter-Chorus in the later version to instruct the audience in the conventions of Noh theater) was part of a larger emphasis on the role of the audience playing out across the poetry world more generally. This was, after all, the era of Donald Allen's "New American Poetry," which challenged academic verse with a living practice that reached audiences directly through performance, including both theatrical productions and poetry readings. Several of the New York poets associated with Herbert Machiz's Artists' Theatre in the mid-1950s had only recently relocated from Boston, where they had been actively involved with the Cambridge Poets'. While Poets' Theatre memoirist Nora Sayre asserts that the group's most lasting influence was its contribution to the development of a "natural speaking voice" for poetry, she also argues that it can be seen as a spiritual predecessor to the later off-off-Broadway movement and midcentury American avant-garde theater companies and experimental clubs, such as La Mama.

Lang's Interpreter-Chorus figure explains that Noh plays are built around situations rather than actions: "The Situation is *described* in lyric circumstances by poetic thoughts and stately movements. The audience comes to see how a story they all know very well is displayed by suggestive verses, subtle and philosophical commentaries and asides, and of course music and dance" (53). A decade later, New York's off-off Broadway and underground theater scene would stage in cafés and makeshift venues highly theatrical performances that were built around a similar central emphasis on a particular moment instead of the development of themes and a linear narrative. As Bottoms describes it, these performances "tended to stay in one place—literally, the small space of the stage—and to view that place prismatically, creating a variety of perspectives on the central dramatic circumstance by 'riffing' improvisationally around it. They keenly felt the need for a central, theatrical image around which a play could cohere," focusing on what they found most visually exciting (125).

As a conceptual merging of poetic language and performance, many of the works produced by the Poets' aimed to disrupt the conventions of both poetry and theater. As theater, they explicitly brought "reality" into contact with "imagination" (as when O'Hara's piece explicitly cited the actors as the characters). They also frequently used bodies as art material, turned spectators into actors and actors into spectators, and drew attention to the conventions of theatrical representation, such as stage, frame, props, and so on. As poetry (building off poetic trends in the 1940s), they explored the arbitrariness of the symbol; made the "subject" of the piece the shifting relations between author, narrator, world, and language; self-consciously explored the evolving processes of art making and meaning making; and employed linguistic artifice and the materiality of language to undermine absorption into the conventions of theater. Many poets of the 1940s saw themselves as agents of cultural change and understood poetry to be a more "real" experience due to its wedding of imagination with reality.

One method of blending the poetic with the theatrical involved incorporating popular theatrical forms with verse dialogue. Modernist poetic drama by such writers as Edna St. Vincent Millay and E. E. Cummings sometimes included images and conventions from popular genres such as commedia dell'arte, popular music, minstrelsy, cinema, and melodrama. Lang's second play to be produced by the Poets' Theatre was built around a community of vaudeville and burlesque performers. *Fire Exit*, a loose adaptation of the Eurydice and Orpheus myth subtitled "Vaudeville for Eurydice," turns Eurydice, or Eury, as she's known in the play, into a performer in training. Eury is being raised after her mother's death by her aunts and uncles, all of whom work on the vaudeville circuit as performers and concessioners. She attends a convent school, but during school breaks the family trains her as a dancer and performer with the hope that she will follow in their footsteps and join the family profession. But Eury doesn't feel that this is work of which she can be proud. When she meets Orpheus, he is a classical pianist working in a hotel lobby, and by the time he returns for her several years later (after she has graduated from school, turned down a marriage proposal, and passed on a chance to join a traveling midget show in order to wait for Orpheus), he has become a hugely successful, "serious" professional musician. Unfortunately, Orpheus is not interested in Eury's career, or even in her desires and happiness. As his fame and fortune increase, he wants her simply to follow him, quietly waiting and doing nothing. Eventually, he leaves Eury behind on an ill-fated bicycle tour through the French countryside, and when he returns to find her, she's gone. He looks for her for years, eventually assuming she's dead, only to learn from a vaudeville comedian that she is working as a chorus girl and occasional stripper in an unremarkable town—Hades as burlesque theater. He comes to take her back, promising that her past doesn't matter, but Eury refuses to return with Orpheus. "Perhaps it was better this way," she remarks at the

Stop Numbers Enliven 'Fire Exit,' New Poets' Production at Brattle

Burlesque takes on avant-garde overtones in the Poets' Theatres' first fall production, "Fire Exit." Showgirls, models, and dancers from Boston have been imported for the strip numbers.

ANNE LANG, right, plays the lead in the play, "an ironic reworking of the Orpheus and Eurydice legend." The show will run at the Brattle Theatre December 1 through 6.

Gaston Courvoisier '53 takes the leading role of Orpheus; Arthur N. Stowe '55, Jim Upham '52, and Lester Kramer 2L, are also in the cast.

Fig. 3. Announcement for *Fire Exit* in the *Harvard Crimson*, November 26, 1952.

end to the comedian who has become a kind of father figure to her. "I wanted him to look at me" (252).

The play was produced by the Poets' in 1952, and Lang starred in the role of Eurydice. In 1951 she had worked a several-month stint as a chorus girl at the famed "Old Howard," the Howard Atheneum, a long-standing Boston burlesque theater, in order to pay off a debt. Even after the debt had been repaid, Lang continued in the chorus for several months, and she wrote *Fire Exit* in part as a tribute to the friends she made there. Her room in her father's home prominently displayed the photos and notes the regular company gave her upon her departure, and her closet held a number of used burlesque costumes. Her friends from the Poets' Theatre all went, sometimes regularly, to see her perform. Lurie described the standard Old Howard evening's entertainments in this way: "A short opening number, often with a patriotic theme, presented the cast, and then the individual acts began: a vaudeville scrap bag of comedy bits, strippers, chorus numbers, and specialties which might include a tap dancer, an acrobat or sentimental popular songs to the accompaniment of candy-box colored lantern slides" (39). In *Fire Exit*, Lang positions such popular theatricality as a foil for "serious" performance, and this clash itself becomes the ethical dilemma of modern life.

Lang's experiences as a chorus dancer inspired the play's themes, especially the conflict between the supposed social betterment encouraged by true "art" and the profane pleasure aroused by popular entertainments. Eury's vaudeville family members love and respect themselves and each other, they take pride in their work, and they take care of their family and community. Orpheus lives in a world of adulation and isolation rather than love and community, and his single-minded pursuit of his art renders him incapable of love and compassion for another person. The difference seems to be not "art versus entertainment" but whether or not you believe in what you are doing. Eury tells her uncle that she'll never be a performer because she doesn't "believe" in it, and she could never be proud of it. Hurt, her uncle explains how he and his wife have built up their bird act, training the birds themselves and creating the show from scratch. Orpheus, by contrast, has talent but little depth. He mocks his own audience, makes career choices out of a sense of competiveness rather than devotion, and seems not to enjoy his own successes.

Like *At Battle's End*, *Fire Exit* thematizes the role of the audience, and it critiques popular audiences of all classes. Eury cringes at her experience with members of vaudeville audiences, who, emboldened by their ability to hide in the darkness, laugh and mock the performers they have paid to see. "I hate the audience," she announces coldly (162). Orpheus, on the other hand, is advised by his manager not to cater to popular tastes. He doesn't, but, bewilderingly, his music is adored by popular audiences, who misunderstand his intentions. "I wrote *The Melancholy Magic of Your Smile* as a joke, do you understand?" he protests, to no avail, as his audience chases him, not comprehending his music but treating him like some sort of prized object (196). Audiences, the play implies, are both ignorant and cruel. And popular performers are caught between the jeering of the working-class spectators and "college boys" who come to "laugh at what is publicly contemptible" (245) and the bafflement of high-society spectators who can't understand why they don't try to "better" themselves. The play might even be taken as a subtle swipe at the behind-the-scenes conflicts of the Poets' Theatre itself, where Lang, O'Hara, Phelps, and others supported the playful theatricals being produced by many of the young poet-playwrights while Howe, Catharine Huntington, and others advocated more "serious" theater.

Whereas *At Battle's End* is written entirely in verse and uses poetry as one of several theatrical elements to heighten the symbolic impact of the play, *Fire Exit* uses poetry rhetorically to emphasize key themes and critiques. When Orpheus returns to Eury to reaffirm his love and marry her, Eury and her family rejoice at the great fortune they feel Orpheus will bring to Eury (which of course later proves to be false). Eury's aunt, Mrs. Robelle, for example, is relieved that they will have to "No longer abide her silly ancillary decisions, / Now she knows where she is. / Reward us her aunts our precipitant persistence, / He is hers, she is his" (178). Eury, too, seems to see Orpheus as a kind of knight in shining armor, crying, "There shall be nothing that I will not understand, / There will be no attention that he will not grant! We shall be cared for and coveted, justified at last, / With all the right what-have-you that we love the best!" (ibid.). But the stilted verse here gives lie to the sentiment it expresses. Part of what we see in this mockery of poetic elevation are Lang's own deeply ambivalent feelings about marriage. Poetry reveals this young "love at first sight" as an overwrought performance of a clichéd story with no substance. Rather than a tale of the beauty of a doomed but undying love, the story of Orpheus and Eurydice becomes here a biting critique of our oversimplified cultural belief in the transformative power of love.

In the end, *Fire Exit* was controversial not for its subject matter but for the way Lang took control of the play, defying other board members and racking up costly bills. Lang directed the play herself because, according to Lurie, she didn't find any other director agreeable enough (a promotional flyer listed the director as "Madeleine Paget," an apparent pseudonym). While Lang was rumored to have argued that the play was worth three hundred dollars in promotion for the Poets' (Accounts n.p.), the one-week run at Cambridge's Brattle Theatre ultimately put the group several hundred dollars in debt,[9] possibly due to unusually high advertising and production costs that Lang had approved. But reviews of the play were positive overall. The *Christian Science Monitor* praised its imaginative dialogue in "the hard task of bringing new poetry to the stage," though it ultimately found both the writing and performing uneven (Nordell 10), and it singled out for criticism the play's "undisciplined" merging of realism and stylized acting. The *Harvard Crimson*, on the other hand, deemed the play "thoroughly entertaining" with a "some very interesting characters," an "original interpretation," and a "fine cast." It was a great improvement on the "spotty poetry and confusing physical gyrations" of past productions, the review asserted, concluding that *Fire Exit* offered renewed hope for the Poets' Theatre (Maccoby).

Lang became ill in July 1953 with what would eventually turn out to be Hodgkin's lymphoma. She was hospitalized for several weeks, lost thirty pounds, and underwent radiation treatments. Meanwhile, the Poets' Theatre, having been nearly driven to financial ruin by *Fire Exit*, abruptly changed tack, avoiding new plays by unknown artists and instead producing verse drama by Harvard faculty and other established authors. Phelps's notes recall three productions during the 1953–54 season, all by established authors—*This Music Crept by Me upon the Waters*, a modern comedic parable warning against the American tendency to work too hard and forget what is important, and *The Trojan Horse*, which used the tragedy of the Trojan people to criticize McCarthyism, both by Pulitzer Prizing–winning poet and Harvard faculty member Archibald MacLeish; and *Agamemnon*, a modern verse adaptation of the story of the murder of King Agamemnon and his wife Cassandra by Harvard literature professor William Alfred, who had studied verse drama under MacLeish. Howe directed all three, and Phelps acted as producer. MacLeish's *This Music Crept by Me upon the Waters* was soon published as the first play in Harvard University Press's Poets' Theatre series, which was meant to represent the group's best work. Lurie also remembers two Yeats plays produced by the Poets' at the Fogg Museum during the winter of 1953. In addition, the group hosted Irish poet and playwright Dylan Thomas for a much-celebrated first reading of his newly finished radio play *Under Milk Wood*. Meanwhile, the Artists' Theatre produced Lang's *Fire Exit* in New York, and "for the first time," Lurie recalls, Lang "seemed to have lost interest in the Poets' Theatre, which was now becoming incredibly respectable" (45).[10]

By the following year, Lang had regained some of her health, and she became active again as director, actor, and playwright. In planning the season's offerings, Phelps, Howe, and Lang apparently decided to meet in the middle with a mix of work by both new and established authors and by international as well as American playwrights. The season included a revival of Phelps's *Three Words in No Time*, as well as plays by the budding American poet James Schuyler, American poet and academic Reuel Denney, French poet René Char, Irish playwright Denis Johnston, and the American literary critic and poet I. A. Richards, though none of these playwrights were active members of the Poets' and they had little, if any, involvement in the productions. The season also included Lang's third and final play, *I Too Have Lived in Arcadia*. In a letter to Bradley Phillips, whom Lang married in 1955, Hugh Amory wrote:

> Without laboring the point, I don't know as she ever regarded the Poets' Theatre as her friend, in the sense that I think they were opposed to much of what she believed in, and still are. The big battle, of course, was over *Fire Exit*, on which the Poets' Theatre has since meanly claimed the credit. All I can say is that she conveyed a sense of honor even in returning to a theatre which had none, and did not regard it as opportunism to have *Arcadia* produced here, the more so, after all, since she did not receive the production she wanted. (Amory n.p.)

Whatever happened behind the scenes, Lang did return, and *Arcadia* was by all estimations her best work.

This time Lang stayed out of the production, which was directed by Phelps—a production that Lurie calls "first-rate, professional but unpretentious" (55). The plot revolves around Damon and Chloris, who have left their "beat," "bugged," "hung-up," and false lives in the city to live on an island near Newfoundland, raising food and sheep and loving themselves and each other. When Damon's former lover Phoebe comes to the island to take him back to his urban life of music, art, and nightclubs, Damon, who is easily swayed and never fully honest with himself, follows her back. The plot is simple, but the play is infused with symbolic musings on the ice age and the extinction of the dinosaurs. It also includes a talking dog named Georges, Phoebe's sidekick (perhaps a former lover who now follows her slavishly, the play seems to imply), who speaks in French translations of American jazz slang—the dog riffs on "dig" with the French words *creuser* and *bêcher* and finds Chloris's naïveté hilarious when she doesn't understand him. Lang wrote the play in part to take revenge on a former New York boyfriend, the abstract expressionist painter Mike Goldberg, to whom she was briefly engaged.

Unlike *At Battle's End* and *Fire Exit*, *Arcadia* neither thematizes nor critiques its audience. Instead, it is Damon's superficiality and lack of self-honesty that are lambasted here. Damon is a trumpet player who gives up his ideals of an "honest" life to return to his unfulfilled de- sires as a nightclub musician. Poetic dialogue heightens the power of the play's conflicts, and expositions and philosophical ruminations replace action. As with *At Battle's End*, the central dramatic circumstance plays out with fantastical elements—in *At Battle's End*, it is the grim reaper figure that causes both Jack and Melpomene to fall dead; in *Arcadia*, it is the talking dog with the Beat vocabulary. A poetic quality imbues all the play's dialogue, but it is neither as symbolic as *At Battle's End* nor as plot-driven as *Fire Exit*. Instead, the play attempts to bring poetry and drama together into a balanced presentation of dramatic situation, lan- guage, and action.

The production, which included recorded jazz interludes and was pre- ceded by a playlet by Alfred de Musset called *A Door Must Be Open or Shut*, premiered to a packed house in October 1954. While the *Harvard Crimson* complained that the straightforward story was "smothered by form and language that was far too complex" (Schoenberg), the *Boston Herald* admired Lang's "originality and genuine poetic talent," though it also felt the play presented "a challenge both exasperating and stimulat- ing" (Hughes). Mixed reviews were the norm for the Poets' Theatre, how- ever, and *Arcadia*, which appeared in the April 1955 issue of *Poetry* and was awarded the magazine's Vachel Lindsay Prize, was arguably the most popular play the Poets' had produced in all of its first five years. "If [Lang] had lived," writes Lurie, "she would certainly have taken her place in the so-called New York School of poets, along with her friends John Ashbery, Kenneth Koch, and Frank O'Hara" (xvi).

Institutionalizing the Poets' Theatre

The popularity of *Arcadia* only underscored what several members of the Poets' already believed—that Lang's work represented some of the best new poetic writing being produced for the theater. Shortly after its successful run, the play was enthusiastically nominated by the Poets' Theatre to be published in Harvard University Press's Poets' Theatre series, which had been founded in 1953 explicitly to publish annually a play that represented the best work produced by the Poets' in the previous year. For such an amateur group, the backing of a high-profile press series may seem surprising, but while the Poets' Theatre was still largely an experimental project aimed at supporting new writing and new forms, its members' affiliations with Harvard gave it a measure of respectability and seriousness it might not have otherwise enjoyed. Its board included such theater and poetry luminaries as Thornton Wilder, William Carlos Williams, Francis Fergusson, and Richard Eberhart. But it may have been Archibald MacLeish's support that had the most material impact.

MacLeish had already won a Pulitzer Prize for poetry when the Poets' Theatre was formed in 1950. He won his second Pulitzer in 1952 for his *Collected Poems, 1917–1952*, and a third for his verse drama *J. B.*, published in 1958. As Harvard's Boylston Professor of Rhetoric and Oratory from 1949 until his retirement in 1962, he was an early supporter of the Poets', twice convincing Harvard to make a five-hundred-dollar donation to the group and offering his own plays for production. His play *This Music Crept by Me upon the Waters* was a safe choice for the first publication of the Harvard Press's Poets' Theatre series—a fully-plotted dramatic parable for the modern era written by a nationally celebrated poet-playwright who was also a noted Harvard professor.

Although the series was a remarkable institutional vote of confidence in the experimental theater company, conflicts between the press and the Poets' over differing goals for the series slowed publication. Following the publication of MacLeish's play, Lang's *Fire Exit* had been recommended for publication in 1954, as the second volume in the series, but it was rejected by the press. Because of this rejection, there was a year's lag time before the second title in the series, Lyon Phelps's *The Gospel Witch*, was published in 1955. *The Gospel Witch* was produced in February 1955 and was the fifth of Phelps's plays to be produced by the Poets'. Written in blank verse, the play told the story of Ann Putnam and the Salem witch trials, a popular dramatic metaphor for McCarthyism in the early 1950s. (A shorter, one-act version of the play was performed by the Poets' as *Speak If You Can!* in 1952, almost a full year before the premiere of Arthur Miller's *The Crucible*.) Unlike *Three Words in No Time*, *The Gospel Witch* offered social critique in a conventionally realist package. For the press series, it offered a highly readable play.

While the Poets' sought to publish works that it felt best represented its vision of poetic theater (though there wasn't yet agreement on what that vision was), the press was, of course, interested in sales to readers of drama. And *The Gospel Witch* proved to be critically acclaimed as literature, listed as one of the *New York Times*' "100 of the Year's Outstanding Books" in 1955 (Janssen 141). But perhaps still disheartened by the rejection of *Fire Exit* and the resulting gap in the series, the Poets' Theatre proposed in 1955 a trial two-year publication selection process that would institute a balanced committee of four members—two submitted by the Poets' and two by the press—as readers of an entire season's plays. The committee was then to choose a play to recommend to the press for publication, with the expectation that the press would accept this recommendation summarily. The previous selection process—in which the Poets' nominated to the press one play per year and if that play was turned down a whole year passed without a publication in the series—was disheartening to writers, they argued; it also misrepresented, they implied, the nature of the work the Poets' Theatre was doing.

Once again the Poets' decided to submit a play by Lang—this time *I Too Have Lived in Arcadia*, one of its most popular productions to date. Perhaps submitting *Arcadia* along with this proposal for a revised selection process was a hopeful calculation. Certainly submitting a second play by Lang after one had already been rejected indicated a particular vote of confidence in Lang's work by the Poets' Theatre. Richard Eberhart wrote a letter supporting *Arcadia*'s publication on the grounds of its contemporariness, pointing out that the Poets' Theatre was especially interested in showcasing plays with modern themes and characters that would appeal to young audiences. Then, too, this was the third play of Lang's to be produced by the Poets', and each had been more critically successful than the last. While *Fire Exit* had run for four nights at the two-hundred-seat Brattle Theatre, *Arcadia* had run for an initial week and then been extended for another week at the fifty-seat Palmer Street Theatre, which had recently become the Poets' Theatre's home. A second letter from the Poets' in support of *Arcadia*'s nomination to the press estimated that "at least 400 of this 800 [who saw the play] wanted to read it, from conversations in the lobby. Their feelings were so new, I think, that they wanted to confirm them to see if they were right" (Wayde n.p.). But once again Lang's play was rejected by the press on "literary" grounds. In his explanation, Peter Davison, writing as assistant to the director of the press, explained that as much as the press wanted to support "high quality" verse plays by new writers, it also wanted to be able to publish works by recognized writers that would be easier to sell. Should the press be aimed at readers or actors? Davison asked rhetorically. In the end, there was, once again, no play published by the series in 1955.

The third and final publication in the series came in 1957 and was written by the third guiding figure of the Poets' Theatre—Howe's *Passages from Finnegans Wake by James Joyce, a Free Adaptation for the Theater*.[11] The play, which had been produced by the Poets' in 1955, was a remarkably skilled adaptation of Joyce's epic novel that managed to achieve both dramatic coherence and progression while still maintaining Joyce's linguistic play and absurdity. While Joyce's multivocality has sometimes been compared to that of Stein, the effect of Joyce's novel is ultimately narrative progression rather than the continuous present of "repeating with a difference" found in Stein. In speech and song, the play moves from death to sleep to birth, with the coffin literally at the center of the stage. Howe's adaptation expertly combined poetic language and theatricality with high-culture literariness by an established and celebrated author. But unfortunately the selection once again proved that the press wasn't interested in the new, experimental works that the Poets' had been initially formed to foster, and the series only widened the gap between postwar poets' theater and "respectable" theater.

Meanwhile, MacLeish had also been working quietly to secure a Rockefeller grant to support a Poets' Theatre artist's residency. A residency program would combine the new and the respectable by lending institutional support to up-and-coming writers. The grant was approved in 1954 and included "money for a tape recorder and travel expenses of poets coming to Cambridge" (Poets' Theatre, September 7, 1954, n.p.). It also included a stipend of fifteen hundred dollars each. In 1956, the first Poets' Theatre residency was jointly awarded to Lang and O'Hara, not only underscoring the hope their plays offered for the future of postwar poets' theater but also reestablishing the Poets' support for new writing. While some complained that O'Hara drank his residency away in Boston area bars and Lang spent half of hers on a honeymoon in Europe,[12] the joint selection of O'Hara and Lang demonstrated the Poets' Theatre's vision of poetic drama as a new form in which poetry served not as merely a "texture" for traditional dramatic form but as a new and promising unity of poetry and drama.[13] Lang died, however, soon after her residency ended. The following year the Poets' reorganized itself as a professional theater.

Over the course of its first six years of plays, under the shared guidance of Phelps, Lang, and Howe, the Poets' Theatre grew in both reputation and respectability, partially through its own efforts and the quality of the works it produced and partially through increasing cultural interest in verse drama. Harvard faculty and students who had previously avoided the Poets' began to flock to its productions. In 1955, Harvard sponsored its own symposium on the verse drama. Although the Poets' had no official ties to the symposium and Harvard did not enlist the Poets' Theatre to present its work, at least some of the symposium panelists were Poets' members. But the play Harvard chose to showcase as exemplary verse drama, *The Hidden King* by British playwright Jonathan Griffin, was an overwrought historical allegory written in turgid verse that took four hours to perform, and in a later interview both Phelps and Howe distanced themselves from the event, claiming that *The Hidden King* didn't represent the kind of work that the Poets' Theatre was trying to do (Phelps, Manning, and Rogers 27). Meanwhile, the Poets' Theatre's reputation was spreading. A local Boston radio station, WGBH, broadcast the Poets' productions of MacLeish's plays in May 1954, and by early 1955 Wheaton, Bard, and Bennington Colleges, as well as the Artists' Theatre in New York, were all requesting permission to produce Poets' Theatre plays.

But, although interest grew, funding did not increase at the same pace. The Rockefeller grant was prestigious and not ungenerous, but it was used to support writers in residence and not the costs of operating the theater itself. There was talk of creating a summer school, in acting, dance, or stage movement, as a way of raising funds. By 1955, the Poets' seemed to be experiencing a crisis of identity as a direct result of its own critical success. In a letter dated December 18, 1955, Howe, Catharine Huntington, and William M. Hunt argued that "the Poets' Theatre has arrived at a crossroads as a logical consequence of recent success and achieving long worked for recognition. We are now in the theatre business with all its responsibilities even if we only operate a 49 seat house" (Howe et. al. n.p.). While some, like Lang, saw the Poets' as primarily a lab for writers, others, like Howe, saw it as a professional theater. The authors of the letter felt that continuing on as a writer's lab was untenable, largely because there were too many conflicting visions.

In the end, the biggest blow to the Poets' early experimentalism was not any single event, not even Lang's untimely death, but a confluence of several events—including Lang's passing, the growing popularity of the Poets', formal recognition from Harvard University Press and the Rockefeller Foundation, and the enormous audience draw of more traditional events and readings, such as Thomas's reading of *Under Milk Wood* and poetry readings by Dame Edith Sitwell and Sir Osbert Sitwell. From 1956 until its demise in 1968,[14] the Poets' produced a wealth of modern theater that included both new poetic plays and "classics" by such figures as Beckett, Eliot, Lorca, and Eugène Ionesco, but its vision of a truly new poets' theater had faded even as its name remained. Direct instruction of the audience and destruction of theatrical illusion were key, albeit contentious, strategies in the early years of the Poets' Theatre, but as the group's productions of new plays by young writers increasingly gave way to stagings of "classic" plays by established artists, its self-conscious attention to audience training and the conventions of theatrical composition began to recede. Still, because of some of its early performances in New York, as well as the relocation to New York of some of its early members such as Ashbery and O'Hara, the legacy of the early Poets' Theatre has lived on.

CHAPTER THREE

From Poets' Theater to "Antitextual" Theater
The Living Theatre and the Rhetoric of the Real

> Breakdown of language equals breakdown of values, of modes
> of insight, of the sick rationale. Breakdown of language means
> invention of fresh forms of communication. Breakdown of language
> means breakdown of computers. Breakdown the language of
> the controlling forces and you breakdown their weary logic, you
> breakdown their tight structure. Shake things up, change, give
> ourselves over to what we do not comprehend, what we think we
> comprehend we don't comprehend anyway, our logic is false, is rigid
> and systematic, open it up. Breathe.
> —Julian Beck, "Three Meditations on Strategies" (1970)

Now emblematic of radical participatory performance and best known for its 1960s experiments in collective creation and ritual theater, including *Paradise Now* and *Mysteries and Smaller Pieces*, the Living Theatre began its career doing poets' theater by such writers as Gertrude Stein, Pablo Picasso, T. S. Eliot, Kenneth Rexroth, Frank O'Hara, and John Ashbery. According to the standard narrative, the group's founders, Julian Beck and Judith Malina, began with challenging literary works, Brechtian alienation and self-conscious antinaturalism, and experiments in poetic drama in the late 1940s and 1950s, and then moved on to plays with more specifically American themes and situations when they discovered Artaudian cruelty, and along with it their own political-aesthetic vision, in the late 1950s and early 1960s. By the late 1960s, this narrative continues, they had largely abandoned (or at least deconstructed) the dramatic script to create interactive and pointedly political performance works before turning to political street theater in the 1970s and beyond. Critics therefore widely treat the Living Theatre's later participatory productions as aesthetically and politically distinct from their earlier "literary" and less directly political plays of the 1940s and 1950s. In this version of events, poets' theater is merely trivial background to collective creativity and participation. But a closer look at the Living Theatre's early productions demonstrates poets' theater's continuity with the later, more overtly political works. In fact, the language politics and collaborative aesthetics of poets' theater helped the Living Theatre develop the strategies of collaborativity and audience participation that became central to its later theatrical activism.

A lack of critical distinction between verse drama and poets' theater is at least partly to blame for this oversimplified account. Christopher Innes, for example, has dismissed the Living Theatre's pre-1959 productions as the work of "a fairly conventional 'little theater' company" (62). Stephen Bottoms offers a more nuanced but still largely dismissive assessment when he writes:

> [T]he Living's productions of poetic dramas had often baffled audiences, and the company itself had never felt happy with much of the work. Loathe as Beck might have been to admit it, even the best poets did not necessarily make good writers for a visual and physical medium like the stage, and indeed many of those who did experiment with dramatic form were really writing "closet dramas"—literary exercises not seriously intended for staging. As some of the Living's would-be successors quickly discovered, theaters dedicated to mounting verse plays ran the risk of seeming esoteric, overly wordy, or simply impenetrable to audiences. The question was how best to find a balance between poetic aspiration and theatrical viability. (61)

According to these critical assessments, the Living Theatre's early experiments in poetic drama were simply the growing pains of a fledgling theater that had not yet discovered its vision.

But a few critics have detected a developing politics in the Living Theatre's early choice to produce poetic drama. Christopher Bigsby, for example, places the Living Theatre's early poetic productions within a wider practice of performance theater that, he argues, "chose to de-emphasize language, partly because of its emphasis on rationalism and partly because, as Pinter, Handke and Albee, among others, have indicated, it is a means for structuring and hence controlling experience" (*Critical Introduction* 65)—and indeed Beck celebrates, in the quotation that opens this chapter, the value of language used against itself to break down the dominant cultural logic. Mike Sell has interpreted the Living Theatre's choice to produce poetic drama in the 1950s as a means of avoiding the reproduction of Cold War ideology by producing plays whose language did not participate in narrative consolidation. As one of the oldest and certainly longest-running experimental theaters in the United States, the Living Theatre was significant, as Alisa Solomon has observed, not only for the iconic *Paradise Now* but also for its endeavors in erasing the line between actor and character and between the stage and reality, as well as for its efforts in collective creation (57)—all of which began with its work in poets' theater.

Examined together, the Living Theatre's early productions of poets' theater, its "transitional" plays *The Connection* (1959) and *The Brig* (1963), and Beck's and Malina's rhetoric on the connections between poetry, dramatic plays, acting, and "real life" indicate a more complex relationship between poetic theater and so-called antitextual theater. While several scholars have discussed the Living Theatre's shift to strategies of improvisation and enactment in its productions of *The Connection* and *The Brig*,[1] these concerns actually begin with the earlier productions of Gertrude Stein, Paul Goodman, William Carlos Williams, Luigi Pirandello, and others. The history of the Living Theatre demonstrates that poets' theater is not a minor theatrical practice that occurred simultaneously with but separate from the development of antitextual theater but is, rather, another important American theater practice that grew directly out of the same collaborative interart scene of the 1950s and 1960s and that, at least in the case of the Living Theatre, led directly to experiments in antitextual theater. In fact, poets' theater and antitextual theater can be understood as two different manifestations of surprisingly similar ideas.

"Gertrude Stein has clues": The Living Theatre's Early Productions, 1951–1955

Malina and Beck met in New York in 1943 and immediately connected. Their early relationship involved attending theater, film, and art exhibits together, reading Stein and Joyce, discussing politics, and immersing themselves in the rich, dynamic, and informal New York artists' scene of the 1940s. As part of a growing community of avant-garde artists, anarchists, and activists, Beck and Malina were introduced to a wide range of beliefs and practices that explored the relationship between aesthetics and cultural politics, and they were especially active in the interart scene, which included writers, painters, composers, and dancers. By 1947, they had founded a theater together (although it would be four years before they staged their first production). Readings, especially poetry readings, and informal collaborations of all sorts were a regular occurrence, and Beck and Malina established a regular Monday night series in which playwrights, poets, and writers met to read and discuss their current projects as a way of supporting new writers and collaborations. The poetry that tended to be featured among New York's underground writers at this time emphasized the performer's presence as a means of producing a kind of unmediated connection between poet and audience, and the frequent poetry readings held by the Living Theatre contributed directly, in Donald Allen's estimation, to the development of New York's "extraordinary poetry scene" (448). It also availed the group of poetry's more developed distribution networks, including mailing lists, small presses, and reading series.

The antiauthoritarian, participatory stance that played out on the Living Theatre's stages was therefore part of a more general melding of politics and aesthetics that characterized the larger New York arts community in the 1940s, 1950s, and 1960s. Beck was an abstract expressionist painter and showed his work in New York galleries in the 1940s, including at an exhibition at Peggy Guggenheim's Art of This Century gallery in 1945, where he shared space with Jackson Pollock, Robert Motherwell, and Willem de Kooning. Meanwhile, Malina studied directing at the Dramatic Workshop at the New School with Erwin Piscator, who originated the "epic theater" style later developed by Brecht.[2] Piscator introduced Malina to left-wing political theater and to, as Erika Munk puts it, the "Jewish/'degenerate'/'Bolshevik' art that he and other refugees from Nazism had brought to America, just when the House Un-American Activities Committee started to purge America of such ideas" (35). Their artistic and social activities brought them into contact with many of New York's most innovative artists and writers. Malina met John Cage, for example, at an art show in 1951, and Cage became an early supporter and collaborator. Beck and Malina met John Ashbery and Frank O'Hara, both of whom had worked with the Poets' Theatre in Cambridge and would later become playwrights and actors for Living Theatre productions, at a party after one of Cage's performances. A few months later Cage brought Merce Cunningham to the Living Theatre's first production, and Cage,

Cunningham, Beck, and Malina soon began looking for a shared theater space at which to produce their various works. Cage also introduced
Beck and Malina to the *I Ching* and the Black Mountain School (Tytell
84), where the influential performance poet and theorist Charles Olson
was a faculty member.

Within this artistic milieu, ideas varied widely about what the relationship between audience and artist should be. For writers like Olson,
abstract expressionist painters like Pollock, and jazz musicians like Charlie Parker, art could express the artist's feeling spontaneously and could
therefore create direct communion between artist and audience. For the
writer, anarchist, and psychotherapist Paul Goodman, art could be a prod
for social revolution and should inspire audiences to act. For other artists,
such as Cage and sometimes the New York poets, art revealed the performativity of everyday life—and the conventions of art could even offer a
frame through which the audience might look at itself.

Beck and Malina were political activists as well as artists, and both
were involved in the peace and antinuclear movements. But it was not
necessarily clear to them how to translate their political commitments
into an aesthetic strategy. As avowed anarchists, they derided the propaganda of conventional "political" theater, wanting instead to leave their
audiences free to think and act for themselves. But their early work was
full of contradictions. Their approach to the audience often wavered between a desire for direct connection on one hand and critical detachment
on the other. Malina's training with Piscator had taught her to keep the
audience at a contemplative distance, while Beck's immersion in abstract
expressionism's spontaneity and direct access to the artist's experience created a preference for erasing the boundary between audience and artist.
But they shared an admiration for Stein, whose work was roomy enough
to encompass both impulses.

Beck and Malina had long been avid readers of Stein, and Stein's use of
indeterminacy, which required the participation of the audience to create
meaning, appealed to their anarchism. In fact, their inaugural production
featured Stein's play *Ladies' Voices*, directed by Beck and starring Malina
and Helen Jacobs, which opened in August 1951, just six months after the
Poets' Theatre was launched in Cambridge, Massachusetts.[3] *Ladies' Voices*
was part of an evening of four short plays performed in Beck and Malina's living room because they were too impatient to wait for their lease
to begin at the Cherry Lane Theater in Greenwich Village later that year.
The venture was called the "Theater in the Room" and accommodated an

audience of twenty, with ten people seated on a bench against the living room wall and ten more on floor cushions. The makeshift performance space was not only a sign of eagerness but also a clear indication, argues Leslie Atkins Durham, of their "rebellion against the constraints of the commercial theater" (164). In addition to *Ladies' Voices*, the bill included Paul Goodman's *Childish Jokes: Crying Backstage*, Bertolt Brecht's *He Who Says Yes* and *He Who Says No*, and *Dialogue between a Young Man and a Mannequin* taken from Federico García Lorca's *If Five Years Pass*.

Together the plays offered a mix of aesthetic experimentation and social critique. Goodman's *Childish Jokes* was "a meta-comedy about the nature of theater" (Malina, *Piscator* 171), while Brecht's *He Who Says Yes* and *He Who Says No* were a pair of didactic plays that explored one's rights and responsibilities when asked to consent to a larger cause. Brecht's paired plays invited audience members to consider what to do not only when the needs of an individual are directly at odds with the needs of the larger community but also when what is right and sensible conflicts with what is customary—a topic that spoke to Beck's and Malina's anarchism, as well as to their disapproval of American involvement in the Korean War. "The audience makes its choice," Malina mused in her diary, "[and] shares his dilemma" (*Diaries* 177). Lorca's *Dialogue between a Young Man and a Mannequin* explored the issue of desire left unsatisfied through a talking wedding-dress mannequin who advises a young man to pursue love that exists in the present rather than dwelling in the past on an ideal image of a love that has been lost. The dialogue's brief exploration of desire, romance, and gender paired well with Stein's *Ladies' Voices*, a poetic play that asked audiences to consider the social rhetoric of gender by asking "What are ladies['] voices[?]" (204).

Beck and Malina idolized Stein, and *Ladies' Voices* helped them make a statement about the kind of theater they wanted to do. Stein's very brief poetic play consists mainly of snippets of a dialogue between two "ladies" that cover such topics as social propriety ("I do not excuse myself. I feel there is no reason for passing an archduke."), social politics ("Genevieve does not know that it is only in this country that she could speak as she does."), and social gossip ("Mr. Richard Sutherland. That is a name I know. / Yes. / The Hotel Victoria. . . . / Masked balls. . . . / Poor Augustine.") (204). Although the play begins by confidently asserting "Ladies' voices give pleasure," it soon becomes a critique of the social rhetoric of class and gender (203). Neither a direct political slogan (for which the Living Theatre would later become famous) nor a purely aesthetic withdrawal

Fig. 4. Judith Malina and Helen Jacobs in *Ladies' Voices* by Gertrude Stein, produced by the Living Theatre in 1951. (Photo by Carl Van Vechten, Gertrude Stein and Alice B. Toklas Papers, American Literature Collection, Beinecke Rare Book and Manuscript Library, Yale University. Copyright Van Vechten Trust.)

from the social world, the brief, non-naturalistic dialogue of *Ladies' Voices* explores cultural politics at the level of language and discourse.

As is the case in most of Stein's plays, dialogue in *Ladies' Voices* is not assigned to specific characters—in fact, there are no characters listed, leaving matters of performance entirely up to the director. Under Beck's direction, Malina and Jacobs played two women of society who wore stylish black dresses and hurled admonishments and innuendos at a dressmaker's dummy. The scene symbolized the world of fashion and upper-middle-class femininity, and Malina and Jacobs offered, in Malina's own estimation, "a perfect duo portrait of *Vogue*-ish chatter in which the dressmaker's dummy is the scapegoat, the outsider. We know well how to treat her" (*Diaries* 180). Yet, despite this scenario, much of the work of deciphering a plot out of the string of poetic wordplay and nonsequiturs that comprises the play's dialogue fell on the audience's shoulders. And it appears that the audience loved it, for the Stein play in particular "drew calls for encores," Malina noted in her diary that same evening (184). Carl Van Vechten, the modernist photographer and Stein's literary executor, was so taken with the production that he requested to photograph it (185).

Taken together, the four plays performed that first night in Beck and Malina's living room explored the nature of storytelling and the role of the audience. The audience was asked to think, to make choices, even to make meaning, but it was not invited into the performance and the performance did not make direct reference to audience members' own social lives. Instead, social life itself was portrayed as a performance, the success of which had more to do with the believability of the performance than with any objective "truth." The production undermined familiar social narratives and spotlighted the manner in which such narratives are learned, accepted, and reproduced. The plays incorporated metatheater, Brechtian defamiliarization, nonnarrative, poetic language play, antirealism, and a focus on the activity of the audience. Even the most conventional of the plays, Lorca's *Dialogue between a Young Man and a Mannequin*, involves a talking dummy. For audiences that had been trained in the seeming transparency and easy consumption of theatrical and cinematic realism, the Living Theatre's offerings may have been discomforting, though whether such discomfort was pleasurable or not depended on one's perspective.

A few months before the living room production, Malina mused in her journal about what a "*living* theater" must be.

Plays should be short enough to be easily rehearsed so that they do
not deaden in the process. The plots simple. The style pure, direct;
not too much scenery; music, but not too much; poetry, but not
too many words; perfect tempo. Attain the perfection of production through the perfection of immediacy. The Noh is a perfect medium, but the Noh is too rigid. Better than Noh's strictness is the
short enacted poem, the active, living poem. Gertrude Stein has
clues. Work on this! (*Diaries* 169)

The clues that Gertrude Stein offered soon became a road map. In December 1951 at their new Cherry Lane performance space, The Living Theatre
staged yet another Stein play, under Malina's direction—*Doctor Faustus
Lights the Lights*, a retelling of the Faustus myth conveyed in Stein's signature
poetic reiterations. In Stein's version of the legend, Doctor Faustus has sold
his soul to the devil in order to invent electric light. Before he descends into
hell, Mephisto offers to make Faustus young again in order to woo a young
woman into hell with him. But this turns out to be a trick, for once he has
changed, the young woman doesn't recognize him, and she sends him away.
With typical Steinian wordplay, the play undermines both identity and causality. Malina described the play as "one of the company's earliest manifes-
tos" (Rosenthal 27), and the two-week run played to packed houses. After
attending the premiere, William Carlos Williams wrote to Beck and Malina,
calling the production "so far above the level of commercial theatre that I
tremble that it might fade and disappear" (qtd in Biner 29).

The "clues" that Gertrude Stein offered pointed toward audience autonomy, and in keeping the production "simple" Malina wanted to resist
too closely guiding the audience. She was especially drawn to its abstract-
ness and "over-simple words breaking the language to smithereens" (*Diaries* 187). She was also drawn to the gender politics of the play, remarking
in her diary that it was crucial to cast "someone who can convey Gertrude
Stein's womanly view of this male legend: a Gretchen who does not re-
deem Faust, but dies in her own innocence" (195). The production emphasized abstraction and indeterminacy over an overtly political message, for
in the Cold War climate of the 1950s, Malina worried that political theater
was "oversimplified as cheap propaganda. . . . [I]t was the sort of thing that
had no subtlety[,] that tried to tell you what to think" (qtd in Durham 76).[4]
But there are also clear thematic resonances between the thirst for technological knowledge that leads an inventor to sell his soul and the Cold
War nuclear climate, as Leslie Atkins Durham notes. Following Stein's

lead, the production, "granted the viewer enormous perceptual freedom," Durham observes, "and . . . avoid[ed] producing propaganda that they believed would affirm the dominant Cold War ideology" (75). The goal of such perceptual freedoms was a radical particularity that would place the performer and audience in a new relation and can be likened to what George Quasha, writing about performance poetry of the 1970s, described as "the freedom of performer and audience to originate an unknown state of attention or to enter an 'anarchistic' social relationship through 'author-less' language" (488). In Stein's work, these new relations and perceptual freedoms were encouraged by the punning rhymes and abstract, looping repetitions of Stein's text, but it was also fostered by Beck's set design of abstract wooden cubes and risers, which offered no hint of location. Although the production took place on a conventional stage and followed a "textbook production process" (Durham 80), the lighting, costuming, music, and set eschewed narrative details. Actors tended to strike poses rather than perform actions, asking audiences to use their own imaginations to make meaning from the cues. The hope was that giving audience members a taste of such freedom inside the theater might also make them thirst for it outside the theater and reject an unquestioning adherence to the dominant cultural ideology.[5] Thus, while it may have avoided direct political proclamations, Malina saw the Stein production not as an escape from politics but as a step on the path to developing a political theater that called on the audience to participate, and hopefully to act, rather than merely making it subject to the work. Moreover, the production presented "a clash," as Sarah Bay-Cheng has observed, "between the technologically advancing modern civilization and the primal forces beneath it" (126), which was to become a key characteristic of the Living Theatre's aesthetic.

With two Stein productions under their belts in just a few months (and a reprise of *Ladies' Voices* to be staged in January 1952), Beck and Malina had clearly set a tone. They wanted to stage innovative works that challenged the norms of theater and dramatic dialogue. They wanted to offer works that scrutinized the politics of language and social rhetoric. And they wanted to activate audience members to break out of the passivity of the one-to-many role, established by conventional realist theater and perpetuated through the dominance of cinematic spectatorship, to become cocreators of the work. They were committed to a set of strategies rather than to a particular style or form, but poets' theater, and especially the clues offered by Stein, helped Beck and Malina establish their vision of what their theater might do.

Like abstract expressionist painters, Beat poets, and bebop musicians, members of the Living Theatre pointedly refused to use their art to make political statements, which, as other critics have observed, was in itself tantamount to making a political statement in the constrictive surveillance atmosphere of the 1950s. They also worked to undermine the dominant Cold War ideology by freeing audience members' perceptions and placing them in an active role. As Jack Wright observed of the Living Theatre's inaugural 1951–52 season, "In each of the five productions, an attempt was made to involve the audience in the action of the play and to seek greater participation. Actors approached audience members . . . in an effort to force members into some kind of activity" (qtd in Durham 79).

Getting the audience involved—whether through direct interaction with actors or through ambiguous plots, dialogue, and set designs that relied on the audience to make creative associations for themselves—was a key goal the Living Theatre shared with other poets' theaters, and productions of poets' theater were central to the Living Theatre's developing ideas and strategies in these early years. Its first year of productions included several poetic plays, including Kenneth Rexroth's *Beyond the Mountains*, Pablo Picasso's *Desire Trapped by the Tail*, T. S. Eliot's *Sweeney Agonistes*, Paul Goodman's *Faustina*, and John Ashbery's *The Heroes*. Some of these were plodding verse dramas in which poetry was treated with too much reverence and served simply as an "elevated" delivery system for largely conventional ideas and actor-audience relations, and these were the season's greatest failures. The production of Rexroth's play, for example, which followed on the heels of *Doctor Faustus*, was an overly long, stiff, and impersonal verse adaptation of the Oresteia. Although it was performed in Noh style, with masks and Noh dancers, this defamiliarizing technique on its own failed to activate the audience, and with a run time of more than three hours, the production was an unequivocal flop.

But fully fledged poets' theater, in which the language, performance, and stage design collaborated to resist both traditional theater and the cultural coercion of dominant social narratives, generally connected with audiences and critics alike. "An Evening of Bohemian Theatre," the shared bill of three short poetic plays that followed the Rexroth, was the Living Theatre's first clear success. Produced for a total cost of thirty-five dollars (Biner 31), the evening included a reprise of Stein's *Ladies' Voices*, followed by Eliot's *Sweeney Agonistes*, and, finally, the evening's featured offering, Picasso's *Desire Trapped by the Tail*. Beck and Malina both believed that poets' theater was not just the Living Theatre's alternative to the staleness of contemporary theater but its remedy. "If this won't save the theater," Beck proclaimed, "nothing will" (Malina *Diaries* 204).

Picasso's *Desire Trapped by the Tail* was yet another investment in non-linear narrative and the disruptive uses of material language. The plot was darkly comical, and Picasso's writing was especially visual: a character heading off for a cup of coffee at dawn, for example, remarks in language that is at once visually poetic and, in performance, comically ornate, "The sash of the veil that hangs from the eyelashes of the shutters wipes pink clouds on the apple-coloured mirror of the sky, which awakens already at your window. I am off to the café at the corner to tear off with my claws the remains of the chocolate colour that still prowls in the blackness of its coffee" (34).[6] The play's use of poetry is ironic rather than sincere, lambasting "high" art's attempts to get at deeper "truth." But the absurdist play also takes on a serious topic—artists and lovers coming together during the German occupation of Paris—and its short scenarios often end in tragedy: picnickers are carried off alive in coffins, one character's obsequious admirers faint down to the ground covered in blood, the smell of potato chips suffocates a roomful of people, and even in the final scene of defiance against the dehumanization of war all the characters are blinded. Clothes, curtains, vegetables, and concepts such as "Silence" and "Anxiety" become personified. And, much to the audience's delight, John Ashbery and Frank O'Hara appeared in the Living Theatre's production as a "madly funny" pair of "Bow Wows," nonspeaking roles that relied on broad physical humor (Malina *Diaries* 210). But underlying the play's humor are themes of loss, anguish, and desire that cannot be fulfilled, and the characters are ultimately survivors. The play offers no political slogans, but its message is clear: war leaves survivors but no winners, and no one escapes.

As with the Stein plays, the audience was called on to actively make sense of the performance via a combination of narrative nonsequiturs and absurdities, the self-consciously satirical use of poetic diction, and non-naturalistic acting that invited the audience to observe the work—and play—of the performance. Writing about the production in her journal, Malina declared, "I will not have any audience: Only participants" (*Diaries* 214). But it was perhaps a painful participation, for the comedy of the play draws audiences in only to crush them with the tragedy of scene after scene. The reviews were generally tepid. One newspaper columnist lambasted the production as "communistic" because of Picasso's political ideas, and he publicly listed the names of the all the theater's sponsors as a way to call out their support (211). But audiences kept coming, and the production made enough money that the actors, who had been performing for free, could finally be paid.

But Beck and Malina were looking for a still greater prod for the audience, and their next production, Paul Goodman's *Faustina*, was their most overt attempt to date to force the audience to act. It also demonstrated some of the limits of fully narrative participatory theater. Playing for four weeks in repertory with *Desire Trapped by the Tail*, *Faustina* was a modern verse adaptation of the story of the wife of Emperor Marcus Aurelius. The audience witnesses a horrific ritual sacrifice of the gladiator with whom Faustina's husband has fallen in love. The murder is meant to appease Faustina's jealousy, and at the end of the play an actor admonishes the audience for not stepping in to stop the brutal onstage murder. Malina was so taken with *Faustina* upon reading it for the first time that she immediately insisted that the Living Theatre perform it, later calling it "the best new play that I know" (*Diaries* 61). When she saw the play performed in 1949 by the Prester John Company, an anarchist group, she noted the young audience's "wide-eyedness," "wakefulness," and "lack of ennui" (82), and she wanted to create a similarly responsive audience. But the Living Theatre's production did not fare as well. Audiences were small and reviews mediocre, and the performers' reverential delivery of the verse dialogue seemed aimed more at elevating than destabilizing the narrative. But most important, the actors were displeased with the blatant audience manipulation of the final scene—so much so that the actor assigned the play's key lines, which scold the audience for not interfering with the onstage murder, refused to speak them and a replacement had to be found to deliver them. Beck later admitted that the lines were "insulting, and could only rile and affront an audience" (Tytell 83). But, while it is disingenuous to admonish a theater audience for failing to halt an onstage "murder," Beck and Malina's understanding of how to foster audience participation was sharpening. Rather than criticizing the audience for responding conventionally to a largely conventional play, they needed to find new ways to incorporate the audience actively into the performance. And if the goal was to resist dominant cultural representations, then the lulling narrative structures to which audiences had become comfortably accustomed had to be undermined.

The final two plays of the Living Theatre's inaugural year—Alfred Jarry's *Ubu the King*, in a translation by Beck and Malina, and John Ashbery's *The Heroes* as the curtain raiser—attempted to critique bourgeois morality, another strategy that would become central to the group's vision.

Jarry's absurdist play was so controversial when it premiered in France in 1896 that it caused a riot and the production closed after only one performance (some say it heralded the start of modernism), but by 1951 it could only raise the specter of scandal as a historical artifact. But its call for a stripped-down staging, using masks, plain backdrops, and cardboard props, appealed to the Living Theatre's bare-bones aesthetic, and Beck made his own set out of brown wrapping paper and his costumes out of rags in a paint-splattered design inspired by Jackson Pollock. The play famously begins with "Merdre!" (the French word for shit with an additional *r*), and though it's not written in verse, the dialogue consists, in a kind of foreshadowing of poets' theater's mashing together of rhetorical registers, of a mix of puns, schoolyard slang, code, and coarse language.

But the play that opened the evening, Ashbery's *The Heroes*, had more immediate resonance (and it would be staged in a new production the following year, 1953, by the New York poets' theater group the Artists' Theatre, directed by Herbert Machiz). Malina described the tragicomic gathering of Greek legends, including Ulysses, Circe, Theseus, Patroclus, and Achilles, now relocated to a modern seaside country house, as "a poetic dissection of the foibles of the figures of the Greek myths, like an 18th century play written by a young 20th century poet whose pen has been dipped in surrealism" (*Diaries* 252). With Wildean affectation, plenty of homosexual innuendo, and self-conscious references to theatrical conventions, the play questions the common association of heroism with masculinity and domination. It also invites the audience to consider how the conventions of narrative clarity might work to support a particular dominant ideology or overly simplified worldview. "I've been invited to see what's to be done," the Chorus explains as she introduces herself, but then she later ups the ante: "So far this play has been easy. From now on it's going to be more difficult to follow. That's the way life is sometimes" (40, 41). The homosexual portrayals of *The Heroes* were either shocking or appealingly subversive, depending on one's cultural perspective, and the play ends with a police officer arriving to break up a party at which men are dancing together. On opening night, the audience response to the production was so enthusiastic and raucous that the stage curtain came down. Unfortunately, the theater was closed two days later, apparently through the machinations of the new building landlord who was skeptical of his tenants' associations (see *Diaries* 240–41).

In many ways, the first year of the Living Theatre resembled the first year of the Poets' Theatre as both experimented with verse drama and poetic theater by new and established writers and both employed Noh stagings, stripped-down sets, and poetic language to break through theatrical illusion and dismantle audience complacency. They even shared Ashbery and O'Hara (and soon Goodman as well), although the Living Theatre produced many more plays by established figures in the avant-garde world. But, while the Poets' Theatre was a workshop for poet-playwrights, the Living Theatre was a performance lab. Its experiments with Stein, Goodman, Picasso, and Ashbery taught its members that there were many ways to break through theatrical illusion, but not all of them created community and none created true freedom. At the same time, performances that defied social convention could have just as much, and sometimes even more, immediate political impact as direct address and sloganeering. As they spent two years looking for a new theater space, their search for theater's liberatory power continued.

Poetry and Cruelty in Repertory:
Many Loves, The Connection, *and* Tonight We Improvise

In 1954, the Living Theatre opened a new theater space at Broadway and 100th Street, and for much of the 1950s it offered an assortment of antirealist and avant-garde theater and poetic drama, including works by W. H. Auden, August Strindberg, Jean Racine, Jean Cocteau, Luigi Pirandello, Claude Fredericks, and Paul Goodman. Several plays featured political messages that appealed to Beck and Malina, but they were not always theatrically innovative, and the results were mixed. Their production of Auden's Pulitzer Prize–winning book-length poem *The Age of Anxiety* addressed cultural paralysis and people's failure to help one another. (Auden's poem, writes Alan Jacobs, "is among the first poems in English, perhaps the very first, to register the fact of the Nazis' genocidal murder of millions of Jews" [xiii].) A Narrator, played in the Living Theatre production by Malina, who also served as director, guides the audience through the story. But the poem, possibly the least read of Auden's major works, is dense, allusive, and alliterative, with long soliloquies and a plodding plot. The production featured a musical score by Jackson MacLow, but Beck "knew that the play was old-fashioned as theatre" (Tytell 105), perhaps in part because the Narrator was too controlling a force, as Malina suggests (*Piscator* 173). Although the theater was initially packed, audiences soon dwindled. A few months later Claude Fredericks's *The Idiot King*, a sadly idealistic morality play about a pacifist king who will not kill even though his kingdom is crumbling, also failed to find an audience, and the last three performances were canceled due to low attendance. But the company's production of *Phèdre*, Racine's seventeenth-century French verse tragedy about a family destroyed by forbidden love, was a clear success, and the run was twice extended. Other productions also fared generally well, but one of the group's greatest successes of this period was the production of Pirandello's *Tonight We Improvise*, a metatheatrical exploration of the audience's role in the theater.

Tonight We Improvise portrays a group of actors improvising an Italian melodrama, a stage adaptation of Pirandello's short story "Leonora, addio!" The director asks his actors to immerse themselves fully in their roles while improvising scenes, but the actors chafe at the director's constant attempts to control the improvisations. As the director and actors argue, the actors begin to transform themselves into their fictive roles. The script being improvised is the story of the La Croce family—wife, husband, and four daughters—and the air force officers the daughters flirt with. The La Croces are lovers of the theater and former performers. The father has fallen in love with a cabaret singer, and before the end of the play he has died defending her honor. One of the sisters, Mommina (played by Malina in the Living Theatre production), soon marries one of the air force officers and they have two children, but he turns out to be abusive and suspicious of her past life in the theater. When he leaves, she discovers among his possessions a playbill for an opera in which her sister, now a famous opera singer, is starring. As Mommina tells her children about the opera, her heart begins to race and, in a merging of theatrical frames, she dies while singing the opera's aria of love, jealousy, and deception. The play ends with the actress rising from her "death" and the director briefly addressing the audience before the final curtain.

The role of the director, Dr. Hinkfuss, was played by Beck (renamed Dr. Beckfuss) in what Malina described as "a satire on himself, as avant-garde director" (*Diaries* 353). In perhaps the group's earliest articulation of antitextualism, much of Hinkfuss's dialogue at the beginning of the play emphasizes the limitations of the playwright's control over the actual theatrical product. A work of art is ultimately fixed and unliving, Hinkfuss asserts in a direct address to the audience, though it is precisely this rigidity that also makes it eternal. In contrast, life is "in an infinitely various and continually changing state of becoming," which is also why it is "doomed to wither and perish" (Pirandello 14). But art may be brought to life, Hinkfuss claims, by a living audience that can give it movement. Then again Hinkfuss is dissembling, playing with the audience by claiming that he and the cast have actually prescripted the actors' rebellion against him as a means of making the performance seem more "authentic." One of the questions raised by the play is whether the audience needs to be fully immersed in the theatrical illusion in order to have an emotional response to the portrayals.

But it is not only the playwright's control that is resisted here. Instead, the play resists control by any single authority—author, director, performer, designer, or spectator. Hinkfuss may have removed Pirandello's name from all promotional materials, but the actors also resist Hinkfuss's control of their performances. Meanwhile, the constant movement back and forth between the internal melodrama and its metatheatrical frame, with "actors" going in and out of "character," raises the question for the audience of what sort of performance is required for audience members to play their own expected roles in the theater. By planting actors in the audience to play the worst kind of stereotypical audience members for real audience members to react against, the play was in some ways as manipulative as *Faustina*. But it also might be seen as a forerunner to contemporary immersive theater: the performance is site specific as audience members watch actors playing "actors" stage a play in a theater. During the "intermission," audience members could either stay in their seats and witness the "director," Dr. Hinkfuss, set up Act III, or could head to the lobby and watch four interrelated scenes involving the La Croce family members, somehow transported to the present-day theater space, playing simultaneously. As a test of the authenticity of theater itself and also in some ways as an exploration of the ways in which role-playing is a part of everyday life, *Tonight We Improvise* was well suited to an era in which J. L. Austin was lecturing about the performativity of language and Erving Goffman was formulating his ideas about social life as a kind of performance. The play was the Living Theatre's most popular production yet, and extra chairs had to be brought in nightly during its four-month run.

Tonight We Improvise was also a key step in the Living Theatre's developing sense of performer-spectator interactions. "It was in Piscator's production of *Tonight We Improvise*," Malina later wrote, "that Julian Beck and I first confronted the question of who the actor is in relation to the spectator" (*Piscator* 147). But the Living Theatre, she felt, was able to take this question much further than Piscator had by creating opportunities for real improvisation between audience and actor: during one particular scene, Malina playing the role of Mommina flirtatiously sits on an audience member's lap. When Mommina's jealous boyfriend protests, she asks for protection from the audience member, who must then make a choice of how to respond. "Faced with the spectator's response," Malina recalls, "neither Pirandello nor Piscator was willing to confront the challenge of the audience's improvisation and potential irresponsibility. To deal with this required the whole ensemble to be committed to the experiment, and greater confidence in the audience than Piscator could muster. The Living Theatre, on the other hand, was committed to just that experiment" (*Piscator* 149).

A few years after the successes of *Tonight We Improvise*, the Living Theatre encountered another formative moment in its development, as many others have noted, when Beck and Malina met Mary Caroline Richards. Richards was a poet, potter, and Black Mountain faculty member who was working on translating the French director, theorist, and poet Antonin Artaud for her now renowned *The Theater and Its Double*, published by Grove Press in 1958 (originally published in French in 1938). Richards offered Beck and Malina an advance copy, and in 1959 she also delivered a guest lecture on Artaud at the Living Theatre. *The Theater and Its Double* soon became required reading for a generation of theater artists. Beck and Malina found in Artaud a kindred spirit who shared their interest in the liberatory power of theater, and soon Artaud's notion of a "cruel" theater began to guide the company. No longer safely set apart from the action and no longer in control via the authority of an all-encompassing gaze, the spectator of cruel theater is subject to the spectacle, dominated by it, and engulfed in it. "An ideally 'cruel' spectacle," David Graver explains, "would be one in which the spectator feels unwittingly implicated as both agent and victim" (52). The idea is not inherently liberatory, as Kimberly Jannarone has noted, and "'Revolution . . . does not always represent a progressive move" (15). In fact Artaud himself was opposed to liberal politics, and he saw his radical theater as apolitical. But, in what might be seen as an extension of poets' theater's merging of materiality and representation, the Living Theatre combined Artaud's emphasis on the body over intellect with Piscator's epic theater into performances that it hoped would catalyze audiences to act against oppression.

Artaud appealed to the company members' interest in destabilizing any single authority—text, author, director, performer, or audience member—an idea that they had already explored in *Tonight We Improvise* and in works such as Stein's. As Graver points out, Artaud wasn't as interested in overthrowing any one specific authority as in cultivating "multiple sources of authority as much as possible without dissipating the powers of the theatrical event" (48)—rather like the way poets' theater sought to free the audience's perceptual powers by employing different theatrical elements to destabilize and undermine narrative and authorial control. Advocating a balance between text, spectacle, and performance, Artaud argued "for a transformation of the text into a hieroglyph, the spectacle into cruelty, and the performance into affective athleticism" (ibid.).

Even before being exposed to Artaud's cry for "no more masterpieces!," American poets and theater artists had become skeptical of external centers of authority controlling their experiences—from the form of the text itself to the smooth façade of the professional impersonating actor. In poetry, for example, Olson's 1950 manifesto "Projective Verse" was taking hold. Projective verse rejected control of poetic rhythm and meter by externally imposed form and instead called for "composition by field" based on the poet's own breath and uninhibited by the editing mind (see the "Introduction" for a more detailed discussion of Olson's impact on poetry performance). Projective poetry was thus processual, as the event of emerging language, rather than as object, and as a vehicle for spiritual connection.

But, although projective verse was controlled not by language or externally imposed form but rather by the "natural" expression of the poet's physicality, some still found it too controlling and too tied to lofty spiritual goals. "Nobody should experience anything they don't need to," Frank O'Hara wrote in his tongue-in-cheek manifesto "Personism," published in *Yugen* in 1961. "If they don't need poetry bully for them, I like the movies too. And after all, only Whitman and Crane and Williams, of the Americans poets, are better than the movies" (498). "Writerly" texts—Roland Barthes's term for texts that turned the reader into a producer rather than a consumer of meaning—such as Stein's, decentered the authority of the text (and author) in ways that echoed Artaud's injunction against masterpieces (even if Stein herself believed in authorial "genius"). The Living Theatre was well steeped in Stein's participatory, performative works before discovering Artaud in 1958. What Artaud offered, then, was not an entirely new vision but a way to bring the group's interest in nonauthoritarian performance to dramatic theater.

Criticizing traditional western theater's emphasis on psychological or emotional conflict created via a privileging of language and dialogue, Artaud advocated a theater that would provoke spiritual conflict via the concrete language of the mise-en-scène, beyond the reach of speech, which would use all elements of the stage, including sound, gestures, lights, and physical objects, to produce in the audience both physical response and revelation. Replacing the "poetry of language" with what he called "a poetry of the senses," Artaud argued that this concrete physical language "is addressed first of all to the senses instead of being addressed primarily to the mind as is the language of words" ("Metaphysics" 37–38). His privileged text was the hieroglyph, by which he meant a text that didn't just signify but performed, a text that both represented and created a world.

But as much as Artaud disavowed speech and language, he also went to great lengths not merely to abandon language but to alter what it could be used to do. Although the language of the senses is primary as a "visual and plastic materialization of speech," Artaud argues that this "does not prevent it from developing later its full intellectual effect on all possible levels and in every direction. But it permits the substitution, for the language of poetry, of a poetry in space which will be resolved in precisely the domain which does not belong strictly to words" ("Oriental" 69, "Metaphysics" 38). While Artaud locates the value of theater in performance that appeals directly to the senses without intellectual mediation, he does not require the banishment of intellect entirely. Although he suggests, "To change the role of speech in theater is to make use of it in a concrete and spatial sense" ("Oriental" 72), he also asserts that the theater "rediscovers itself precisely at the point where the mind requires a language to express its manifestations" ("Theater" 12). As he further clarifies in his essay "Oriental and Occidental Theater," speech may be conceived of on a "universal level" as "an active force springing out of the destruction of appearances in order to reach the mind itself," but the West tends to treat speech as completed thought, "which is lost at the moment of its own exteriorization" (70). In this formulation, speech functions nonsymbolically to inspire creativity. The thought that is produced by such speech is emergent rather than completed.

The political force of this shift from speech-as-completed-thought to speech-as-destruction-of-appearances lay in its potential to reconfigure modes of perception via theatricality. As a phenomenon of perception, theatricality depends, as Josette Féral puts it, "on the overlap of representation (ostension, fiction) and presentation (reality, the real)" (11).

Certainly Olson's notion of projective verse as an indication of physicality free of semantic reference satisfies Artaud's notion of the "truly theatrical." In "An Affective Athleticism" Artaud writes about the importance of breath in supporting the actor's body, arguing that the tempo of the breath corresponds to a particular emotion: "It is certain that for every feeling, every mental action, every leap of human emotion there is a corresponding breath which is appropriate to it. The tempos of the breath have a name taught us by the Cabala; it is these tempos which give the human heart its shape, and the movements of the passions their sex" (134). Through a kind of somatic synchrony, audience members experience within their own bodies the tensions and rhythms enacted in the stage spectacle. Making a related argument about poetry performance, Olson asserted that the emotional response to poetry came not from its form or sound (which involved the mind) but rather directly from the heart through the breath.[7] While Olson was writing about the breath of the writer, he was also offering instruction for reading, which works more actively than theater to put the audience's (reader's) breathing patterns into harmony with the rhythms of the work. And yet, while Olson's emphasis on performance as way of creating emotional response via breathing rhythms resembles, in some ways, Artaud's affective athleticism, it lacks the spiritual goals of Artaud.

Most critics have located Artaud's legacy in an explosion of "antitextual" theater in the 1960s.[8] Associated with happenings, unscripted spontaneity, and an emphasis on the event "itself," antitextual theater is frequently characterized as openly hostile toward the traditional textuality of the commercial theater. But "antiauthoritarian" theater might be better descriptor than "antitextual" for a practice that was largely aimed not at eradicating texts but at destabilizing all centers of authority. Such antiauthoritarianism was hardly limited to Artaud—it could be seen in the paintings of Jackson Pollock, in the infamously participatory readings of Beat writers, and in the chance compositions of John Cage. But what Artaud offered Beck and Malina was a theory of the theater that helped focus their aesthetic strategies and experiments into an ethics.

The most critically acclaimed of all the Living Theatre's productions of poets' theater was William Carlos Williams's *Many Loves*. The large audiences that lined up to see *Many Loves* helped to sustain an initially much less successful play that opened in repertory with it a few months later—Jack Gelber's *The Connection*, which won a small following despite opening to initially terrible reviews. In November a revival of *Tonight We*

Improvise was added to the repertory rotation, in a new translation by Claude Fredericks. Together *Many Loves, The Connection,* and *Tonight We Improvise* showcase the multiple approaches by which the Living Theatre attempted to bring theater into everyday life and to bring everyday life into the theater. They also demonstrate the connections between poets' theater and "cruel" theater. Each of the plays uses the same central trope— the audience is witnessing the staging of a scene and actors play both characters and "themselves," with different degrees of pretense apparent to the audience. As a self-conscious alternative to the passivity of the commercial theater, each play strove to create a deeper and more authentic experience by making the audience part of the play itself. Indeed, in his notes for *Many Loves,* Williams wrote "The audience is the play: the play is to be written looking from the stage, not at it, into the minds of the audience where it is really taking place. That is the thing to represent on stage as it occurs" (qtd in Bay-Cheng and Cole 214).

Many Loves uses verse as a counterpoint to the naturalist dialogue of conventional drama. In this play about a play, a poet-playwright, who is betrothed to his leading lady, tries to win the support of the middle-aged male financial backer who is not so secretly in love with him. This frame story is intertwined with three short internal scenes, which depict play rehearsals that are taking place in the theater. Watching each scene rehearsal, the two men discuss the merits of different kinds of theater and their expectations of the audience. Both the interior scenes, written in naturalist dialogue, and the frame structure, written in free verse, depict the darker underbelly of love as emotional manipulation and sexual exploitation. The poetry of the frame might be expected to offer an attractive alternative to the brutal naturalism of the interior dramatic scenes, in which lovers use and abandon one another with a survivor's impersonal cruelty, but the frame characters, too, selfishly manipulate one another even as they seek a higher beauty. Hubert, the poet-playwright, aspires to create a more authentic theatrical expression through the use of a modern verse that has not yet been discovered in the theater (a desire that particularly resonated with Beck), but he also hides his betrothal so as not to damage his chances of financial support from the wealthy dandy, Peter. Meanwhile, Peter believes theater is best built with romance and illusion, and he thinks Hubert's interest in verse (as well as his interest in Alise, his fiancée) is naive and precious.

The play contains very little action, and the conflicts center on ideas: the interior scenes are built around emotional disagreements over sexual relationships, fueled by desire, fear, and the wish to control another person, while the frame story foregrounds debates about the role of theater, and especially of poetic drama. Hubert argues, for example, that poetic language itself should be the action, "words in love, / hot words, copulating, drinking, running, / bleeding!" and the action of these words should take place in the minds of the audience. But Peter reminds Hubert that commercial theater audiences are more practical and are often "made up of / boredom" come to be entertained. "So, by God, you're / going to make them swallow poetry— / for your amusement," Peter scolds him. "You won't get / away with it, Hubert" (Williams 34). In thematizing the audience, the play makes the audience aware of its own expectations and conventions of spectatorship that it brings to the theater. Are you like Hubert, who believes that a truly modern theatrical verse will have the power to present audiences with a higher truth, the play seems to ask its own spectators, or are you like Peter, who believes in the appeal of an easily consumable narrative?

In the end, the play sides neither with Hubert nor with Peter, and no truth rings out more authentically than any other. Believing in the power of poetry to offer a "higher truth" is just as coercive as being passively absorbed into narrative, since both approaches subject the audience to its version of reality. If there is a central character, it is Alise, Hubert's leading lady and fiancée. Williams's stage directions stipulate that the role of Alise and the lead female role in each of the interior scenes are to be played by the same actress (played by Malina in the Living Theatre production), and as we watch Alise move from cuckold and jilted lover to independent, childless businesswoman to seductress, and as we see her as both a solid supporter of Hubert's vision of the theater and an able defender against Peter's dismissive attacks, her agile shape-shifting becomes the clearest action of the play. The play's final message is that all communication is performance, which, like theater, relies on illusion and persuasion. Like other works of poets' theater, *Many Loves* uses verse to explore the power and cultural coercion of conventional language, social rhetoric, and narrative forms.

Many Loves opened on January 13, 1959, to an enthusiastic reception, and Malina received eleven curtain calls (Tytell 151). Brooks Atkinson of the *New York Times* called the production "original in form, exhilarating in content and alive with knowledge about human beings," adding that "everything about the acting . . . is honest and intelligent" and the play "makes no concessions to the conventions of theatre." "Bow down, bow down, you hardy revivalists of O'Neill, Shaw, even of Chekhov," proclaimed Jeffrey Tallmer in the *Village Voice*, for "the frenzied few of the Living Theatre, for all their long-haired intramuralism, have charted out new worlds to conquer." Afterward, at a party attended by Jack Kerouac, Gregory Corso, Paul Goodman, and Jackson MacLow, Allen Ginsberg praised Beck's direction by kneeling at his feet (Tytell 152). Williams himself was in ailing health when the play premiered, but he attended a matinee and commended Malina's acting. The show ran for more than two hundred performances, a remarkable success in the world of experimental theater.

As a way of orienting audiences to its artistic goals, the playbill for *Many Loves* included a short 1925 essay by Martin Buber entitled "Drama and Theater: A Fragment." Beck and Malina had been reading Buber's work for several years, and in this essay he discusses the power of drama as poetry and the artistic independence of dialogue. As a place where action occurs, the essay argues, dialogue has the power to bridge the "I" and the "Thou," Buber's terms for the partners in human relationships that give meaning and spirituality to experience. Lying somewhere between fiction and ritual, the poetry of dramatic dialogue not only represents a scene or tells a story, Buber argues, but it can create a world, as well as real experiences and emotions, for both actors and audiences. As a guide for the audience of *Many Loves*, the essay adds a spiritual element to the play's test of the power of language to communicate truth.

When *The Connection* opened six months later, its playbill also included an essay, this one a brief piece by Artaud entitled "The Theater and Culture," the introductory essay in *The Theater and Its Double*. Artaud's essay contains echoes of Buber in its call for the "language" of theater to touch and bring forth real life. Artaud writes that art should be useful, for "If confusion is the sign of the times, I see at the root of this confusion a rupture between things and words, between things and the ideas and signs that are their representation" (7). Here Artaud seems to be arguing in part against the *art pour l'art* movement. But, notably, he does not suggest that representation should be banished but that it should be used like a totem—that is, as something that has a shadow or "double" and that can also, like magic, bring something new into being. If Artaud is ambivalent toward theater's use of representation, it is an ambivalence born out of his specific critique of an inwardly oriented theater, a theater separated from everyday life. The antitextuality with which Artaud is so commonly associated must be understood in these terms—as a break not from language, or even representation itself, but rather from language cut off from life. *The Con-*

nection particularly appealed to Beck and Malina in this sense because it challenged the division between theater and everyday life. And it did so by focusing attention not on the theater itself but on the cruelty (and painful monotony) of the everyday lives of social outcasts such as drug addicts.

The Connection was, in some ways, an attempt to achieve a level of "honesty" in the theater—something that Beck spoke of frequently in his lectures of the period. The play, which opened in repertory with *Many Loves* on July 15, 1959, is about heroin addicts in pursuit of their next fix, and it compares drug addiction to bourgeois consumerism and wage labor while offering no easy answers. The production's depiction of the suffering of addicts was inspired by Malina's recent experience with addicts during her imprisonment in the New York Women's House of Detention.[9] According to Malina's own account, both Beck and Malina were detained in 1957 for refusing to report to a fallout shelter during an air-raid drill. During their thirty days of incarceration, they got to know some of their fellow inmates, many of whom were prostitutes and drug addicts. "This crucial moment in [Beck's and Malina's] political educa-tion," Sell notes, "ratified for them a lesson first taught to them by Allen Ginsberg: artistic revolution was inseparable from bodily revolution" (71). The goal was to confront audiences with real suffering in order to inspire them to act toward social change.

Like both *Many Loves* and *Tonight We Improvise*, *The Connection* is framed as the fictionalized staging of a work in production (in this case, a producer and writer are employing real addicts in their documentary about addiction), but it also breaks through this frame, both in the actual use of drugs by actors onstage and, more important, in the music of actual jazz musicians improvising together onstage. *The Connection* has often been seen as a turning point in the Living Theatre's career precisely for this merging of art and politics into an "authentic" audience experience. Bradford Martin asserts, for example, that, whereas in previous produc-tions the company relied heavily on aesthetic innovation that referenced very little outside of itself, *The Connection* drew, like Beat poetics, on the cultural influence of jazz improvisation to support its arguments.[10] In fact, many of the performers in *The Connection* were actual jazz musicians whose improvisational musical interludes were incorporated directly into the stage performance as a jazz "jam" session.[11] The "jam" is not a concert or show but just a gathering of musicians who wish to play together, and its existence outside market structures allowed individuals to do and say what they pleased, as Sell has argued (94). Jazz jams were not, however, intended to be public spectacles. Instead, they were lessons in listening that brought the performers themselves together into an interactive community. The jam was therefore a social structure performed in the theater, and it became, Sell suggests, part of the political strategy enacted by the Living Theatre (ibid.).

The poetic language spoken by the play's "junkies" became a kind of pleasurable and interactive performance as well. When stoned, the characters of *The Connection* put language together in ways that don't always proceed rationally—in ways, in fact, that are poetic, such as in the character Solly's address to the audience.

> As you have gathered, we are, as they say in the tabloids, dope fiends. We are waiting. We have waited before. The connection is coming. He is always coming. But so is education, for example. The man who will whisper the truth in your ear. Or the one who will shout it out among the people. I can't generalize and believe it. I'm not made that way. Perhaps Jaybird [the producer of the play] has chosen this petty and miserable microcosm because of its self-annihilating aspects. This tells us something about Jaybird, but nothing about me. Hurry, hurry, hurry. The circus is here. Suicide is not uncommon among us. The seeking of death is at once fascinating and repellent. The overdose of heroin is where that frail line of life and death swings in silent breeze of ecstatic summer. The concept of this limbo you can hold in your palsied hand. Who else can make so much out of passing out? (Gelber 40)

Sell aptly describes the play's druggy speech, which wanders at times into the sounds of agony, as "a kind of sound poem . . . what we would now call a deconstructive performance that troubles the distinction between text and performance" (120). That is, the Living Theatre dramatized the rejection of the text by making the script itself an object of struggle between the junkies and the "producer" of the play, rather like Pirandello's *Tonight We Improvise*. Sell has argued that while Pirandello's *Tonight We Improvise* and Williams's *Many Loves* both displayed an ambivalence toward the written text that he characterizes as antitextuality, it wasn't until *The Connection*'s discovery of jazz as a structural component—what Sell refers to as a "jazz epistemology"—that antitextuality became more than a thematic in the work of the Living Theatre (78). *The Connection* in this sense might be characterized as a "deconstructive" performance, and its use of live jazz improvisation begins to make the transition toward the use of nonmimetic performance—that is, unscripted, improvisatory, and nonrepresentational performance—which was to become a central concern of the Living Theatre in the latter part of the decade and which has become the company's greatest legacy.[12]

Unlike *Tonight We Improvise* and *Many Loves*, *The Connection* wasn't entirely scripted. The play combined prewritten dialogue with improvised action to create a version of realism as the performance of actual events unfolding in the present moment (Martin 58). The monotony of "a theatrical event that depicted more than two hours of 'real time' in the lives of junkies waiting for a fix" (ibid.) achieves on some level the temporal conditions of real life. Demanding real silences, real dirt, real jazz, and real speech, Beck aimed for, as he put it, a "resurgence of realism" because "what had been passing for realism was not real" ("Storming" 26).

The plot of *The Connection* revolves around a group of heroin addicts who have been hired to add authenticity to a piece of documentary theater about the lives of "junkies." Using a play-within-a-play structure, the characters also include playwright, Jaybird, and producer, Jim. The audience is told that some of the actor-junkies are off procuring drugs, and it is implied that, in an experiment with unscripted, improvisatory theater, the audience will get to witness the junkies actually getting high when the others return (though Jim offers the rather tongue-in-cheek assurance that "we are not actually using real heroin. You don't think we'd use the real stuff? After all, narcotics are illegal" [19]). But the heroin delivery is delayed, and the junkies grow increasingly agitated and less subject to Jaybird's authorial control as they wait for Cowboy, their "connection," to return with their drugs.

The producer, meanwhile, has his own plans for the play, and he announces, to the surprise of both the actors and Jaybird, that he has hired a two-man film crew to record the performance, arguing that it contributes to the theme of improvisation and that it also means "money." The filmmakers certainly add another level of framing to the production, but they are positioned outside the "play" and they do not improvise. In fact, over the course of the performance, the two cameramen, or "photographers," as the play refers to them, slowly "exchange, piece-by-piece, their clothing and personalities," suggesting that they are interchangeable types, or categorical representations, rather than authentic individuals (22). The cameramen are also presented as simple-minded: the 1st Photographer counts on his fingers while the 2nd Photographer, when asked how much money he's being paid to film the play, stumbles in his response, explaining, "I'm visual, you see. I'm not able to express, ah, myself" (25). Simple, inexpressive, and primarily interested in money, the cameramen, regardless of their avant-garde credentials, symbolize the naïveté and inadequacy of film as a medium for expressing life.

The critique extends not only to the limits of film as an expressive medium but also to the ideology of spectatorship associated with those representations. The 1st Photographer invests fully in the believability of the onstage performances, as he sits in the audience and offers the same unchanging comment "That's the way it really is" over and over again. The first time he says this, it's easy to agree that the performance has really captured some sort of fundamental truth, but soon the repetitions begin to sound rehearsed, or at least superficial. Each repetition creates increasing distance from the photographer's simple faith in the transparency of representation, which prevents him from seeing the world's complexities. The limits of seeing are also underscored by the character of Sister Salvation, who accompanies Cowboy when he returns with the drugs in Act II. Cowboy explains to his curious friends that after he made his purchase he saw the police closing in. While his friend was stopped, he managed to escape by starting a conversation with the sister and then inviting her to accompany him home. But Sister Salvation doesn't understand that she's been used as a cover, nor does she see that all the junkies, now heading in and out of the bathroom in pairs, are busy shooting up heroin. Unable to see what's happening right in front of her, Sister Salvation, like the cameramen, demonstrates that vision is easily deceived. In this sense, filmic spectatorship—symbolized by the cameramen but built into the structure of *The Connection* as an ideological counterpoint to the kind of engagement fostered by live improvised musical performance—functions via what Martin Harries has termed "dismediation," or the portrayal of "what happens when a medium becomes part of the 'content' of another medium, when film in all its perceived totalizing force becomes part of the substance of theater" (350). In fact, Harries argues that postwar theater, from the 1950s to the 1970s, is defined by this characteristic dismediation of cinema. Faced with the cultural dominance of film, which interpellates and creates a distanced, abstracted mass public, Harries explains, postwar theater "worked to negate a model of the spectator associated with mass culture" (352). It also tended to abandon the conventions of neat storytelling, not because of "some transhistorical suspicion of narrative," Harries asserts, but as a rejection of "the pleasures of cinematic narration in particular" (352).

Critics have tended to focus on *The Connection*'s use of jazz, not just as incidental music but, like Sell, as epistemology. While this is an important and fruitful reading, the play's critique of spectatorship is just as crucial to understanding its arguments. Positing a dichotomy between seeing and hearing, *The Connection* offers sound as a political alternative to the ocularcentric logic that organizes not only conventional filmic spectatorship but also conventional realist theater spectatorship. Indeed, scripted theater, too, is indicted in *The Connection* for relying on an ideology of normative spectatorship that subjects its audience to its particular version of the world. After all, Jaybird's vision of improvised theater gives the actors improvisatory freedoms only within very clearly delineated boundaries. He is not ready to relinquish conventional plot structure or narrative exposition, and when, after playing a Charlie Parker record for two minutes, the musicians themselves begin to improvise together live, he runs in from the audience shouting "Cut it! Cut it! You are murdering the play" (33). Jaybird embraces the thematization of improvisation, via the recording of Charlie Parker, but not actual improvisation as a structuring and performative element of the play. As in *Tonight We Improvise*, the actors have been asked both to play characters and to play themselves—that is, Jaybird has given the junkies character identities with appropriate biographies from which he has asked them to improvise "confessions" and "capsule moments" (34). But "There are to be no realistic body movements[,] as we rehearsed," Jaybird reminds them. "No longer is your hand your own hand. You are part of something infinitely larger" (33). "Man," the junkie Sam replies as he chafes at the contradictions, "you've been telling us to act natural. Now we don't own our own hands" (34).

Like both of its repertory counterparts, *Many Loves* and *Tonight We Improvise*, *The Connection* thematizes the issue of authorial control in the theater. And, just as the Living Theatre's production of *Tonight We Improvise* offers the audience a moment of participatory improvisation when Mommina asks for protection against her jealous boyfriend, *The Connection* also momentarily goes beyond authorial control by offering actual unscripted performance as a structuring counterpoint to conventional scripted theater. As the producer, Jim, emphasizes at the start, the entire play is a fiction except for the jazz, which is authentic: "We do stand by the authenticity of improvised art" he assures the audience (19). Authenticity here means improvised rather than predetermined and possessing an aura of individuality and originality. *Many Loves* and *Faustina* thematize this question of authenticity, but *Tonight We Improvise* and *The Connection* also perform it, if only in a limited way. Onstage from the beginning, the musicians are both "characters" and "themselves." They perform "actual" (not prescripted) jam sessions that go on for several minutes, giving the audience the experience of attending a miniconcert where the music is not incidental but is in fact the event, the thing the audience is meant to pay attention to. These jazz jams test the audience's sense of theatrical attention. Can audience members rest their attention and chat to each other, as they might do in a music club? Should they tap their feet, nod, snap? Should they listen quietly and reverentially? The extended jam sessions ultimately raise the question of what it means to think of the music as plot. Not as *part* of the plot—that is, not merely as symbols of a certain type of performance or as representations of other narrative media—but as plot itself. What does music *do* and how is that fundamental to what the audience experiences and what the play is about?

The Connection's use of jazz certainly resembles some of the ways in which other Living Theatre productions used poetry. Both Stein and Gelber, for example, challenged the usual conventions of storytelling—the clear exposition, plot development, and tidy ending that Jaybird wishes for—in order to create a less passive audience experience. Both Stein and Gelber created plays that were subject to change with each performance, though Stein's writerly script invited active audience participation in ways that Gelber's script did not. Jazz functioned in *The Connection* more as a metaphor for participation than as a prod to it, and in this sense *The Connection* is more closely aligned with *Many Loves* and *Tonight We Improvise* than with Stein. Williams employed poetry to rhetorically structure his play device, and Gelber, too, used jazz as a structuring device.

On November 6, 1959, a new production of Pirandello's *Tonight We Improvise* opened in repertory with *Many Loves* and *The Connection*. Claude Fredericks provided a new translation of the play, but reviews of the production were mixed, perhaps because reviewers were distressed by the staged heckling or possibly by the fictional rebellion of the actors (Tytell 160) or perhaps because they felt, like Brooks Atkinson, that the metatheatrical inquiries of the play, while "interesting," were ultimately "valueless" because they were trained entirely on the theater itself ("Tonight"). Meanwhile, *The Connection* was becoming ever more popular, and celebrities such as Leonard Bernstein, John Gielgud, Lauren Bacall, Salvador Dalí, and even Dag Hammarskjöld came to see it. Increasingly, the idea and problems of "audience" occupied Beck and Malina, as heckling and even occasional fistfights broke out. The problem was how to engage the audience, give it freedom to react and even participate, but also, as Beck wrote in his journal, to "move that audience in such a way and imbue that audience with ideas and feeling that transformation and genuine transcendence can be achieved" (qtd in Tytell 161). "None of the actors," Beck wryly reflected, "know what I'm talking about" (ibid.).

"A Resurgence of Realism": The Rhetoric of Antitextuality and Authenticity

Beck's ideas about the relationship between poetic language and authenticity were developing rapidly at this time. In a 1959 speech entitled "Why Avant-Garde?" Beck asserted that the future of theater must involve the language of poetry, for "only poetry or a language laden with symbols and far removed from our daily speech, can take us beyond the ignorant present" (n.p.). Beck wasn't referring to the poetry of Elizabethan drama, nor to nineteenth-century prose drama, which he felt had forced audiences to look at "important truths" but had become stale by the mid-twentieth century. Instead he was talking about a contemporary poetic voice that could speak for the present time. "But a reform of language is not enough," he continued. "For the spectator to achieve a full synthesis of experience, he must become totally involved as in a dream or a religious ritual" (n.p.). The following year, in a speech entitled "Feelings on the Theatre," Beck reflected on his youthful hubris, observing that ideas such as catharsis, transcendence, and "uncovery [sic] of the subconscious . . . no longer [have] meaning to me" (n.p.). What he now wanted more than anything was "honesty," created through "the art of creation, not of representation, not of imitation" (n.p.). And the only way to achieve this honesty for the audience was to present not a fiction but an event in which the audience would participate. Shortly thereafter, in a speech at the Artist's Club, Beck predicted that audience participation would be the next crucial development in theater (Tytell 162).

In notes for an untitled 1961 lecture on avant-garde theater, Beck observes that "my feelings have changed with time" (n.p.). He recalls that he used to think avant-garde was "cubism, Stein, Surrealism, Neo-Plasticism, the ballet of Diaghileff, Graham. Noguchi" (n.p.). But now he thinks that "vanguard theatre must develop in a different way" and must be "a theatre which has a kinship with Abstract Expressionism" (n.p.). At the same time, Beck faulted abstract expressionism for not having enough empathy, feeling, and human connection, and he had come to believe by this point that plays such as *Many Loves* and *Tonight We Improvise* were "unable to achieve" honesty and connection. "It has struck me," he argues, "that one of the reasons why Abstract Expressionism has become so much the plaything of the rich[,] and it has become that[,] is because of its impersonalism[,] a mirror of the cold and heartless" (n.p.). In contrast, Artaud offered a theater of feelings created in response to an actual event. Yet, despite this change of heart, and despite also claiming that the Living Theatre was not controlled by "mammon," the Living Theatre's first European tour, that same year, featured a revival of *Many Loves* alongside *The Connection* and Brecht's *In the Jungle of Cities*.[13]

Beck's own changing accounts and sometimes contradictory rhetoric surely have something to do with why critics tend to identify a "break" between *The Connection* and the group's previous work. Drawing a line between the "text-based, even highly literary" plays prior to 1959 and those that came after, Innes argues that, while the first Artaud-inspired works, *The Connection* and *The Brig*, were, like the earlier poetic plays, defined by written dialogue, "their documentary quality encouraged an extreme degree of actuality in performance—corresponding on one level to Artaud's principles, but by intensifying the naturalistic illusionism he had rejected" (62). Of course, this documentary quality can also be seen in the metatheatricality of *Many Loves* and *Tonight We Improvise*. The goal of these productions was to merge fiction and reality until they were indistinguishable. Both *Tonight We Improvise* and *The Connection* kept actors in character during the intermission, but in *Tonight We Improvise*, the audience was in on the fiction, whereas in *The Connection* the naturalization of actor and character was so successful (and therefore it was unclear to observers where one ended and the other began) that the police intervened on one night because they thought actors were actually doing and selling drugs onstage (ibid.).

What Beck called a "resurgence of realism" might therefore best be thought of as authenticity, a presiding concern of the theatrical avantgarde in the 1950s, 1960s, and 1970s. We might even think of the "realism" of *The Connection* as a generativity that sought to create experience in the present moment through performance that drew on both narrative and material presence in unstable relation to each other. Such authenticity was most often attempted through improvisation and amateurish expressiveness that was seen as offering a more "real" truth than the rehearsed smoothness of the professional actor. Texts were considered antithetical to this notion of authenticity, and some have even criticized avant-garde performance groups for taking unscripted performances and codifying them as texts, as the Living Theatre did with its 1969 performance *Paradise Now* (see, e.g., Innes 74). But, while a text certainly cannot capture the live experience of *Paradise Now*, and the desire to do so goes against the very goals of the performance, there is a conservative notion of what a text is in these critiques that also needs to be unpacked.

The idea that a text controls, codifies, and fixes a performance relies on a belief in the stability of the text and on the assumption of the monovocality of language that says more about cultural beliefs about texts and language than about the way they actually work. Innes, for example, employs a rather conventional idea of a "core text" as something that is "reproducible" (58). But actors certainly recognize the instability and multivocality of a script when they explore emphasis, gesture, and intonation as means of changing the meanings of words and phrases. Of course, poets rely on the polysemy of language as well, though in a very different way from actors. An actor, noting different possible meanings of a single phrase, often makes a choice, and in doing so conveys a *particular* meaning, one that will best serve his or her characterization or the director's interpretation of the play. Poets, on the other hand, embrace polysemy. Rather than making a choice to convey a particular meaning, poets rely on the multivocality of the text to engage multiple, flickering meanings simultaneously. Artaud, too, hints at the fundamental multivocality of texts in "The Theater and Culture" when he writes of the "confusion" that results from the "rupture between things and words, between things and the ideas and signs that are their representation" (7), before he launches into his discussion of language that precedes text.

The pre-1959 work of the Living Theatre was far from uniform, both in its use of "texts" and in its attempts at authenticity. But from the very first night of plays in Beck and Malina's living room in 1951, poetic theater was a key element in the exploration of how an authentic audience experience could be achieved. What the Living Theatre was deposing was not texts themselves but any single authority controlling the performance— whether the authority was seen as residing in the playwright's script, in the director's vision, in the actors' professionalism, or in some combination. Its next production, *The Brig*, replaced the authority of the text with the authority of the performers: "Group-created texts replaced or upended scripts by playwrights," Erika Munk observes of the Living Theatre's transitions, and "the performer's body became a central source of meaning;

interactions with the audience grew 'cruel'; social and political themes were expressed as ritual. In rehearsal, rehearsal itself eclipsed results" (43). Still later, radical participatory works such as *Paradise Now* decentered the performers' authority as well.

In its production of *The Brig*, which opened on May 15, 1963, the Living Theatre took its reformulation of realism one step further. The play depicts the terrifying discipline and order of an actual Marine Corps brig in Japan in 1957—a horror, the play's notes explain, that was "feared and ignored by members of the unit not directly connected with it" (Brown 43). The production involved audience members not by placing them in the midst of the action—as productions of *Tonight We Improvise*, *Many Loves*, and even *The Connection* tried to do—but rather by enforcing a separation between audience and performers. Embodied in the barbed wire fence at the edge of the stage, this barrier was intended to submit the audience to the pain of coerced divisions and ultimately lead to them to action, the storming of the wire barricades, born of a desire for union. The villain of *The Brig* is therefore not a character but rather, as Malina put it, the "Immovable Structure" itself, embodied in the prison, as well as in the separation of performers from the audience that reinforces the social structure of bourgeois society ("Directing" 83), though the hope that the audience would respond by storming the brig was as idealistic as the hope that the audience would stop the onstage murder in *Faustina*.

What the members of the Living Theatre tried to do with *The Brig* was more than mimic the confinement, monotony, and cruelty of a military prison. All their rehearsals were aimed at creating similarly cruel conditions, conditions that were almost as genuinely constricting to them as prison life was for the characters of *The Brig*. The pain created by the performance is therefore not a strictly mimetic representation but a re-presentation, an enactment inspired by actual experiences but relocated into a new context. If it's not possible to take audiences to an actual military brig, the production implies, it *is* possible to give them a similar emotional experience of witness through the re-presentation of the pain of the confinement, control, and routinization of all human activity in the space of the theater.

In order to accomplish this, Malina prepared a set of "Rehearsal Regulations," which she modeled on the play's "Brig Regulations," which were themselves modeled on a US Marine Corps manual. The rehearsal regulations included strict adherence to a rigid schedule, to be determined by the stage manager; the prohibition of eating, joking, or conversation unrelated to rehearsal; a dress code; and substantial penalties for misconduct, tardiness, or absence. The rules were so unlike the usual operation of the company that members had to take frequent "breaks" to relieve the tension. More important, the strict rules about formal address and respectful silence and the prohibition of joking left the normally intimate company with a distinct feeling of separation from one another. The rehearsals therefore paved the way for a strangely naturalistic performance, in the sense that the emotions and conditions that the actors portrayed onstage were in fact the actual emotions and conditions effected by the rehearsal regulations.

Given this emphasis on the communal experience of the actors rather than on the playscript, it may seem surprising that Beck returns again and again to the importance of poetry in his introductory essay to the published acting script for the play. In this essay, entitled "Storming the Barricades," Beck repeatedly reworks the term *poetry*, revealing in the process his own contradictory ideas about the power of poetic theater. In the beginning of the essay, Beck assesses the group's early productions as "failures" in aesthetic terms. They simply didn't work, he laments, and the fault lay both in the difficulty that poets have with writing for the theater and in the difficulty that actors have with delivering poetry (13). Musing that the productions were "perhaps too much Schumann and not enough Cage" (ibid.), Beck implies that there was too much emphasis on intellectual and emotional appeal and not enough on listening to the sounds of the everyday. But the model of Cage here is also perhaps contradictory, for Cage was not interested in the union of audience and performer but rather in making a spectacle of the very activity of the audience. As the company matured, its goal became the creative collaboration between poetry and theater, conceived of as a process rather than a product, and as an ethics—"joining," as Beck put it, "as opposed to separation" (22). Reading Richards's translation of Artaud, he asserts, had inspired the company "to create that spectacle, that Aztec, convulsive, plague-ridden panorama that would so shake people up" by putting them back in touch with real feeling (24). And it was the separation from "real feeling," Beck reasoned, following Artaud, that had led to wars and atrocities. Reconnecting with our feelings would make such suffering intolerable, so that "we might put an end to it, and then, being able to feel, we might truly feel the job, the joy of everything else, of loving, of creating, of being at peace, of being ourselves" (25).

Perhaps paradoxically, Beck implies that both real feeling and social critique were to be achieved by "a strict formalism in the very nature of action," a formalism created by attending to improvisation and pursuing the effects of chance events as an alternative to authorized, predetermined relations. "In the reverence for truly spoken speech, the reverence made clear by the absence of just such speech and the few phrases of friendly conversation," Beck writes, "[are] thick hints of the new poetry we are seeking" (33). Beck's return to the term *poetry* here is informed by contemporaneous poetic practices that sought out the rhythms of "real speech." Unlike Artaud, whose "mistake," Beck argued, "was that he imagined you could create a horror out of the fantastic," the power of *The Brig* was the insight that "horror is not in what we imagine but is in what is real" (35). Communicating this reality relied on the exposure of the controlling power of a range of institutional and social conventions, including those of language—conventions that created the reality of everyday life. The solution to social ills lay not so much in abandoning language and other conventions of authority and control but rather in reorganizing them so that the relations they produced were not predetermined.

Beck's essay makes a case for the honesty of emotion in plain speech that is not just a matter of speaking plainly but of scripting language accordingly. Arguing that "language is the key. It opens the doors that keep us locked in confining chambers," Beck derides the script publisher's decision to make more than six hundred revisions to his original text without his approval, a decision that erased Beck's idiosyncratic use of typography and punctuation, which he intended, perhaps partly in the spirit of Olson's "Projective Verse," to distinguish "passion from affectation and me speaking to you from me writing an essay" ("Storming" 3, "Mister Beck" v). "Honest" language, for Beck here, resides in what he termed "speech" but might be better described as oral performance, in "the poet reading aloud, the actor speaking the word, not on the page, but in the ear" ("Storming" 4).

Beck's own characterization of his writing as a form of resistance to the "ancien regime of grammar" suggests that he locates in nonconformist uses of language a means of liberating not only literature but also the world.[14] And in fact Beck makes the connection between writing and theater explicit when he says of the publisher's revisions that he has "the feeling I might have if the barbed wire that separates the audience from the action in *The Brig* had been removed, because somebody thought the spectators could see better that way" ("Mister Beck" v). To Beck, then, *The Brig* does not serve as a departure from the company's earlier devotion to poetic theater. In fact Beck claims that the Living Theatre's first major production—of Stein's *Doctor Faustus Lights the Lights* at the Cherry Lane Theater in 1951—and the 1963 production of *The Brig* "are like mirrors locked face to face. . . . Both are concerned with examining minutely a moral sensibility and both are concerned with identity. Both are deeply formed by the rhythms they create" ("Storming" 8). The history of the Living Theatre's growth from *Doctor Faustus* to *The Brig*, Beck suggests, might best be understood in terms of "development" rather than "change" (9)—a development that led the company from its earlier "revulsion . . . against sham" to its current interest in "poetic action" (6). "Nothing can get closer to life than verse," Beck insists, "and nothing further away, nothing further away as when the verse strays into representing that kind of life which never ought to be" (11).

The published text of *The Brig* also included a concluding essay by Malina entitled "Directing *The Brig*," and the divergences between Beck's and Malina's essays embody the emerging separation between poetry and physical theater in the rhetoric of the Living Theatre's cofounders. Beck's emphasis on plain speech supports an egocentric understanding of language in which writing is used to create the best approximation of the natural oral expression of the speaker/writer. This is a rather different understanding from Malina's theatrical description of the actors, who, she observes, "play[ed] themselves" (qtd in Innes 63). In Malina's essay, the framing of the theater transforms identity from a "natural" manifestation to a performative enactment. As Biner describes it in his history of the Living Theatre, "Instead of saying, as a traditional actor, 'I am the embodiment of Richard III,' or as a Brechtian actor, 'I am Mother Courage, but I am also Helen Weigel playing Courage,' the actor in the Living Theatre says, 'I am Julian Beck and I play Julian Beck'" (170). The intent is not to suggest that all identity is mere "play" but rather that the relationship between identity and performance is complex—in fact, it may not always be clear whether one is watching a representation or an enactment or that there is necessarily a clean distinction between the two.

Increasingly what it meant to "play" one's "self" was open to debate. Within the frame of the play, the "self" takes on the contours of character, even if the goal of the acting is to communicate a lack of pretense. And as experiments in presentationalism reached their investigative limits, both poetry and theater began to shift in the 1970s away from a contrapuntal relationship between representation and presentation and toward the idea of a continuum between the two, with each pole—"pure" representation and "pure" presentation—as philosophical, rather than actual, possibilities. These poles correspond to the two ends of the acting continuum posed by Michael Kirby in "On Acting and Not-Acting," published in *TDR: The Drama Review* in 1972, in which Kirby abandons the opposition of representation and presentation and instead portrays acting as a continuum that holds the two in a productive relationship. At one end of Kirby's continuum is "nonmatrixed performing," in which a performer "is not embedded, as it were, in matrices of pretended or represented character, situation, place, and time"; at the other is "complex acting," in which multiple elements of pretense are employed by the actor (4). The complex combinations of the elements of impersonation increase the degree to which actors are seen to represent specific character identities. Thus, as the complexity of the acting increases, so, too, does the degree of representation attached to their bodily presence on the stage.

Part of what Kirby emphasizes here is the status of actors not as objects but in their relation to each other, rather like what was described in poetry as the verbal "field" of relations. As performers embedded within a matrix of impersonation who are simultaneously involved in nonillusionist performance, the actors in *The Connection* raise questions about the boundaries between art and everyday life—questions aimed not only at exploring the reach of artistic practices themselves but also at challenging the very boundaries subscribed to by many academics and practitioners. How do we "play ourselves" and how is language a part of that performance—complicit, critical, or somewhere in between? Where does speech slip into "art" and how is communication itself already a scripted performance?

In describing the actors as "play[ing] themselves," Malina implies, intentionally or not, that such representations can be critical, that they have the potential, like poets' theater, not just to reinscribe identity but to raise awareness of how identity is communicated, passed on, and reinforced. By the end of the 1960s, actors playing themselves had become a key element in the Living Theatre's signature style of political theater. And poets' theater had led the way to the destruction of the barrier between audiences and actors for which the Living Theatre has become known.

CHAPTER FOUR

Sounding the Revolution
Amiri Baraka's Black Arts Poets' Theater

In 1961 Amiri Baraka helped to found the New York Poets Theatre (later known as the American Theatre for Poets, Inc.) with Diane di Prima, Fred Herko, James Waring, and Alan Marlowe. Over its five years of existence, the New York Poets Theatre offered not only plays but poetry readings, dance performances, musical compositions, films, happenings, and art exhibits, and its list of collaborators included such names as Yvonne Rainer, Trisha Brown, Robert Duncan, Michael McClure, John Weiners, Frank O'Hara, Archie Shepp, Allan Kaprow, and Muddy Waters. The inaugural program of plays featured Baraka's *Dante*, an early version of *The Eighth Ditch* (adapted from a chapter of *The System of Dante's Hell*), but it was actually Baraka's 1967 Black Nationalist play *Home on the Range*, written after the New York Poets Theatre had closed up shop, that best represents his most fully realized poets' theater. Combining poetic multivocality and black cultural music and voices, *Home on the Range* redirected meaning away from dominant cultural narratives and the conventions by which they are secured and reinforced. Instead, the play invited audience members to participate in the making of a new black world.

Home on the Range opens with a "typical" domestic scene: a white middle-class American family—Father, Mother, Daughter, and Son—are seated in their living room watching television, eating popcorn, and talking. This domestic ritual is observed by a black Criminal, who appears at the window looking in on the scene as an outsider, marked both by his location outside the home and by his skin color. This clichéd depiction of the cultural marginalization of racial minorities, who are relegated to peering in on "America" (coded white) from the other side of the window, is complicated by the play's challenge to corresponding norms of language usage. While the black Criminal speaks in clear English, the white fam-

122

ily's chatter is incomprehensible, a nonsensical string of repetitive expressions such as "Gollygolly" and "Mamarama," sounding vaguely like the soundtrack of a wholesome 1950s family sitcom twisted into unintelligibility. Although the black Criminal is racially, spatially, and even linguistically marginalized from the white family's performance of domesticity, it is the Criminal outside the home, rather than the white family inside, with whom the audience is encouraged to identify.

The white family's "unintelligible gibberish," composed, according to Werner Sollors, of "meaningless word fragments reminiscent of Ionesco dialogues" (208), has largely consigned this Black Nationalist one-act to the critical waste bin. And if critics don't dismiss the play for its unusual language, they bypass it as an anomaly in Baraka's general development as a playwright. Kimberly W. Benston has called it a "baffling piece," a "collage of absurdity, farce, social satire, mythology, and apocalyptic vision . . . designed to make a series of quick, catching, and only loosely related impressions on a large audience" and "probably the least powerful of Baraka's agit-prop pieces" (*Baraka* 219–20). Sandra G. Shannon has flatly summed it up as essentially "based upon tongue-in-cheek inversions of the usual negative principles of black behavior assumed by whites" ("Evolution" 277).

But in 1967–68 the play seemed destined for a more auspicious career. First read publicly in San Francisco in the spring of 1967 as part of the Black Communications Project, the play was given a full production in 1968 at Newark's Spirit House and taken on tour to Boston, Chicago, Los Angeles, Detroit, and New York courtesy of the Spirit House Movers and Players.[1] The New York leg of its tour opened before an audience of twenty-six hundred at the Fillmore East Theater as part of a high-profile Black Panther benefit, to raise bail money for Eldridge Cleaver and six other Panthers in California jails.[2] That event was covered by two newspapers, including the *New York Times*, and was taped by three national television networks, as well as the radical film group Newsreel.[3] The play was also published as a model of black revolutionary theater in the celebrated 1968 *Black Theatre* issue of *The Drama Review*, an important event in the worlds of both avant-garde drama and black theater. And yet it soon fell into obscurity, with no productions on record for forty-five years and no reprint for thirty.[4] So what happened?

The fact that a play would disappear is not in itself remarkable. The economics of theatrical production and dramatic publishing, to say nothing of changing audience interests and critical tastes, ensures that most plays are lost to history. *Home on the Range* enjoyed a moment precisely because it captured a scene. And more than most plays, perhaps, *Range* is both product and victim of its particular historical, social, and aesthetic moment—a clash of poets' theater, agitprop drama, ritualist performance aesthetics, Black Nationalist ideology, and the emerging sense of cultural performativity Baraka championed, all coming together at a particularly activist moment in African American cultural history. Meanwhile, the rise of environmental theater, which shared some of the same aims as poets' theater, pulled Baraka in new directions.

But the fate of the play may also have had something to do with its particular mix of poetry, drama, and politics. As a work of poets' theater, *Home on the Range* used the discursive and material features of language to critique more broadly the power of language, narrative, and discourse to control social identity. Like any systems-immanent critique, which we might say uses the master's tools to dismantle the master's house (despite Audre Lorde's warnings to the contrary), the struggle is to simultaneously use and subvert a single coherent narrative. Poetry is defined, in part, by its layering of discursive and material texts, so that sound, visual appearance on the page, and discursive meaning together create a multivocal poetic experience. Bridging popular culture, the literary avant-garde, and Black Nationalist political activism, Baraka embodied what many critics have too rigidly characterized as competing impulses. The text, performance history, and ultimate critical fate of *Home on the Range* demonstrate both the ways in which the poetry of poets' theater has been used as a critique of western epistemological structures and the difficulties of using poetic multivocality to stake a clear critical claim.

Baraka's Art and Politics in the 1960s

The years 1967 and 1968 were a pivotal period in the development of Baraka's Black Nationalist consciousness. The second National Black Power Conference, with more than a thousand people in attendance, had been held in Newark in 1967 on the heels of the Newark Rebellion in which Baraka had been arrested and eventually sentenced for inciting violence. A few months later Baraka and Harold Wilson founded the United Brothers (later the Committee for a Unified NewArk and, still later, the Congress of African People) to promote cultural nationalism and black political unity (Woodard 89). In 1968 Baraka also founded the Black Community Development and Defense Organization, whose members were Black Muslims, wore African dress, and conversed in Swahili. As many critics have noted, he thereafter abandoned the "slave" name LeRoi Jones in favor of the African-identified Imamu Amiri Baraka as a way of both claiming and performing his Africanist identity, a change that Jerry Gafio Watts characterizes as "Baraka's dramaturgic approach to politics" (310).[5] For Baraka the Black Nationalist, culture was political and "all activities were cultural" (Van Deburg 177), and he famously advocated the performance of black culture and the expression of black life through politically committed artistic practice as elements in bringing about a Black Nationalist revolution. This emphasis on cultural performativity was also instrumental in his developing approach to poets' theater.

But Baraka's appeal to performativity can be traced even farther back, before his black cultural politicization, to his participation in the fertile avant-garde artists' scene of New York's Lower East Side in the late 1950s and early 1960s, where ritual performance groups, underground dramatic theater, and text-based, performance-oriented avant-garde poetry flourished side by side. Baraka himself was both actively involved with the Beat poets and associated as a sort of mentor figure and political colleague with the black writers of the Umbra Poets' Workshop group. Many of the poets in both groups employed a textual aesthetics that featured elements of live performance, and both were influenced by the orality and musicality associated with African and African American cultural traditions and especially by the rise of jazz.[6] But the Umbra and Black Arts poets associated jazz more specifically with black resistance and liberation.

Most critical narratives identify a shift from symbolic to revolutionary action in Baraka's abandonment of the downtown avant-garde scene for Harlem, where he founded the Black Arts Repertory Theatre/School (BART/S) in 1965, shortly after the assassination of Malcolm X, and later for Newark, New Jersey, where he founded a black cultural center, Spirit House. This move also established Newark, with an estimated black population of 220,000 in 1967,[7] as the center of Black Arts and black nationalism on the East Coast. But Baraka's migration from Greenwich Village to Harlem to Newark reflects not so much a break with his past as an increasing political allegiance to black culture that had begun much earlier. Moreover, as Jimmy Fazzino succinctly observes, "Black cultural nationalism is not incompatible with the legacies of the European avant-garde" ("Amiri" 84). The question was how avant-gardist strategies could be put to Black Nationalist use in an attempt to achieve what Werner Sollors has deemed, in Baraka's own terminology, a "populist modernism" (8). Andrew Epstein has argued that Baraka's increasing cultural nationalism went hand in hand with a turn away not from avant-garde poetics in general but from the Emersonian pragmatist orientation of American poetry in the 1950s, exemplified by figures such as Frank O'Hara and John Ashbery and characterized by individualism, nonconformity, and detachment from community, a disavowal of absolutisms, and the separation of art and politics. Epstein suggests that while Baraka embraced racial essentialism as a political necessity, his range of poetic styles demonstrates his use of writing as "a space where the problems of American individualism and experimental poetics, liberal and radical politics, racial identity and the communal avant-garde, are all tested and critiqued" (*Beautiful* 170).

Baraka's dramas of the 1960s experimented with a range of dramatic styles. At the same time, Baraka increasingly selected black-identified venues for their staging. Prior to 1965, virtually all of Baraka's plays debuted within what might be thought of as New York's off-off-Broadway theater scene, situated downtown and populated largely by liberal white artists. Following on the heels of the New York Poets Theatre's production of *Dante*, *The Toilet* was presented in 1962 by the Playwright's Unit, founded by Edward Albee and Richard Barr, which also premiered *Dutchman* in 1964. *The Baptism* (1964) was performed by the Present Stages company in the East Village in a double bill with Frank O'Hara's *The General Returns from One Place to Another*. Even the first of Baraka's overtly black revolutionary dramas, *Experimental Death Unit #1*, was staged at an East Village venue—St. Mark's Playhouse, home to Theatre Genesis, where Sam Shepard began his playwriting career in 1964—though Baraka explains that this was largely an arrangement of convenience: "We charged $20 a ticket, the audience was mostly white, and we used the money to pay down on the brownstone and help put the building [for BART/S] in some shape" (*LeRoi* 370). But Baraka abandoned off-off-Broadway with his next play, *A Black Mass* (1966), which was first performed at the Proctor's Theatre in Newark. *Great Goodness of Life* (1967) and *Home on the Range* (1967) both premiered at Newark's Spirit House, while *Madheart* was first staged at San Francisco State College in 1967 with a Black Arts alliance cast. Such a migration not only of Baraka's creative home but also of his collaborative and audience networks, and their attendant aesthetic and political expectations, changed the potential impact of these performances.[8] Baraka notes, for example, that although his most famous play, *Dutchman*, received an Obie for Best American Play when it was produced at the Cherry Lane Theater in 1964, when it was performed by the BART/S on Harlem street corners the authorities called it racist and tried to shut it down. These struggles with the authorities are seen by many as one of the reasons BART/S funding was withdrawn, and the loss of funding helped contribute, ultimately, to its demise (Sell 33).

In his infamous "Revolutionary Theatre" manifesto, published in the *Liberator* in 1965, the year after *Dutchman* was first produced, Baraka calls for a theater that communicates black revolutionary spirit through the playwright's use of ordinary language "tightened by the poet's backbone," suggesting the poet's ability to transform ordinary language into a cultural weapon (4). Placing performance at the center of cultural revolution, Baraka's vision of revolutionary theater resembles Artaud's "cruel" theater, "full of wild, convulsive gestures, dissonant sources and violent action all meant to stir the audience into action" (Fazzino "Amiri" 90), and indeed Baraka himself has acknowledged his debt to Artaud. But, as Fazzino points out, it was Artaud's anticolonialist critique that particularly resonated with Baraka (*World* 80). Aligning his revolutionary theater with Artaud's rejection of European imperialism, Baraka called for a *world* revolution: "Even as Artaud designed *The Conquest of Mexico*," Baraka wrote, "so we must design *The Conquest of White Eye*, and show the missionaries and wiggly Liberals dying under blasts of concrete. For sound effects, wild screams of joy, from all the peoples of the world" ("Revolutionary" 5).

Combining Artaud's Theater of Cruelty with Black Nationalist politics, Baraka employed the sounds and sights of cultural revolution. Many theater artists of the era employed ritualized performance that immersed the audience in the mise-en-scène, but whereas most other ritual theater groups foregrounded the relationship between the performer and spectator as a model for, and opening into, more egalitarian social relationships, Baraka took this relationship in a different direction. Spectatorship was for Baraka a sign of political passivity, an ideological trap largely associated with white middle-class rituals, such as the "American" family ritual of watching television together in the opening scene of *Home on the Range*. In seeking to transform Artaud's Theater of Cruelty into concentrated social action, Baraka emphasized rituals associated with African American culture, such as dance and jazz improvisation—performances that enacted not the liberatory power of personal interactions but rather the potency of community and cultural traditions.

Baraka's poetry of the 1960s exhibits these developments. The poems in the 1964 collection *The Dead Lecturer*, for example, perform a cultural and political transformation as the poet shifts from a tone of self-hatred to one of racial pride. The 1966 Black Nationalist poem "Black Art" melds form and meaning into a hybrid poetry-performance that is, simultaneously, both cultural critique and an ethics of action. First published in the *Liberator*, this poem was later included in the 1969 collection of poems *Black Magic*, which ridicules the American way of life and seeks to destroy it and replace it with Black Art. "Poems are bullshit," the black voice of the poem announces, "unless they are / teeth or trees or lemons piled / on a step" (*Black Magic* 117). Black Art, the poem makes clear, is concrete and almost antipoetic in its drive to kill the abstraction and escapism of European American poetic traditions. Advocating "'poems that kill,'" the poem performs its own destruction of universalized introspection as it slides into the pure sounds of airplane engines and gunfire, "rrrrrrrrrrrrrrrr / rrrrrrrrrrrrrrrr . . . tuhtuhtuhtuhtuhtuhtuhtuhtuh / . . . rrrrrrrrrrrrrrrr . . . Setting fire and death to / whities ass" (ibid.). No longer interested in poetry as a critique of bourgeois excesses, the poem's speaker wants poems that inspire communal action and impel communal destruction—that is, that incite a revolution.

> We want a black poem. And a
> Black World.
> Let the world be a Black Poem
> And Let All Black People Speak This Poem
> Silently
> or LOUD (ibid.)

"Black Art" adopts the direct diction and concreteness of the European American poetic avant-garde, but its violent images are an explicit appeal to black audiences to recognize themselves and rise up. Its language is performative, not only in its use of sound, which raises voices in a performance of gunfire, but also in its performative destruction of a lyrical expression of subjectivity.

Similar developments can be seen in Baraka's plays of the 1960s. *Dante*, later revised and published as *The Eighth Ditch* and produced by the New York Poets Theatre in 1961, is set in a Boy Scout camp that at times also seems to be a Marine barracks. It portrays the seduction, and rape, of a character known only as 46, "a middleclass Negro youth," by 64, "an underprivileged negro youth" (85). Different but also complementary, 46 and

64 are two sides of the same personality; 46 is younger, literary, intellectual, white-identified, naive, and existing largely in his head rather than his body, while 64 is more worldly, physical, and politicized. Typically understood as a dramatization of Baraka's own internal conflict between his younger, Beat-identified self and his growing sense of social commitment to Black Power, the interactions between 46 and 64 are telling. 46 likes "Jazz at the Philharmonic. Flip Phillips. Nat Cole," while 64 is a "bellyrub man" who likes "R & B & those quartets" (84). 64 derides 46 as an "honorable poet" who "hear[s], exclusively, what you want" (85), while 46 warns 64 that he's lucky "you don't wipe your ass with newspapers or disappear into the marine corps" (82). In one of the few critical commentaries about the play, Epstein writes that "Baraka uses these two characters to pit tendencies within himself—the bourgeois and the avant-garde—against one another. On the one hand, the precious, innocent boy with literary pretensions, and on the other, the jaded bohemian longing to break away from his friends and their stifling literary community" (*Beautiful* 215).

This portrayal of a divided self is a continuation of a theme that occupied much of Baraka's early poetry. But the turn to drama is new, and the play stands as an important bridge between Baraka's poetry and drama. "To move from poetry to drama," observes Sollors, "Baraka had to radicalize his introspective stance to the point at which lyrical monologue becomes lyrical dialogue" (95). The conflict of a divided self here becomes externalized in such a way that it depicts not only an internal but also a social conflict. At the end of the play, the intimate aggression between two characters becomes more outwardly violent and aggressive, as in *Dutchman*, with the introduction of a group of outsiders—in this case, three boys who walk in on 64 having sexual intercourse with 46. 46 seems to have given himself over to 64's advances, asking him, "What other blues do you have . . . How many others?" as the other boys jostle with one another and urge 64 to hurry up so they can "get some too" (90). While the play is not written in verse, its language is lyrical and antirealist, conveying, as in so many other instances of poets' theater, a kind of heightened truth amid the realities of an ugly world. "What do you feel," 64 asks when he first announces himself to 46.

Grass? Games? False muscles cut thru water, thru precious sanity. Your earth is round & sits outside the world. You have millions of words to read. And you will read them. (*Loudly*) So buy expensive clothes and become middleclass that summer after college. But don't sneak away! You can't. I'll never know you, as some adventurer, but only as chattel. Sheep. A "turkey," in our vernacular. (80)

This lyrical interaction between the two main characters soon gives way to grunts, groans, and short exclamations as the play ends with a gang rape.

While Baraka did not give up poetry in favor of drama, the language of both his poetry and his drama became less symbolic and introspective and more direct and concrete as his aesthetics and politics developed. And the use and thematization of sound—as cultural expression, as the counterpart of the written word, as a means of undermining received narratives—became increasingly important. The short, pre–Black Nationalist play *The Toilet* (1962), for example, is an early work that depicts the painful isolation of an individual struggling to understand the world around him. Its action revolves around a group of black boys who beat a white boy for writing a kind of love letter to the head of their gang. Raising issues of power, privilege, race, and masculinity, it ends with a surprisingly tender scene in which a black gang leader cradles the head of the white boy, who is so beaten and bloody that he cannot rise off the floor. *The Toilet* shares both thematic and aesthetic affinities with works produced by the Artists' Theatre in New York the late 1950s, written by Ashbery, O'Hara, and others, which tended to depict, in the words of founder Herbert Machiz, "the private landscape of tormented souls living in an environment they never made" (9). For this reason, Sollors has argued that *The Toilet* "never completely transcends the individualistic 'love story' reading. It is an unresolved fusion of aesthetic protest (as the abstract sentimentalized affirmation of individual beauty against the brutal social order) and emerging ethnic protest" (116).

But as Baraka honed his poetic-dramatic style, the aesthetics and politics of his plays began to cooperate. His 1964 one-act *The Baptism* features a teenage boy who goes to church to be baptized and forgiven for his sins of masturbation. It turns out that the boy is actually the son of God, but he's been a total failure in saving the earth. Refusing to leave the church, he is hit over the head and carried off by a messenger. Meanwhile, a homosexual, who has witnessed this entire encounter and realizes the world is doomed, chooses selfish escapism rather than action and heads off to spend his last few hours before earth's destruction partying away at the bars. While the plot comes off as too intentionally shocking, blasphemous, and adolescent, its punning, indeterminate, "perverse" language linguistically performs the play's themes of hypocrisy and perversity, successfully wedding theme to form. *The Baptism* can be read not only as an indictment of religious perversion but also in part as a critique of apolitical bohemianism (and for Baraka and other Black Nationalists, homosexuality was seen as another perversity of the white avant-garde). And yet neither *The Toilet* nor *The Baptism* performs anything that can be called black culturalism.

That changes, however, with the 1964 play *Dutchman*, a work explicitly concerned with US race relations and devoted to the communicative limitations of language and to the political limitations of art. The protagonist, Clay, is a prerevolutionary poet, afflicted with DuBoisian double consciousness, who chooses speech over action. But, although Clay's murder at the end of the play can be read as a call to action for African Americans, *Dutchman* does not exhibit the racial separatism of Baraka's next play, the overtly Black Nationalist *A Black Mass* (1965). *A Black Mass* relates a Black Muslim mythical story critiquing the individualist values of European America (while the music of Sun Ra plays in the background). When the black scientist Jacoub creates a creature that is half (white) beast and half (black) humanity, another character accuses him, "You made them. Human. You made them. And now they roost in the human mind" (26). As the word *Human* slides here from its reference to Jacoub into the suggestion that Jacoub made the beasts themselves human, the boundaries of humanity performatively slip. And in this single poetic, performative ambiguity, the text encapsulates the play's fear of racial mixing and the threat, once again, of double consciousness. A similar, more cutting poetic slippage occurs in *Madheart* (1966) when the white Devil Lady, depicted as a "free enterprise" prostitute who has been killed, in part, by a spear thrust into her "hole," comes back to life and speaks: "Enter the prize. And I am the prize. And I am dead. And all my life is me. Flowing from my vast whole, entire civilizations" (6). The aural slippage from "hole" to "whole" implies the cultural emptiness at the core of white civilization. The Devil Lady's w/hole is not a "whole" of cultural accord but rather a "hole" that prevents black unity. As the white-identified black Sister and Mother mourn the Devil Lady's loss, they also mourn an America divided and unwhole without recognizing, the play makes clear, that the wholeness they seek comes only at a price devastating to black America.

White Voices, Black Voices

While Baraka's plays increasingly employed poetic strategies that relied on aural excess, *Home on the Range* represents his first full-fledged attempt to put these strategies to cultural nationalist use. It is, above all, a play that must be *heard*, a fact that is apparent as soon as the white characters, watching television in the living room, speak their opening lines.

> FATHER: Red hus beat the trim, doing going.
> MOTHER: Yah, de 89 red garter shooting.
> FATHER: Siboom, das blows.
> MOTHER: Coil. (107)

Because most of this dialogue consists of recognizable words and not merely sounds, both a reader's and an audience member's first inclination is to try to decipher the language. The dialogue's syntax mimes familiar structures, further supporting the feeling that the "language" can be decoded, perhaps as some sort of dialect.

Baraka was interested in the ideological processes at work in all dimensions of expression, and the language of the white characters is, in fact, a carefully crafted nonsensicality rather than the mere "unintelligible gibberish" Sollors has deemed it. The rhythm of the words suggests a conversation, which is further emphasized by the phonic echoes present in the Criminal's own intelligible speech. The recognizable words and conversational structure and the identifiably Germanic phonemes such as *hus*, *yah*, and *das* all work together to give the impression that attention to the language will eventually unlock its meaning—after all, it sounds like speech. Perhaps, for example, "de 89 red garter shooting" refers to a significant local event, like "the blizzard of '78." The Father then responds to his wife with a general expression of discontent or critique, to which she rejoins in agreement. While the specific meaning of the dialogue cannot be translated, the rhythm of the language creates the *experience* of a conversation despite the fact that the utterances are semantically undecipherable.

In a 2003 interview with Kalamu ya Salaam, Baraka described this experience of language rhythms as "onomatopoetic."

> SALAAM: Like in *Home on the Range* and *Experimental Death Unit*, you have people talking all kinds of stuff. How did you write that? I'm asking a technical question. Did you put words in a hat and just pull them out?

Fig. 5. Unidentified cast members perform a scene from *Home on the Range* by Amiri Baraka in 1968. (Photo by Fred W. McDarrah, Premium Archive, Getty Images.)

BARAKA: No, I got the rhythms of what I thought they might be saying.

SALAAM: What do you mean by rhythms?

BARAKA: Well, the kind of people I was creating, their personalities would make them go (*does a chipper sing-song rhythm*).

SALAAM: So you heard the sound of what they would sound like, but how did you get the words?

BARAKA: That's what I heard. You just try to make an onomatopoetic representation.

SALAAM: Onomatopoetic? Is that a technique you use often?

BARAKA: Yeah, always. That's what bebop is. You take the rhythm and make it into a vocal sound.

SALAAM: So the rhythm becomes the melody and the harmony?

BARAKA: Yeah, which it is anyway, to me, always, but that's another thing. (225)

For Baraka rhythm functions as a kind of ideological contouring of language. Speech rhythms reflect not just physiological differences but also "personalities" and cultural identities. But note as well the final turn of this discussion from onomatopoetic rhythms of speech associated with particular people to music and then, more specifically, to melody and harmony. Whereas early jazz and blues performers such as Louis Armstrong used instruments to imitate the sounds of the human voice, Baraka uses scatlike language to imitate the sounds of human speech, thereby insinuating absence precisely through the medium traditionally associated with notions of presence—the white characters, all form and no substance, are talking but they're not saying anything.

Later in the same scene, the white characters are shown to be controlled from the outside through the static repetition of external forces—and language—they have internalized. This critique of the mass media and more generally of the modern scientific-technological state wasn't just specific to Baraka. Many social activists in the 1960s, and especially those associated with the student free speech movement, leveled similar critiques and championed alternative forms of education and information. But *Range* turns this into a racial censure.

> *Laughter is coming from the television set. A cold hideous sustaining laughter. That backs the CRIMINAL unintentionally into the wallpaper.*
> CRIMINAL: Goddam. *He waves gun at television.*
> *Laughter goes on, rising. Then broken by explosions, of great dimension. Screams. People in violent turmoil. The laughter rises again above it. Now the FAMILY, the MOTHER starting it, passing it to the SON, to the DAUGHTER, then the FATHER. They all begin to imitate the laughter on the television screen. They are wiggling and shaking, slapping each other and grabbing themselves in a frenzy of wicked merriment.*
> FATHER: HAHAHAHAHAHAHAHA! (107–8)

Despite the explosions, screams, and images of devastation coming from the television set, the family responds not with action or even with concern but with laughter, which echoes the laughter of the news commentator. Associated with white middle-class capitalist consumption and media indoctrination, the language of the white characters suggests that they have been brainwashed. Their words are empty and devoid of any power for critique or cultural change, and the characters have no agency of their own. America's idealized "home on the range" is an ideological trap, an embodiment not of the individual freedom associated (by some) with the frontier spirit but rather an empty imitation, effected through the static repetitions of propaganda piped in through the mass media with the power to constitute and control one's identity and create distance from oneself and from one's community.

Because the white characters produce sounds that only *mimic* language, a system of meaning that is in itself arbitrary, they are, the play suggests, more removed from the world's realities than the black characters are. In emphasizing absence, such mimesis creates not identification but rather the marked failure of identification. This effect relies on poetic excess, in the layering of discursive language with its material sounds and shape, which creates multiple simultaneous subject positions through generativity. Performed in what W. B. Worthen has called the "mise-en-page" (*Print* 11), the multivocality of the dialogue creates competing alternatives of identification through a kind of theatricality that relies more on the ear than the eye. The use of the page as a field of performance can be seen in works by figures ranging from Harold Pinter to Suzan-Lori Parks. But in Baraka's plays, and in *Home on the Range* especially, the materiality of language on the page acts in collaboration with the stage performance to mobilize competing subject positions.

Such competing subject positions can be seen in one of the play's most emblematic moments. As the Daughter prepares to open the door in response to the Criminal's knock, the Mother cries "Achutung swachtung" (107). While the words might appear to be merely a bit of nonsensical sound play, read poetically they become illustrative of the play's aesthetic and cultural politics. In his original typescript, Baraka has corrected the apparent typographical error *actung* to conform to the German *Achtung*.[9] The Germanic overtones in the Mother's call for attention, echoing the play's opening lines and drawing on images of the Third Reich, imbue the white characters' language with the terror of fascism and genocide (a variation, perhaps, on the cultural erasure of the Plains Indians implicit in the play's title motif). *Achtung* is not just a warning to be disciplined and to pay attention. It's also an epistemological approach to the world, a belief in an unbiased empiricism that will render everything clear. Pay attention and learn, the Mother seems to instruct her Daughter. The ways of the world are about to reveal themselves to you.

But of course the Mother's remark isn't simply "Achtung"; it's "Achtung swachtung." Both words are overdetermined, but unlike *Achtung*, *swachtung* is not easily translated. Read poetically and with a German inflection, the first syllable suggests *schwarz*, indicating perhaps a warning of the black Criminal who is about to appear at the front door or, more broadly, an echo of the overall racial theme of the play.[10] Phonemically and visually, *tung* echoes *zunge*, meaning "tongue," and suggesting perhaps language, sound, or voice, but it also resembles *tunen*, "to tune." Together in the same word, this cacophony suggests black music or black voices, crookedly foreshadowing the moment a few lines later when the Criminal speaks his first words.

Aurality functions as Baraka's cultural weapon, creating dialogism through poetic strategies. As Bottoms observes, much off-off-Broadway theater emphasized a particular moment rather than the development of themes and a linear narrative. Baraka employs a similar singular emphasis but instead of visually riffing on a central image, he uses a central musical element and aural slippages that riff around it to create competing perspectives. Beat poets, too, were known for their use of scat-like language and musical sounds, but Baraka's target is not simply uptight bourgeois literary culture but white cultural expressiveness in general. Performing blackness as a means of cultural transformation, Baraka presents black music and cultural sounds as antidotes to American culture's ocularcentrism and dominant cultural ideology. How one looks—in the sense both of how one appears to others and of how one looks at others—is inseparable from how one sounds.

Like Baraka's references to the "w/hole" of civilization in *Madheart* or the slipping boundaries of humanity in *A Black Mass*, "Achtung swachtung" poetically captures the play's central theme. Foregrounding black cultural forms of performance, the play undermines the univocality, white power, and western epistemology of *Achtung* with the multivocality and black performative power of *swachtung*. Recalling the expression "fancy schmancy," which works recursively to trivialize the first term in the pair by phonemically parodying it so that "fancy" is no longer fancy at all but rather, mockingly, fancy *schmancy*, "Achtung Swachtung" ridicules the idea that compelled attention will reveal univocal meaning by subjecting it not merely to singsong deconstruction but rather to the specific parodic power of black voices. The phrase's resistance to translation and ridicule of the assumption that attention simply to words and grammar will unlock meaning spits readers back out into the realm of aural experience, particularly the experience of black language and black music as performative antidotes to European American cultural ideologies. In this way, the play portrays language not as a transparent conveyor of meaning but as cultural enactment that can both express and control.

Despite his declaration that he has come "to commit a crime," the Criminal is not engaged in the theft of material possessions. Baraka struck the next line from the original typescript, "I just want your valuables," rendering the crime more ambiguous, more along the lines of the "fugitive spirit" discussed by Nathaniel Mackey in "Other: From Noun to Verb," an essay whose title was inspired by Baraka's writings on black music. Allied with the history of fugitive slaves, the fugitive spirit refers to the "flatted or bent notes of the African American's altered scale," which, perhaps like the blackness in "Achtung Swachtung," evades detection by white ears (55). Or, as Fred Moten describes it, it "is the sound of the resistance to slavery; the critique of (private) property and of the proper, and it is, in the radical transformationality of all of its reproduction and recording, its commodified dissemination and circulation, irreducible and ongoing" (qtd in Rowell 963). The "criminality" of fugivity appears only in reference to white laws and notions of propriety, just as here the Criminal is marked as such not because he steals (which he does not) but rather because he is outside normative white family institutions. He is a black American fugitive whose survival, the play suggests, depends on the aurality lurking just outside (the window of) the prison house of meaning. The effect is both parodic and generative. The white characters are perhaps dangerous in their madness, but they are merely clowns. Meanwhile, the power of blackness comes not through overt force but through the ability to subvert normative modes of representation, thereby changing how meaning is produced and policed.

Breaking down white normative codes and infiltrating them with blackness, the play denormalizes whiteness through aesthetic processes that allow for disidentification with European American rhetorical structures and aesthetic conventions. This was further aided in production by casting black actors in white masks to play the white characters, a strategy that recalled the controversial New York production of Jean Genet's *The Blacks* in 1961. Genet's play dramatized black revolt and the use of ritualized violence against white colonial power. For the American premiere, director Gene Frankel added American jazz music to the original score, adopted an abstract set design, and cast professional African American actors, many of whom were politically active, thereby locating the action of the play in the immediate cultural context of the civil rights movement and American social unrest. Theater historian John Warrick notes that prominent African American writers such as Lorraine Hansberry and Langston Hughes worried that Genet, a white European avant-garde playwright, "endangered the progressive aims of an indigenous black theater movement" (132). Hansberry further cautioned that the play, which Genet explicitly intended to be played for white audiences, "prevented communion between actors and spectators" (136). But, while many white audience members were offended by the production, they kept coming back for more, and it ran for 1,408 performances before closing in September 1964, making it "the longest standing serious drama in the history of New York theatre" (Warrick 139). Several African American playwrights produced subsequent plays that might be seen as responses to *The Blacks*—including Adrienne Kennedy's *Funnyhouse of a Negro*, Hansberry's *Les Blancs*, and Baraka's own *Great Goodness of Life*.

While *Home on the Range* is not a direct response to *The Blacks*, its use of an all black cast donning stylized white masks in a play about black revolt against white European American cultural indoctrination may be seen in part as a deliberate challenge to the arrogance of what Hansberry called white paternalism—that is, the idea that a white writer could presume to speak for black lives and experiences. In Baraka's play, cross-racial casting served to further the parodic critique. Marvin Pancho Camillo, a black and Latino member of the Spirit House Movers and Players, played the white Father and Baraka enthused, "His portrayal of a 'Dad' of one of the average American families in *Home on the Range* convinced me he knew madness! He could imagine himself to be the thing he hated!" ("Marvin" 106). In playing "the thing he hated," and playing it straight rather than as caricature (the strange language notwithstanding), Camillo performed whiteness and blackness simultaneously, capturing the dialogism of Baraka's script and parodically disrupting the conventional "invisibility" of whiteness through racial cross-dressing. Camillo's portrayal of the white Father layered competing subject positions to create for the audience multiple critical identities. But the audience is not left free to explore multiple identifications as equally valid. Instead the play suggests that black voices and black music can offer a means of slipping past European American culture's surveillance structures, infiltrating white spaces and white normative conventions with an uncontrollable blackness.

In layering black voices and values in the white characters' speech (which is itself depicted simply as a regurgitation of media propaganda), Baraka creates in his white characters a kind of dual identity that enacts a dynamics of subjection. Ideological state apparatuses and the altered scale of black values and voices vie for control over the white characters. But the black characters, too, are subject to external control by social discourse, political propaganda, and cultural coercion. Consider, for example, the final two scenes, beginning with the play's most Artaudian moment—a party of black people who mistakenly look to conformist music and dance as antidotes to the passivity of the white family's media consumption. By this point in the play, the Criminal has destroyed the loudspeaker that externally controls, Big Brother–like, the voices and lives of the white family, yet the effects of internal colonization continue, at work not only in the white family but in the black Criminal as well:

> CRIMINAL *comes over. Then he, as if from a pre-signal, jams his gun into his breast pocket, and takes a collapsible baton out of the other pocket. He begins, with great fanfare (tapping on a chair as if it is a music stand, calling for attention with his head and now very haughty demeanor, turning to acknowledge an invisible audience) to conduct the* FAMILY *singing: first a version of "America the Beautiful," then a soupy stupid version of the Negro national anthem, "Lift Every Voice and Sing," which comes to a super-dramatic climax, with the* CRIMINAL *having been moved to tears, finally giving a super-military salute. As they reach the highest point of the song, suddenly a whole* CROWD OF BLACK PEOPLE *pushes through the door. The* CRIMINAL *wheels around, at first, startled, then he lets out a yell of recognition, and there is a general yowl from all the* BLACK PEOPLE, *and they proceed to run around and once they all take in the* FAMILY, *with second takes, over the shoulder jibes, and stage-whispered insult-inquiries, they race around and begin getting ready for a party.* (110)

This scene swings on the moment in which the black Criminal appears, if only briefly, brainwashed or controlled by a "different set of vibrations." He suddenly puts his gun in his pocket, takes out a baton, and begins directing the family in songs of national patriotism and racial assimilationism. Although both are musical, neither "America the Beautiful" nor "Lift Every Voice and Sing" offers a way out of dominant American cultural ideology. One celebrates the victory of European America over indigenous populations in its ideal of an America that spreads "from sea to shining sea"; the other has been critiqued for offering hope for African Americans through long-suffering assimilationist strategies that look to God and Heaven for true freedom.[11] The play suggests that the alternative to all of this mind-less mimicry—white and black alike—lies somewhere else, in the music of Albert Ayler, which plays in the background during the whole of the play.

Unfortunately, the black Criminal seems unable to hear this music or understand, through it, the improvisatory process that will free him from the bonds of (white) American nationalist ideology, which has internally colonized him. Transformation comes, if at all, in the form not of individual resistance but of the controlled chaos of the ensemble, whose "dancing, singing, cursing, and fighting" is "the cool takeover in the midst of strong rhythms, and grace" (110). The wild party indicates an attempt to get beyond the ideology of language altogether, replacing it instead with more fundamental cultural expressions that are communal in nature—lyricless music and dance. And yet, the play suggests, when musical expression takes the form of cultural anthems and popularized dance moves, when it exists within a colonizing system of representation and mimicry, it, too, stands in the way of presence. As the play cycles through various modes of representation—"ethnic" language, dramatic impersonation, cultural anthem, and even dance—it dismisses each in turn, suggesting that cultural revolution cannot be brought about by performing self-identity through rituals that are externally imposed and assimilated, either consciously or unconsciously.

Performativity and the Jazz Aesthetic

Cultural nationalist aesthetics were for Baraka just one element of a broad revolutionary program of "nation-becoming" that included participation in black political conferences, voter drives, community education, and agitations of all sorts.[12] Working on multiple fronts simultaneously, the goal was to instill pride in African American traditions while at the same time critiquing European American culture and to provide an alternative that celebrated and enacted self-actualizing identities—relying not on mere performance (the realm of representation) but on performativity, which for Baraka constituted an ethics. For Baraka, the political nature of revolutionary theater lay not merely in its depiction of black heroes or in its thematic exposure of black oppression but also, and, Baraka suggests, more importantly, in the "aesthetic" of the plays: "Wittgenstein said ethics and aesthetics are one. I believe this" ("Revolutionary" 4). In arguing for the unity of ethics and aesthetics, Baraka points to the ideological processes by which art is created and critiques the European tradition of separating art from lived experience, which tradition Larry Neal has critiqued as "symptomatic of a dying culture" (31). The black aesthetic, both Baraka and Neal argued, wed aesthetics and ethics as a means of intervening in the cultural ideologies that lead to oppression. In *A Black Mass*, for example, the black scientist Jacoub performs increasingly dangerous experiments despite the protests of his fellow scientists. He eventually creates a white Devil, the embodiment of evil, who represents, Neal suggests, "the aesthetic impulse gone astray" (36). Taken as a parable for artistic creation, the play argues that acts of creation must have a function, must not be meaninglessly separated from the world into which they are created. Art becomes both action and moral value and functions as an alternative to the idiotic passivity of the white family in *Home on the Range*.

Baraka has written extensively on the ethics of music as cultural expression and as an ideological intervention that emphasizes process over product. In *Blues People*, he argues that music is a way of emphasizing the "swing," or verb force, of the artistic process, a process to which he refers elsewhere as "art-ing": "Art is like speech . . . in that it is at the end, and a shadowy replica, of another operation, thought. . . . Art-ing is what makes art, and is thereby more valuable" ("Hunting" 175). For Baraka, western art is too focused on nouns, or objects. Social change can only come about by intervening in the ideological processes of meaning making itself. Black music is therefore both cultural expression and cultural critique, and musical performance can be a form of social action, a means of expressing cultural allegiances, as well as a model for intervention into oppressive social ideologies.

Baraka's specific model for cultural expression and intervention in *Home on the Range* is the improvisatory jazz of Albert Ayler. Ayler had moved to New York in 1963, just as free jazz, introduced by Ornette Coleman in 1959, was taking off. "By abandoning chords, the harmonic foundation of Western music," writes jazz historian Mark Richardson, "free jazz opened up new avenues for improvisation but also suggested the possibility of chaos" and "was closely identified with the black liberation movement, serving as both metaphor—culture that breaks free of oppressive structure—and through its sound, a direct expression of pain, anger, and redemption" (n.p.). Ayler was not only a political colleague of Baraka's, but he also provided him with a musical model for his own cultural aesthetic. In 1965, Ayler played a benefit for Baraka's BART/S, sharing a bill with John Coltrane, Sun Ra, the singer Betty Carter, and others, and Baraka wrote admiringly of Ayler's music in the liner notes for Ayler's album *The New Wave in Jazz*, which developed out of the evening's performance (Richardson).

Ayler's signature song, "Ghosts," begins with a jazz transformation of popular white "folk" songs, such as "Oh Susanna," which, like the song "Home on the Range," was used to celebrate American westward expansion.[13] Yet for Baraka cultural ideology lay not just in the lyrics but in the musical form as well. Western musical traditions esteem the regularity of pitch, tempo, and so on and seek clarity and cultivation, he argues in *Blues People*, while African American traditions value imagination and circumlocution (29–30). Clean western melodies emphasize the artifact whereas African American jazz improvisations emphasize the playing itself, with the music as an expression of the self that cannot be separated from the final product. Just as Ayler's "Ghosts" moves from simple, "regular" melodies grounded in western traditions to a free jazz improvisation that transforms but never entirely abandons those melodies, *Home on the Range* attempts to voice its resistance to white ideological systems of meaning by transforming but never entirely abandoning the language of white cultural oppression in the United States. Ayler's musical accompaniment isn't just mood or background to Baraka's play but works as "an added dramatic dimension—as narrator, as actor" (Shannon "Amiri" 427). "Music, to me," Baraka asserts, "is as much alive as the actors" (ibid.).

Much has been written about Baraka's use of "jazzification," but, as Kalamu ya Salaam points out in his interview with Baraka, "Many critics and cultural observers have said that Baraka is very much influenced by black music, and they start looking at the obvious things like [he uses] music when [he] performs the poetry, but they don't look at what it means temperamentally and structurally to be influenced by the music" (233). For this, we have to go beyond the simple recognition of music as a performance element and instead to see it, as Baraka suggests, as an *actor* in the play.

Both Harris and Sollors have noted the "murderous" character of Baraka's Black Nationalist aesthetics. Based on the deconstructionism of prominent jazz musicians such as Charlie Parker and John Coltrane, the idea was to take a familiar, often sugary song like "My Favorite Things" and tear it apart through increasingly discordant repetitions.[14] "Baraka also wants to take weak Western forms," Harris has argued, "rip them asunder, and create something new out of the rubble. He transposes Coltrane's musical ideas to poetry, using them to turn white poetic forms backwards and upside down. This murderous impulse is behind all the forms of Baraka's aesthetic and art" (15). But to characterize Baraka's jazz aesthetic as "murderous" obscures its performative goal (which Harris himself hints at when he argues that Baraka wants to "create something new")—after all, Baraka's weapon of choice is not a gun but jazz.

Home on the Range encourages audience members to identify with the blackness that has infiltrated the portrayals of the white characters (through wordplay and cross-racial casting) but not with the white characters themselves. In parodying European American language and rituals, Baraka repeats them with a difference—a "black" difference based on a jazz model that both critiques the original (in the empty onomatopoeia of the white characters' "sounds") and infiltrates it with an alternative (in the blackness hidden in the white characters' "language"). Blackness is presented as performative while whiteness is presented as unproductive, unethical, and alienated reiteration. Baraka employs avant-garde strategies in order to undermine white ideologies. And, ironically, audience members are likely to identify not only with the blackness of the black characters but also with the blackness in the white characters, for, although the relative normativity of the black characters is attractive, it is the projection of black values onto the white characters that is most striking, most notable, and most gleefully amusing.

Baraka's use of music as an actor might be likened to Coltrane's jazz performance, which Benston describes as simultaneously deconstructive and self-presentational, as both "structural critique" and "phenomenological inflection" (*Performing* 132). Coltrane's deconstructive method points up the limitations in, and the ideology of, the use of harmonious notes and melodies. As the performance grows increasingly discordant and the gaps between notes seem to disappear, something new emerges—something that is no longer deconstructive but has morphed into the constitutive reiterations of performativity. It asks us to consider, Benston suggests, how we might "measure the authority of 'rendition' as against 'original,' and by way of that question, how to construe the relation of interpretation to invention" (131). Baraka's performances, like Coltrane's, are not merely inversions of originals. Via their repetition with a difference, or what Baraka calls the "changing same," they also have the potential to create new relations.

The white characters in *Home on the Range* are victims of their own culture of alienation. As self-absent voids, they do not inspire identification but rather create the possibility for *dis*identification, an important symbolic break in the historical chain of identifications on which double consciousness is based. As the white characters' "presence" recedes, we are faced with the "absences" that constitute white identity—the blackness in whiteness. Of course, this is still a parodic mimesis, presented from the antinormative position of Black Power in American society. But it creates a new relationship to whiteness that is less oppositional than mere resistance, more powerful than ridicule and denunciation, and potentially more transformative than speechmaking. Like Stein's "insistence," here retuned as the enactment of a community ethics, Baraka's "changing same" is a *generative* reiteration. In re-presenting, rather than reproducing, whiteness, Baraka addresses the politics and power of representation. His characterizations are not mimetic in the traditional sense of reinforcing normative themes, concepts, and so on—the "performance" (musical, staged, written, or otherwise) is not secondary, does not simply reflect "the real" or refer to "the world" but rather generates new identifications.

Baraka's performative poetics employs an oscillation between reference and immediate experience that might be best described as "generative mimesis," a term for which I take my inspiration from Elin Diamond's notion of "feminist mimesis." Unlike conventional mimesis, understood as imitative, feminist mimesis "take[s] the relation to the real as productive . . . geared to change, not reproducing the same. It . . . explore[s] the tendency to tyrannical modeling (subjective/ideological projections masquerading as universal truths), even in its own operations" (xvi). Thus, feminist mimesis might be thought of as a *performative* theatrical strategy in that it re-presents, seeking not only to expose subjective and ideological projections disguised as universal truths but also to produce the real in new ways. Diamond's term is aimed at denaturalizing the relation between actor and character that works in concert with ideology. The generative mimesis of Baraka's performative poetics exposes the ideologies inherent in those usages as well as the collaboration between language, texts, and bodies that produce those ideologies.

The Tone of America: Framing the Text

Home on the Range was published in the special 1968 *Black Theatre* issue of *TDR,* the foremost American journal on avant-garde theater edited by

Richard Schechner. For this special issue, Schechner turned editorial authority entirely over to the African American playwright Ed Bullins.[15] "In this issue we sought a precise measurement of a certain aspect of black awareness," Schechner wrote in an introductory comment. "To achieve that, we removed the white hands from the blue pencils. . . . If this issue was to be unavoidably subjective, whose subjectivity should it reflect? I chose Bullins' over my own" (25–26). Yet, as Harry Elam notes, Schechner's reflections are not entirely ingenuous, for he asserts his own editorial control via a brief comment (entitled, pointedly, "White on Black") in which he suggests that the *Black Theatre* issue is "long on plays and short on articles" and that "he didn't like some of the plays" (qtd in Elam "TDR" 47).

Bullins's editorial title "The King Is Dead" may therefore be understood, as Elam indicates, both as a reference to Martin Luther King Jr.'s assassination and the policy of nonviolence that died along with him and as a proclamation of the overthrow of the king of the avant-garde himself. Certainly, Bullins's role as editor, not only of *TDR*'s *Black Theatre* issue but also of the later journal (supported by the New Lafayette Theatre) simply entitled *Black Theatre* and of several drama anthologies, and as the artist-in-residence at the New Lafayette rendered him an extremely influential figure in the black theater movement. And, although Bullins was, perhaps, not as wildly outspoken as Baraka, he was no assimilationist. Six months earlier, in *Liberator* magazine, Bullins had pulled no punches in disparaging western avant-garde theater as ineffectual and "pretentious" (16). "Its characteristics may only be bizarre, e.g., penis worship, masturbation, incestuous narcissism and ego projection," he continued. "And often avant-garde mannerisms are a collection of rediscovered conventions of a forgotten era, newly foisted upon the new generation to become clichés in themselves" (16). Criticizing contemporary European American avant-garde theater for recycling past conventions and thereby remaining within a particularly western tradition, Bullins argued that such theater offered nothing new and was therefore only "so-called" avant-garde. More to the point, Bullins argued that "it is the white man's vision of reality that is most identifiable in his drama, and Black dramatists are not heir to that type of madness" (17).

Given the anti-avant-gardism of *TDR*'s guest editor, the decision to publish Baraka's play in this issue may be understood as a claim for the play as an alternative to, and an implicit critique of, (white) avant-gardism. This in spite of the fact that Schechner's introductory comments identify Baraka's work firmly within the avant-garde tradition: "Surprisingly, among the writers who have maintained a steady relationship with the avant-garde is LeRoi Jones. His militancy has not militated against his powerful use of new forms. As he has used them, these forms are also traditional. Tom Dent of the Free Southern Theatre pointed out to me how dear black culture holds participation, song, tragic and triumphant celebration" (27). Although Schechner characterizes Baraka's work as avant-garde, his own comments also suggest why that label may not fit. As Baraka puts it in his poem "Western Front," "Poems are made / by fools like Allen Ginsberg, who loves God, and went to India / only to see God, finding him walking barefoot in the street, / blood sickness and hysteria, yet only God touched this poet, / who has no use for the world" (*Black Magic* 81).

Contextualized within this larger cultural politics, one of the messages of *Home on the Range* begins to take shape. Generative mimesis is marked by a fundamental tension between a shared system of meaning and an audience member's personal experience of the play's poetic language—that is, between the collective and the individual, or what Fred Moten designates "totality" and "singularity" (89). Despite his emphasis on the collective, Baraka eschewed mere adherence to prescribed conventions, white or black, and he parodies not only the white family's mindless repetition of television propaganda but also the black Criminal's display of American patriotism in the mechanical reiteration of the American national anthem and "Lift Every Voice and Sing." Other critics have noted Baraka's rejection of civil rights and the legacy of Dr. Martin Luther King Jr. as assimilationist and complicit (see, e.g., Elam *Taking*). As an ethical alternative to (white) American individualism, Baraka's emphasis on the collective is mindful, informed by a knowledge of African American cultural history and with a renewed pride in African American cultural traditions. But it is always, ultimately, the individual who must act, who must make choices not simply for his own good but for the betterment of the African American community as a whole, which is achieved, *Home on the Range* argues, by unchaining oneself from convention, by breaking out of representation and entering into *experience*. In the mixing (rather than opposition) of the individual and collective, Moten explains, "You linger in the cut between them, a generative space that fills and erases itself. That space is, is the site of, *ensemble*: the improvisation *of* singularity and totality and *through* their opposition" (89 italics original). Just as Ayler, Baraka's musical inspiration, moved toward an ensemble approach in the mid-1960s, so, too, Baraka's performative cultural nationalism seemed to advocate an ethics of the poetic ensemble as an antidote to traditional narrative structures.

And yet *Home on the Range* ultimately relies on narrative, thereby seeming to undermine its own political message. Turning his back on the dance party scene, the Criminal derisively declares, "This is the tone of America," and shoots his gun out over the audience several times before the scene goes "Black." When the lights come up again the stage is riddled with slumbering bodies in a way that appears to be not merely postparty but postapocalyptic. The Criminal and white Father are the only figures fully awake, and they are engaged in a kind of language lesson. The Criminal is instructing the Father how to speak in normal English, essentially reprogramming him by teaching him how to narrate his personal history: "I was born in Kansas City in 1920," he recites. "My father was the vice-president of a fertilizer company. Before that we were phantoms . . . *Waving at his FAMILY*. Evil ghosts without substance" (111). In this new world of black revolutionary America, whiteness is still "evil," but it is no longer the norm. With the postparty fallout, the play has shifted from one black voice among several white voices to one white voice amid several black ones, and the white voice is, notably, being taught to mimic the now normative language of the Criminal. In this moment, *Home on the Range* may most explicitly manifest Baraka's call, in "The Revolutionary Theatre," for "[a] play that will split the heavens for us . . . THE DESTRUCTION OF AMERICA" (6), and this destruction is realized largely through new language and new performance. While jazz improvisation may serve as a model for evading European American ideologies, ultimately he who controls representation—linguistic or otherwise—has the power.[16]

The play's almost antipoetic ending, with the group of black people speaking in lucid language and greeting a kind of postapocalyptic sunrise at the end of the play, seems to produce a photographic negative of the white-dominated American landscape. This is, in fact, one of the difficulties of trying to create politically activist work with avant-garde techniques, and it suggests why most critics consider *Home on the Range* a failed agitprop play. The play works on one level, through its use of free jazz, to critique the very structure of representation. But critiquing not just a particular representation but the very structure of representation makes it impossible to take up a cogent, defensible, practical political position. In the end, however, the power of the black characters comes from their ability to establish a recognizably *black* identity, as a precursor to political action, by controlling the means of representation. On this point, the play seems divided. It advocates improvisational jazz and poetic multivocality as cultural epistemologies that can undo dominant narratives, but at the same time it also advocates for rather conventional control of narrative, merely from a black perspective. While it explores multiple political standpoints, *Home on the Range* is ultimately unable to integrate them into a coherent strategy.

It is for this reason that the infiltration of black values into representations of whiteness is so key. In the stage directions for the final scene of the play, the family is now referred to as "grays," notably the only such reference in the play. Infiltrated, indeed stained, by blackness, the family is no longer white but gray. Recalling Baraka's description of black America as a "no-man's land, a black country, completely invisible to white America, but so essentially part of it as to stain its whole being an ominous gray" ("Myth" 114), the previously white family and its culture has been fundamentally altered by the performativity of blackness. When Baraka argues that "What a culture produces, is, and refers to, is an image—a picture of a process, since it is a form of a process: movement seen. . . . [and t]he Black artist, in this context, is desperately needed to change the images his people identify with, by asserting Black feeling, Black mind, Black judgment" ("Legacy" 166–67), he indicates that representation is a weapon to be wielded. In order to understand the play's final image, this quotation suggests, we must look at the *process* of cultural transformation it depicts, for the final image neither inspires nor even makes sense without understanding how we got there. The play's vision of America is no longer a "home on the range" but a no-man's-land—a place ironically constituted by absence. It is the location of the abject that blacks have come to inhabit and improvise—creatively, generatively—into a cultural home. Ultimately, it is this generative process that determines the meaning of the play's final image.

When the play ends with a Black Girl announcing, "Hey look, the sun's coming up. *Turns around, greeting the three brothers.* Good Morning, Men. Good Morning" (111), what emerges is a new, postapocalyptic black America that indeed appears to be an inversion of white-dominated society. But when Shannon writes that Baraka's "strategy for developing an effective cultural nationalist message in [*Home on the Range*] is based upon the repeated practices of inverting an original stereotype and thus giving blacks the moral and philosophical advantage over whites" ("Evolution" 283), she omits the seismic shift in the processes that have led to this depiction of the American landscape. The cultural structure has not been merely inverted; it has been turned inside out to redirect identifications and renegotiate desires. It is now the white characters who exhibit a kind of double consciousness by giving voice to the black values that have penetrated their very means of making sense of—and thereby controlling—the world. Audience members are presented with opportunities for identification outside the ruling surveillance structures. When the white Father recites his new history in the final scene, the play demonstrates that history is not fact but construction, produced and controlled by whoever has enough power to direct the narrative. But Shannon's assessment is not entirely wrong: while much of the plot of the play revolves around narrative critique, and while the play's performative strategies point to the improvisatory subversion of conventional structures through poetry's double voicings and bent notes that turn language into music as the way out from under the control of the dominant culture narratives, the play ultimately ends with an inversion of the present world, with black voices using the same old narrative structures to create a world in which black voices and characters are now dominant. Ultimately, the play fails to make good on its own vision.

The Demise of a Black Nationalist Poets' Theater

Without a consideration of *Home on the Range*'s generative mimesis—through which double consciousness is dismantled by the voicing of black cultural values—it is certainly possible to see the end of the play as a simple inversion of racist stereotypes. Moreover, the play's final abandonment of generative mimesis in favor of fairly straightforward agitprop realism seems to produce a photographic negative of the white-dominated American landscape. The play works on one level to critique the very structure of representation, making it impossible to take up a cogent, defensible, practical political position. And yet, in the end, it attempts to establish a recognizably *black* identity, as a precursor to political action, in a cultural aesthetic based in part on the improvisatory model of jazz. But there's more to the story.

The year 1968 was also pivotal in American theater history, the year in which the Living Theatre returned from Europe with four ensemble pieces (including the now infamous *Paradise Now*), which, according to Arnold Aronson, "served as the final catalyst for the destruction of conventional performer-spectator relationships and of traditional literary texts" (137). Although, as I argued in chapter 3, this characterization of American theater as antitextual is exaggerated, there is no doubt that ritualist theater appealed not only to European American practitioners but to Baraka's sense of Black Nationalist theater as well. And indeed Baraka's own most antitextual play appeared around the same time—the ritualist *Slave Ship*, penned the same year as *Home on the Range* and described by Neal as "a play which almost totally eliminates the need for a text. It functions on the basis of movement and energy—the dramatic equivalent of the New Music" (37).

Like *Home on the Range*, *Slave Ship* critiques the conditions of white-dominated society and seeks to create a political and aesthetic alternative, relying heavily on sounds and music to create what Baraka here calls "atmos-feeling." Employing music, dance, nonverbal expression, and even odors, the play moves metonymically between the Middle Passage, a slave uprising, and the contemporary civil rights movement, uniting myth, history, spiritualism, and critique toward Black Nationalist goals. Engulfed in darkness for long periods to experience a total sense-assaulting theater, including the sounds of crying and screaming, the smells of urine, excrement, and death, and the feeling of a rough wooden bench beneath them, audience members are immersed in *Slave Ship*'s performance. In the end they are invited to dance with the actors, until the event turns into an "actual party," taking it past the wild stage party of *Home on the Range* into the realm of physical participation by the audience. Only after the dancing "starts for real"—in other words, only once audience members feel fully integrated into the performance, which is no longer a representation but an event—does the play actually end, with the severed head of the play's assimilationist preacher thrown into the middle of the dance floor, then "Black." Like *Home on the Range*, *Slave Ship* advocates the destruction of white America. At the end of the play, the offstage White Voice ends up pleading for its life, but "The black masses literally destroy and disempower the White Voice," writes Elam, "symbolically deconstructing its representational authority" (*Taking* 89). Both plays depict the overthrow of white representational practices by the power of black community, though *Home on the Range* indicts the cultural power of linguistic structures alongside other representational and communicative practices, while *Slave Ship* critiques American social history and black assimilationist political strategies.

Given their similar starts and critiques, the differing production and publication histories and fates of the two plays are remarkable. Both were written in 1967, and both had their initial productions at Spirit House.[17]

But after its production in March 1967 and publication in *Negro Digest* the following month, *Slave Ship* seemed to founder. While *Home on the Range* was taken on tour across several cities nationwide, performed at the high-profile Black Panther benefit, and selected for publication in the celebrated *Black Theatre* issue of *TDR*, *Slave Ship* lay dormant until 1969—notably, *after* the return of the Living Theatre—when it became Baraka's most successful crossover play since *Dutchman*, with a six-week run directed by Gilbert Moses and produced by the Chelsea Theater Center at the Brooklyn Academy of Music. Occupying a space somewhere between the experimentalism of off-off Broadway and the commercialism of off-Broadway, the Chelsea was known for producing "realized radical scripts, off-beat revivals, or the plays of Europe's avant-garde" (Gottfried) and the fifty-thousand-dollar grant it received from the National Endowment for the Arts (NEA) in 1971 testifies to its mainstream acceptance (see "Papp").[18] Given Baraka's separatist politics at this point in his career, it is not entirely clear why he gave the play to the "white" Chelsea, but it may have been, as theater critic Martin Gottfried has asserted, because Baraka "simply hadn't forgotten that the Chelsea had done 'Black Quartet,' which included one of his plays and that [Chelsea founder Robert] Kalfin had done black plays and used black directors long before it was fashionable."[19] Perhaps because of the theater's location on the border between Brooklyn and Bedford-Stuyvesant, the show managed to pull in 60 to 70 percent black audiences on most nights (Gottfried). After the Chelsea moved the production to the Theater in the Church on Washington Square, it was twice shut down by cast members, unhappy with the conditions at their new venue, who demanded, among other things, that the company "move the play to a black community" ("'Slave Ship' Closed"). Baraka backed the actors' demands.

Elam points out that the shared values and beliefs of *Slave Ship*'s audiences were important to the audience functioning communally, "as a congregation," and responding collectively to the play's ritualism (*Taking* 121). Other aspects of the production also reinforced this privileging of black audiences. After one performance of *Slave Ship*, for example, Wole Soyinka recalled that the black cast shook hands only with black audience members (119). In privileging black spectators in this way, Elam argues, the goal of the production was not to convert audience members but rather "to rededicate [them] . . . to the struggle" (120). Audience responses to *Slave Ship* varied, but Elam notes that audience members nearly rioted following a performance in Baton Rouge and were held back only by the locked theater doors; after a performance in Mississippi, audience members joined the cast in chants of "We gonna rise up!" (122). Following its tour through the south in 1970, director Gilbert Moses noted a sharp rise in "the numbers of black people participating in voter registration efforts . . . in certain cities immediately following the performances of *Slave Ship*" (124).

Of course, several aspects of *Home on the Range*'s production, including the use of an all black cast, the reputation of the Spirit House Movers and Players, and sometimes also the reputation of the venues where the play was performed, were similarly aimed at inspiring black audience members to respond communally. At least some productions of *Home on the Range* also employed a ritualistic prologue that immersed audience members in a vocal and musical soundscape. A Los Angeles production in 1970, directed by Jita Hadi and performed by the PASLA Players, for example, opened with what one reviewer described as a lengthy prologue "of weird percussion, barking dogs and other cacophonous sounds" (Jones 18).[20] And reviews of the Black Panther benefit performance in New York suggest that the introductory soundscape may have been the only part of *Home on the Range* that was actually performed at that event (see Sullivan and Velde). Unlike the musical and percussive sounds and chanting that were performed as part of Black Nationalist political demonstrations, this introductory soundscape was longer and more expressive, though it was also designed to build a communal black cultural experience through aesthetic means. White reviewers did not respond favorably. In the *New York Times*, for example, Dan Sullivan remarked, "I must stop saying 'Negro': if the evening taught me anything, it is that the word is 'black.'" Backhandedly conceding that "to criticize this poem, or incantation, or harangue, or whatever it might be called, as if it were a piece of literature is to miss the point," he argued that "Jones uses words as weapons; he is a propagandist. If he stirs up an audience, he had done [*sic*] what he is trying to do, and he did exactly that last night," although "it is a profoundly boring thing to hear the word 'black' repeated what sounds like 25 times." In a similar fashion *Commonweal* critic Paul Velde commented that the title *Home on the Range* "apparently drops with sarcasm on the right ears," making it clear that his were not the "right" ears (440).

What these reviews suggest is that *Home on the Range*, or at least some productions of it, may have simultaneously encompassed both a kind of ritualistic, incantatory communal experience and the generative mimesis of Black Nationalist poets' theater in a single production. But it seemed to do so in a way that pit the two approaches against one another instead of bringing them together into more collaborative harmony. Interestingly, Velde criticized the prologue performed at the Panther benefit for not being ritualist enough, though it appears that what he really meant was that it wasn't universal enough. He argued that the performance was its best when it produced not a clear message so much as an *experience* of racial history, and he considered it too caught up in African American racial conflict to function as a celebration of the essence of blackness (revealing that his critique is not entirely aesthetic). Complaining that Baraka was "trapped by his reliance on English," he asserted that "if national and cultural histories have to do with exploits, defeats and accomplishments, racial histories with their primordial expansions and contractions carry the weight of the sheer misery of existence" (441). Velde wants racial history to transcend geographic boundaries, and, as with so many white reviewers, his liberalism was offended by a play that angrily and aggressively condemns white people. Still, his assertion that the production was too confined by the American idiom is telling, since the play's condemnation of specifically American racial conditions, and even antagonism toward white people themselves, is most often located in the play's use and critique of language. After 1968, amid the changing political and aesthetic climate that Velde's critique highlights, Baraka's aesthetics splintered into an all too familiar separation between poetry and theater.

Certainly, the disappearance of *Home on the Range* and simultaneous revival of *Slave Ship* reflect in part the post-1968 trend in American theater (especially in New York) toward a more ritualist, participatory, environmental style, and Baraka stated in a 1970 interview that this was where his own theater aesthetic was headed (Hudson "Conversation" 76). It is not that Baraka's aesthetic became more conservative—indeed, *Slave Ship* was considered by many his most challenging and innovative play to date—but ritualism in particular appealed to the BAM's community ethic. In the end, however, the disappearance of *Home on the Range* should probably be blamed on a number of factors, not all of them related to the play's particular cultural aesthetic strategy. Despite Baraka's hope that the play would compel black audiences to political action, there is evidence that some black leaders had a different response. The play's Chicago production was a highly anticipated event in the city's black newspaper the *Daily Defender*, for example, but on the day following the production, the paper published not a theater review but instead a heated reproach of Baraka's prefatory anti-Christian and anti-black-middle-class vitriol (see Calloway). The play itself was ignored entirely, leaving not only no account of how Chicago audience members responded but in fact no descriptive evidence of the production at all. Whatever the impact of the play, it was deemed less noteworthy than Baraka's introductory remarks. Around this same time, Marxist Black Panther Party leaders were expressing their own doubts about the political value of radical aesthetics, a critique that was also leveled by some prominent cultural nationalists themselves, including Sonia Sanchez, Haku Madhubuti, and John Oliver Killens (Murray 300–301). Meanwhile, Ayler, whose music was so central to the play's musical aesthetic, had begun to transform his style into a more commercial rock and R&B sound, so that by 1969 Baraka considered it to be a reflection of the "corny self-consciousness" of white life and, ultimately, "bullshit" ("Fire" 120), which may have contributed to his own decreasing interest in the play.

The story of Baraka's overall growth from the lyrical dialogue of his earliest play, *Dante*, to the poetic aurality and musical soundscapes of *Home on the Range* offers another perspective on the critical history of American poets' theater in the second half of the twentieth century. While the multivocality of poetic language is an especially apt tool for undermining narrative, it is less suited to taking up a committed position. And as Baraka's own personal activities became more political he increasingly turned from dramatic theater to staged agitations, such as "Board of Education" (1968), protesting the poor conditions of black education in the United States, or agitprop revues such as the "Black Power Chant" (1968) dance and stomp performance designed to accompany political protests and fund-raisers. After 1968, Baraka mentioned the play just once in publication, in Camillo's eulogy.

As only one element in a much larger black culturalist campaign to alter the consciousness of African Americans through performative strategies, *Home on the Range*'s individual impact is difficult to assess. But as Michael Omi and Howard Winant have argued in their influential study of new social movements and racial formation in the United States, "The persistence of the new racial identities developed during this period stands out as the single truly formidable obstacle to the consolidation of a newly repressive social order" (91). African American racial consciousness and identity—developed, performed, advocated, and indeed constituted via a variety of performative means during the 1960s—can be seen not just as an accomplishment of black culturalism of the 1960s but also as a resource for contemporary African Americans continuing to agitate for social change (Buechler 132). And, while Baraka's Black Nationalist poets' theater may not have moved audiences toward organized action, its combination of avant-garde aesthetic strategies and African American cultural advocacy certainly managed, according to the reviews, to stir its audiences up. The larger program of cultural nationalism of which it was a part hoped to offer African Americans new ways of conceiving their place in the world, a goal that could only be achieved by first dismantling the European American ruling structure from within. With its complex marriage of performative language and embodied theater, and of simultaneous deconstructive critique and generative possibility, *Home on the Range* used poets' theater to renegotiate and re-present "black" identity in a telling moment in the interrelated histories of African American cultural ideology, the new social movements, and the aesthetic politics of American poetry and theater.

CHAPTER FIVE

Carla Harryman and the Ethics of Performance

I live in a fabrication near something I have never said before.
—Carla Harryman, "Property"

In the 1950s, Julian Beck and Judith Malina encountered in poets' theater crucial lessons that would help them probe the separation between audience and actor. In the 1960s, Amiri Baraka detected in poets' theater the potential to undermine received conventions of racial identity, social communication, and artistic expression. But in the end, Beck, Malina, and Baraka were each unable to break free of their own desires to guide the audience. They wanted audience members to recognize and shed coercive conventions of social communication and cultural identity and to respond freely with their own alternatives to received narratives, but they also wanted those alternatives to align with their own "liberated" political views. In contrast, poet-playwright Carla Harryman locates in poets' theater an ethics rather than a politics. Her contemporary poets' theater grapples with the ways in which identity and relationships are structured and figured through both language and performance, and it asks the audience to explore those identities and relationships with it. The result is a radically non-normative performance ethics that can be seen as one of poets' theater's postdramatic developments.

In "The Ear of the Poet in the Mouth of the Performer," an essay-play that works through the politics of poetry-performance in the post-9/11 United States, Harryman recalls a performance in which she participated in the early 1990s: the wearing of a pin designed by the artist Daniel Davidson, which bore the deceptively simple message "Iraqi." Responses to Harryman's wearing of the pin oscillated between "largely friendly looks and pleasantly unanticipated conversations from mostly Arab immigrant and Arab American shopkeepers of various religions and nationalities" and the confusion of "literal minded American types," who took the pin as a confession, as a "coming-out as Iraqi" ("Ear" n.p.). As a performance, wearing the pin was not simply a personal expression of solidarity. It was also a demonstration of the ways in which meaning can mutate in different contexts and for different audience members. And, significantly, the power of the performance came just as often in the moments of confusion and misrecognition it created.

While the Arabs and Arab Americans in Harryman's account may have gotten it "right," the more "literal minded" observers, too, found ways to identify with the performance, though not perhaps in expected or intended ways. Harryman recalls, for example, that one woman took the pin as "an invitation to exchange confidences, hers being that she had an excess of facial hair and that she was terrified that her husband would find out about it" ("Ear" n.p.). While the woman was mistaken in her assumption, the identification makes some sense to Harryman, who points out that in this interpretation both women "had something to hide until this private moment of mutual outing, even if I hadn't been deliberately hiding something like she had" (n.p.). Although the woman was interpellated by the performance, the performer was not in control of that interpellation.

As the wearer of the pin, Harryman felt a political responsibility to the responses it provoked. The purpose of the performance, she explains, was

> to diffuse the theater of war and to dramatize the real life conflations that lead to the targeting of Iraqi subjects as enemies. As a performer of the pin, one becomes responsible in a local context to major world events. The performer citizen engages in a dialogic meditation that exceeds the limits of conventional narrative and argumentation as she becomes aware of her personhood stripped of reductive theatrics and narratives of identity. As with much performance art of the 70's, Davidson's work is partly about the performer's experience itself; and like the performance values of the modernist avant-garde, it assertively provokes a response to emerging states of affairs. (n.p.)

The performer of the pin circulates, but is not in control of, the meanings of language already embedded in social and political narratives. In this sense, I would argue not that the performer's "personhood [is] stripped of . . . narratives of identity," as Harryman puts it, but rather that the pin clasps the performer to already circulating narratives, which may then be embraced, rejected, identified with, or disidentified with. Harryman is wearing not a pin that states "I claim solidarity with Iraqi victims of war," which would be a speechlike assertion of her political beliefs and identity—a self-narration—but rather a pin that appears to declare an identity that is not self-evident. In order to make sense of the pin, observers must interpret it within the range of their own experiences and understandings. And in subsequently interacting with the performer, they project those identifications onto her body in social exchange, thereby enacting new narratives.

Harryman's own performance writings take up similar questions about the relationship between language, narrative, social identity, and meaning. Her work is associated with the avant-garde poetry movement known as "Language" writing (or "L=A=N=G=U=A=G=E" writing, borrowed from the title of the poetry journal edited by Charles Bernstein and Bruce Andrews) and the San Francisco Poets Theater (aka Poets Theater) that emerged from it. Drawing inspiration from such modernist writers as Gertrude Stein and William Carlos Williams, as well as objectivist poets, Black Mountain writers, and others, Language writing challenges mainstream poetry's notion of the poem as the natural expression of the poet and instead explores the ways in which the reader participates in the creation of meaning. The Poets Theater, founded by Eileen Corder and Nick Robinson, existed from 1980 until 1987, producing more than twenty plays, including works by Harryman, Corder, Bob Perelman, Alan Bernheimer, Kit Robinson, Jackson Mac Low, Bob Grenier, Johanna Drucker, Larry Eigner, and Leslie Scalapino. Steve Benson, Lyn Hejinian, and other area poets also participated as actors.[1]

The goal of the Poets Theater was not plotted drama but an exploration of the conventions of meaning making in performance, and many of its productions denaturalized character and even largely rejected narrative in favor of experimentation with the performative effects of language. For the play *Collateral*, produced in February 1982, for example, Kit Robinson (Nick's brother) gleaned lines from his notebooks and then placed scenes and characters on top of them. Characters, in particular, were developed out of the tone established by different bits of writing, and then the characters were assigned names. During the course of the play, most of the dialogue was repeated at least once in a new context, often by a different speaker. Props were used to "extend rather than illustrate the meanings of words" (K. Robinson 125). What the play therefore explored was not a story or characters but rather the ways in which language functions to create both. The relationship of language to both story and character was denaturalized, yet the effect was to show how language tends to cohere into both. As a line from Leslie Scalapino's performance work *How Phenomena Appear to Unfold/The Hind* puts it, "There's no necessary relation to speaking here" (qtd in Cole et al. 282).

In Harryman's account of the Iraqi pin performance, the "event" of the performance takes place in the interaction between the performer and the audience, or, perhaps more accurately, in what the audience does with the performance. The wearing of the Iraqi pin is a speech act with unpredictable effects, and in this sense both Harryman and her observers become performers of its meaning. Harryman's role in the performance is one of responsibility to her interlocutors, but it is, in some respects, a nonnormative responsibility carried out as generously listening to and considering a range of possible identifications. While she mobilizes the structures, Harryman does not lead the interpretations. And, although she hints that the Arab and Arab American observers got it right, she does not accuse others of getting it "wrong" but rather of getting it different. In wearing the pin, the performer becomes responsible to this difference.

Of course, the performance must remain peripatetic in order to succeed since success relies on individual responses not subject to the pressure of collective social interpretation. One of the ways Harryman tries to retain this peripatetic quality in her own plays that are staged in the space of the theater is to construct a dispersive theater in which meaning is allowed to oscillate rather than being tied to a single dominant interpretation. The oscillation of meaning, Una Chaudhuri reminds us, is "an open space or aporia in the political 'known'"—the space of revolution (163). Harryman suggests that the ear of the poet is tuned to such oscillation, and in her poets' theater it is the job of the performer to keep this oscillation alive. In "The Ear of the Poet," for example, Harryman juxtaposes the discussion of the Iraqi pin performance with an excerpt from a Gertrude Stein play, leaving audience members to interpret for themselves the relationships between the pieces. While Harryman acknowledges that "the discussion [of the Iraqi pin performance] preceding the extract from [Stein's] play would infect the semantic meaning of [Stein's] work—an inference would be brought forth that at this present moment a poet behind a locked door, a no longer living poet, Iraqi, and people are connected and that there is a simultaneity made between the word 'Iraqi' in my exposition and the word 'people' in Stein's play" (n.p.), this is not the "right" or even intended interpretation but rather the result of habituated interpretive practices themselves. Dispersive theater places under scrutiny not only the structure of interpretive practices but also the very impulse to interpret. The space of dispersive theater is therefore an ethical space in the sense that it is a space "where thought itself experiences an obligation to form a relation with its other—not only other thoughts, but other-*than-thought*" (Harpham 404).

I discuss this example here at length because it offers a relatively self-contained way into thinking about some of the strategies and preoccupations of Harryman's poets' theater, which is both like and unlike Davidson's performance art piece. Harryman's use of Davidson as an element in her own essay-play demonstrates her ongoing engagement with intertextuality, hybrid genre, and art and/as analytic discourse, but she also uses Davidson to think through her own artistic practice. Davidson represents here a use of performance not merely as a provisional testing ground in moments of impasse but as a kind of permanently provisional space,[2] "one that in part fulfills an open-ended, non-objective mobile role that is exploratory, improvisatory, and that takes language as a medium as seriously as it does the other mediums of innovative theater that have superseded language" (n.p.). Like Davidson, Harryman is interested in the relationship of narrative to nonnarrative and in the way this relationship figures and is figured by physical bodies. Also like Davidson, much of Harryman's theater is conceptual, though it is usually written as scripted dramatic theater. And as Harryman's own commentary makes clear, in the last twenty years she has become, like Davidson, interested in the social and political consequences of her artistic experiments. For Harryman, this shift in interest from her own "art activity and its genre excesses" to something else not clearly identified but characterized by "a sense of a loss of form-desire" was precipitated by US militarization against Iraq as a response to 9/11. Viewed through this prism of art-activism, Harryman's poets' theater becomes, like the wearing of the Iraqi pin, a kind of "homework assignment" that allows both artist and audience to think through their relationships to form, media, discourse, embodiment, and identity.

Asking what comes first, the poetry or the theater, narrative or nonnarrative, subject or object, muscle or skeleton, Harryman muses, "I would prefer to emphasize the skeleton. I would prefer the movement to be the movement of the muscles lifted by the skeleton. When the muscles are not lifted by the skeleton they become athletic. One becomes aggressive and competitive. The theater becomes a theater of conflict. And somebody has to win" (n.p.). While I want to be careful not to tie Harryman's ideas down to a simple metaphor, part of what she is suggesting here is that bodies are inseparable from the social forces that animate them. While both muscles and skeleton are components of bodies, they serve different but overlapping purposes, one mainly structure, the other mainly force. An illustration accompanying the essay depicts a knife held between teeth and lips, a cooperation of skeleton and muscle that can be read, simultaneously, as both defensive and aggressive. This is a depiction not of an oral weapon but of an aural weapon, both spoken and heard, suggested by the ear in the mouth of the work's title. In the historical moment of the post-9/11 US "War on Terror," Harryman implies, muscle force has been recruited into insidious service, sculpting language and narrative into weapons of social conflict. Yet, just as both muscles and skeleton are necessary to movement, so narrative is necessary to communication. The solution, Harryman writes, is "to distribute narrative rather than deny it" ("Toy Boats" 107).

Language Poetry, Poets' Theater, and the Body

Harryman has composed numerous works of poets' theater, including *Third Man, Percentage, La Quotidienne, There Is Nothing Better Than a Theory, Performing Objects Stationed in the Sub World, Memory Play, Mirror Play, Gardener of Stars, an Opera,* and *Hannah Cut In,* as well as works for voices, instruments, and electronic media. Her poets' theater has been produced across the United States and in bilingual productions in Canada, Germany, and France. The infiltration of performance studies into literature departments has sparked a more performance-oriented interest in hybrid works such as Harryman's in recent years, and this critical turn to performance has also precipitated more opportunities for productions. In 2008, for example, *Third Man* was staged in San Francisco as part of a San Francisco Poets Theater retrospective;[3] *Memory Play* was produced in Chicago with the support of the Renaissance Society at the University of Chicago; and a weekend of poets' theater plays directed by Harryman, including her own *Mirror Play,* Frank O'Hara's *Try! Try!,* and an adaptation from Barrett Watten's *Bad History,* was presented in Chicago as part of a festival of poets' theater. During this same period, *The Grand Piano* series began to credit Harryman's work in particular and poets' theater in general as a fundamental part of the history of Language writing (see, especially, vol. 6). Several new stagings of Harryman's writings have been produced in the last five years, and her most recent performance work,

Hannah Cut In, was performed in 2017-18 in Berkeley, Detroit, and Paris (in a bilingual staging).

While other Language writers were experimenting with poetry, Harryman had already begun writing plays (*Percentage* was first produced in 1978 and *Third Man* in 1979). The story of the San Francisco Poets Theater began when Harryman and her friend and collaborator Steve Benson approached Nick Robinson and Eileen Corder about putting on a play together, which resulted in a one-night performance, in 1979, of O'Hara's *Try! Try!* at the Grand Piano coffee shop on Haight Street (Cole et al. 277). Robinson recalls being inspired by the engagement and enthusiasm of the audience, and he found himself hoping to build a collaborative community in which performers might be audience members another night and vice versa. "So in a way," Robinson observes, "the audience came first in my personal history of Poets Theater" (ibid.). Corder, a costume and scenic designer, performer, and playwright, and Robinson, an actor and budding director with an interest in poetry, had moved to San Francisco the year before and wanted to stage more fully produced and fully rehearsed performances over multiple nights like the ones in which they had participated in college. Drawn to improvisation and "plays that were quick on their feet, light and mysterious," Robinson initially turned to Jarry, Stein, Brecht, Dada, and surrealist plays (278). But of these only Stein felt sufficiently contemporary, so Robinson sought out the community of writers who would produce plays "that used language in ways that the theater would have to grow into" (ibid.). They found a group of interested poet friends, and, inspired by nonverbal improvisatory theater, started working on physical and vocal experiments.

While some of the plays of the San Francisco Poets Theater have been published (almost exclusively in small journals), the group itself has received little critical attention.[4] Language writing in the 1970s and 1980s was focused almost exclusively on material textuality, which left performance work far out on the margins of an already marginal artistic practice, and critics tended to respond to the performance works in similarly text-bound ways. In a 1986 review of Harryman's plays *Percentage* and *Property*, for example, Jean Day addresses the dramatic form of these hybrid works not as actual performance but rather metaphorically, as a *theatrum mundi* in which "'We' are acting out aspects of a common drama through language, not just in the sense that we're using the same tools, but in the sense that it is language which makes the private public, makes the passion of the revolutionary *charge*" (120–21 emphasis original). Steve Benson—Harryman's close friend, fellow performer, and frequent theater collaborator—refers to the published text of Harryman's play *La Quoti-dienne* as "the play itself," folding the entire work under an umbrella of textual interpretation when he argues, "The lack of any stable context or prescribed behavior indicates no means or property other than discourse by which the figures can gain leverage in the struggles for authority and autonomy" (24, 23). Focusing exclusively on discourse, such an interpretation skips over the complex ways in which the physicality of the actor-characters may also give the play's figures an authority and autonomy (however unstable) via the presence of live bodies in performance—in phenomena that are part of but not equal to discourse.

The critical neglect of the San Francisco Poets Theater has come not only from poets, however. The disciplinary divide obscuring the Poets Theater was, if anything, worse on the side of visual artists. Ann Vickery writes that the arts "were strongly differentiated in the Bay Area during the seventies. Although performance-based poets like Carla Harryman encouraged visual artists to attend readings and talks, poetry was still presumed to be too tied to the page and thus limiting. Harryman recalls a young and prominent artist dismissing Language writings as 'just a version of surrealism'" (33). This work was thus trapped, like so many other instances of poets' theater, in both a practical and a critical disciplinary blind spot.

In an essay published in *Poetics Journal*, Alan Bernheimer suggests that poets' theater consists of works "written towards production . . . work[s] with then two lives to lead, one self-evident and the other potential" (70). But there is often very little that is "self-evident" in a work of poets' theater. Bernheimer sees words as agents, which "left to their own devices . . . tell stories by themselves, resolute (resonant in the evolving history of their use)" (ibid.), but of course it is this latter assertion—that words are "resonant in the evolving history of their use"—that points out the falsehood of the former suggestion that words have their own agency, for the assertion of both Language writing and the Poets Theater is that the "stories" of words are constituted in their social use. Certainly, unintended meanings and histories can (and often do) arise when we use language, but to characterize this as an act of words "by themselves" obscures the ways in which meaning both constitutes and is constituted by bodies and embodied identities both on the stage and in social exchange.

Acknowledging the work of Language poets such as Ron Silliman, Charles Altieri, Bob Perelman, and Charles Bernstein, who engage the performativity of material language, W. B. Worthen, too, considers the work of the San Francisco Poets Theater as a textual phenomenon, interesting for its similarity to printed drama (which he indicates in the title of a book chapter is "something like poetry") but not engaged *as* drama or theater. But Worthen's discussion of antitheatricality in both poetry and theater in his 2005 book *Print and the Poetics of Modern Drama* was an important step in opening the relationship between two fields normally considered to have very little overlap. Most significantly for my purposes here, Worthen observes that

> the materiality of the mise-en-page, the precise construction of printed words in space, does not operate as a kind of stage direction, an authorized and authoritarian effort to govern subsequent performance (though some authors may intend it that way), nor is it complete in itself, a container or "can" of perfected meanings waiting to be emptied by performance. Instead, Language poetics implies the incommensurability of these two modes of writing's "thickness." The poem's physical design on the page, and its physicalized performance cannot be collapsed into one another so that the script grounds the performance or the performance realizes the script. . . . Language poetics reframes the page as a distinctive field of play, insisting that words can and must be joined in ways beyond the habits of conventional speech. (138)

Indeed, in "Aesthetic Tendency and the Politics of Poetry: A Manifesto," a collaborative essay on the political and aesthetic practices of Language writing, Silliman, Harryman, Hejinian, Benson, Perelman, and Watten critique the expressivist lyric, institutionalized in literary and creative writing programs in the United States, as responsible for "the scenario of disinterested critical evaluation reinforcing the alleged moral autonomy of the poem" (Silliman "Aesthetic" 269).

Language writing reworks narrative as a political principle through such tactics as foregrounding the conventionalized function of the "I" and of other narrative tools. Such tools mark relationships of location, antagonism, causality, intention, and emphasis and "provide the illusion of movement, direction and location for the reader," Michael Davidson points out, "but when they lose their indexical function, they point at the conventionalized nature of writing itself" ("Framed" 79). When "I" tell a story from memory, who is the "I" that speaks, and who is the "I" that is spoken of? What is the overlap between the two and in what way does each help to constitute the other? Bringing these questions into the space of embodied performance, Harryman puts further pressure on the conventionalized function of linguistic markers as indicators of identity presumed to be natural.

Harryman's *Memory Play* (1994) explores the narrative and performative construction of the "I" via memory, played out differently by the play's three main characters, Pelican, Fish, and Reptile.

> REPTILE: If I tell you one thing that I remember, you will think I'm an idiot for remembering only one thing. This is one thing that makes theater different from real conversation. If I provide you with several of my most esteemed memories, you will probably believe there are more where those came from, and I will have earned your respect. This will make theater a little more like real conversation.
>
> PELICAN: I have a job and it is virtually all I can think about; however, I think this: memory is nothing but words stored up in an inefficient computer. What you will remember of this conversation will be nothing like what went into its construction. Such understanding promotes success in business.
>
> . . .
>
> FISH: I had suffered for a long time from the illusion that remembering inhibited one's experience. Now the illusion is almost my only memory. . . . [Later] I will remember something else and not this. I will have forgotten the story to which I currently refer. Each person has his or her own theater. I propose this as an exhibit or a symptom of my personal stage. (9–10)

Reptile is a chameleon, disguising himself in the camouflage of social discourse. And yet his disguise is not aimed at deception. Although Reptile suggests that whether or not we are respected or maligned depends on the strength of our (storytelling/conversational) performance, he seems to move beyond Goffman's notion of impression management to suggest that social discourse is all the truth there is. Pelican, on the other hand, focuses on the "misinformation" that occurs between what one says and what another hears, and he promotes a notion of performance as information processing, mechanical and morally indifferent. Meanwhile, Fish appears to recognize the necessary relationship between discourse (remembering) and experience while at the same time acknowledging that the "backstory" of identity is often forgotten, that identity is assumed without realizing what that identity is built on. Fish might be taken as an example of contemporary performance studies notions of identity and performance: while we may understand that identity is performative, we experience it as natural. Despite their differences, what Reptile, Pelican, and Fish share is a notion of memory as performative, produced by and in narrative.

Memory relies, then, on the doubling of creative narrative and social discourse, a doppelgänger that first appears in the "stage directions" with which the prologue opens: "A bedtime story/conversation in a little tent town out in the salt flats" (9). What one first notices about this direction is its generic ambivalence. While there would be little difficulty producing the visual elements of such a scenic design in performance (a small tent town, salt flats, bedtime), how would the difference and sameness indicated by the phrase "story/conversation" be performed? The slash is itself a radically textual performance that suggests the imbrication of social discourse with storytelling, with narrative, and indeed this relationship is the play's central investigation. Worthen has argued that "modern drama in print typically frames a dialectical tension between the proprieties of the page and the identities of drama" (*Print* 62). Harryman's slash turns this page-stage tension outward, toward social life. Art (story) is different from, but inextricably bound to, social discourse (conversation). Storytelling is both oral and literary art. Harryman's printed play alludes to the chiasmus of literary textuality and social discourse by putting the play's status—as literary artifact, as embodied performance—into question.

While Harryman makes use of what Worthen has called the "accessories" of modernist dramatic publication, or what I refer to throughout this book as the paratext—"page design, typography, act and scene numbering, speech prefixes, and stage directions" (Worthen *Print* 13)—she does not do so in order to control the stage performance from the page. Despite Chris Stroffolino's assertion that *Memory Play* "works at least as well as a closet drama as it does in theater performance," the page and stage versions of the play are not correspondent but collaborative, together investigating the performativity of memory (177). This is to say not that each version cannot stand on its own but rather that the play's textual-theatrical ambivalence proliferates its identity across genres and forms of reproduction, undermining the final authority of any single version. Readers of the play may not have access to performance, just as audience members may not have access to the written text, and thus all versions are necessarily contingent and incomplete.

In bringing the language of the text into the space of performance—performing "as language event the fluidity between public and psychological space," as Harryman puts it ("Site" 158)—Harryman's plays investigate the social activities of language within a context of actual human relations, of the audience members and performers within a specific social space (that of the performance at a particular moment in time) and in relation to specific objects. Language writing on the page explores language in individual interaction with readers, while the performance of Language writing in poetry readings is bounded by the conventions of a touring authorial performance that rhetorically position the event (albeit falsely) as site and audience nonspecific, if not actually transcendent. In contrast to this, Harryman's poets' theater emphasizes embodied identities at the same time that it deconstructs them. These identities are not incidental, and they are not nonspecific; rather, they are fluid. The character list of Harryman's play *Performing Objects Stationed in The Sub World*, for example, specifies a "White woman," "Child," and "Black man," but, as the author's notes for performance explain, "The categories of gender and ethnicity are mutable in this play, based on whatever circumstance of the performance" (ibid.). This is accomplished in part by having multiple actors play each character but also by leaving the gap between character and actor visible: "For instance C3, the Black Man, reads the newspaper but that doesn't mean that C3 becomes a Black Man who reads the newspaper, but rather C3 performs a reading of the newspaper: his identity or identities such that it is or they are, migrates through activities" (162). In this way, the objects with which the actors interact "do not serve as extensions or illustrations of subjectivity nor do they appear with autonomous luminosity . . . [but they are instead] constitutive of an instability of social encounters and uncertain boundaries between interior fantasy and exterior fact, whether they are sentient or inert" (ibid.). This does not, however, preclude psychological depth. Rather, characters are defined not by the moral challenges they face but rather by the communication they perform and are performed by.

In *Memory Play*, the playing through of multiple discursive and gestural registers in the formation of identity drives the action. As bodies and spoken language self-consciously jostle one another in performance, the relationship between discourse, identity, and embodiment takes center stage. Reptile's lines quoted above appear to interpellate audience members into a self-conscious suspension of disbelief: he explicitly acknowledges our tacit agreement to let one memory in "art" stand in for the multiple memories of "real" conversation.[5] In art, he suggests, a single story or image (memory) can take on a variety of symbolisms and resonances;

in conversation, however, we may question such overdetermination of a single moment in one's life. But the "I" who speaks this line is shifty, posing as a social interlocutor and literary-dramatic character simultaneously. On the page, Reptile's "I" seems to remain consistent, a distant observer of the relationship between theater and conversation. Spoken by an actor onstage, however, the "I" oscillates between actor and dramatic character. Is this line a rehearsed but direct address to the audience by an actor who will soon become a character in the play, or is the actor already in character? And how does this ambiguity position audience members in relation to the play?

This last question raises the issue of what poet Joan Retallack has called "reciprocal alterity"—the "ethical and epistemological destabilizing principle" that I am never fully knowable to myself or to others, just as others are never fully knowable to themselves or to me (5). Is the "I" who, according to Reptile, can earn "your" respect a "fictional" character or a "real" actor? It makes no difference, for either way the "I" is a construction based in part on the speaker's performance and in part on the audience's conclusions in relation to that performance. The matter is both grammatical and epistemological, since pronouns are a necessary part of communication despite their radical insufficiency and contingency. Pronouns suggest independent subjectivity and in doing so contribute to a model of individualism. In order to "move away from models of cultural and political agency lodged in isolated heroic acts and simplistic notions of cause and effect," as Retallack suggests we do, we must therefore think through our tools of communication at their most basic level (3).

Both Retallack and Harryman propose a new kind of realism, one that echoes Stein, with its emphasis not on representations of reality but on the processes of representation themselves. Retallack approaches this new realism by appealing to the essay form, because, she argues, the essay writes from the position of an "I" understood as selfsame, whereas the lyric "I" of poetry is already understood to be a persona. The theater, however, presents an unusually apt arena for an investigation of representation, for the presence of bodies on stage always simultaneously evokes both the characters being portrayed and the actors "themselves."

If the humanities emerged from the turn to language only to enter into the turn to performance, then Harryman's work provides an apt vehicle for exploring our negotiations of these turns. Language writing arose simultaneously with the rise of linguistic theory in the 1970s, and the relationship between the two has always been seen as collaborative—Language writing *as* theory. Some saw Language writing as the perfect object of the new theory and saw developments in theory as supporting the sense that Language writing had a cognitive and social use. But not everyone agreed on the role of theory in Language writing.[6] In *There Is Nothing Better Than a Theory* (given its first full performance in 1989), Harryman satirizes what she sees as a tendency toward theory fetishism. In *Memory Play* she similarly pokes fun at theory's drive to dominate, this time in the figure of a child's toy, satirically named the Miltonic Humiliator. Meanwhile, recent productions of *Mirror Play* seem to indict theory as the production of knowledge removed from lived experience. In debates about representation and gender, the body has become the vanishing point of theory. Perhaps the return to the material body is, as Julia A. Walker suggests, "a kinetic form of political resistance" (171).

Operating from the belief that we are initiated into the/a world by language, Language writing resists closure, conventional syntax, and sedimented meaning as a way of mobilizing against ideology as it resides in language and polices/constructs our subjectivities. If the script on the page is subject to multiple interpretations in the imagination of the individual reader, these interpretations can be trained into submission on the stage via a single dominant character portrayal, set design, voice direction, and/or scenic coherence. But in poets' theater embodied—and especially vocalized—performance also sometimes works in the opposite direction, increasing polysemy by creating aural alternatives not seen in the impaginated text. Poets' theater thus balances the ocularcentrism of theater and the "turn to the visual" with the text-in-the-body of aurality. I use the term *aurality*, following Charles Bernstein, "to emphasize the sounding of the *writing*, and to make a sharp contrast with *orality* and its emphasis on breath, voice, and speech—an emphasis that tends to valorize speech over writing, voice over sounds, listening over hearing, and indeed, orality over aurality" (13). Aurality might be thought of as a particular condition of literate society, which proliferates multiple versions of a text (manuscripts, printing, readings, performances) with no sole authority.[7] Although aurality is fundamentally linked to the body—"what the mouth and tongue and vocal chords enact" (ibid.)—the body does not control the performance. Rather, it is the body's engagement with the text that performs, enacts, and materializes the work. In referring to the bodily grounding of language as its "animalady" (22), however, Bernstein unfortunately removes it from the context of (human) social performance. Poets' theater restores this emphasis on language's social function, welding voice and speech together into a social weapon that cuts both ways.

What Harryman's theater adds to Language writing is a consideration of the ways in which the presence of bodies affects our understanding of language politics, particularly in the different ways language and bodies mark a threshold in interrelated processes of speaking, enacting, and knowing. It may be helpful here to recall Pierre Bourdieu's conceptualization of the body as a kind of "living memory pad" onto and via which not only behaviors but also beliefs and values are inscribed (68). Childhood learning leads to a kind of automatically enacted belief that is not a state of mind but rather "a state of the body" (ibid.). As practical sense becomes naturalized, the source of the practices becomes obscured. "It is because agents never know completely what they are doing," Bourdieu argues, "that what they do has more sense than they know" (69). But, whereas for Bourdieu acting and theater become ways of recalling these automated, naturalized thoughts and feelings,[8] Harryman sees theater as a means of defamiliarizing the social ideologies inscribed onto bodies—ideologies that are, for Bourdieu, obscured by time and naturalization and are, for Judith Butler, denied in the necessary construction of subjective autonomy.

Poets' theater is a collaborative performance between generative language and physical gesturality that can help us understand the complex linguistic and embodied performativities that constitute and materialize identity. Gesture is a bodily act that, in the realm of the social, becomes a sign of communication. Martin Puchner, who has written thoughtfully on arrested movement in modernist drama, describes gesture as "the praxis and labor that go into the production of language and linguistic communication, the labor that is more or less erased in the finished, linguistic product" (28). Isolated and disjointed, individual gestures can only be amassed into an aggregate rather than organically connected into a whole.[9]

Puchner notes that both Nietzsche and Adorno maligned gesturality as that which prevents actors onstage from presenting organic wholes. Postmodernism's valorization of the aggregate, however, offers a new kind of pro-theatricalism that celebrates precisely the gesturality disavowed by these theorists of modernism. Harryman's theater embraces the aggregative quality of gesture by using denaturalized acting to create paratactic (rather than syntactic or hypotactic) structures. In rehearsal for a 2008 production of *Memory Play*,[10] for example, the actor playing Fish needed help slowing down her speech, so she was given an activity to perform:

writing a note on a piece of paper. This practical solution to an acting problem soon became an interpretive issue, however. What should the actors then *do* with the note? Director Catharine Sullivan wanted Fish to hand the note to Child, but Harryman (who was present at rehearsals) was adamant that this was not possible, presumably because it transformed the activity of note writing into the narrative gesture of passing on instructions. In the end, it was agreed that Pelican would intercept the note without (oral or gestural) comment. In preventing the note-writing gesture from cohering into narrative meaning, Harryman and Sullivan created a paratactic structure—one gesture and another gesture and another gesture that do not bear any clear narrative relationship to one another. At the same time, Sullivan and Harryman's disagreement over what to do next demonstrates the tendency of gesture to aggregate into character identity and narrative meaning.

As an embodied act with the potential for social meaning, gesture both is and isn't language.[11] Gesture reaches simultaneously inward toward the construction of subjectivity and outward toward the construction of social identity, but it also relies on bodily impulse, understood within a system of discourse but not reducible to it. As both being and representation, gesture reveals what Peggy Phelan has called the body's metonymic relationship to the subject. While the real exceeds representation, representation also exceeds the real. The identity produced in and through this reciprocal excess is not only a marker, Phelan argues, but an ethics.

> Identity emerges in the failure of the body to express being fully and the failure of the signifier to convey meaning exactly. Identity is perceptible only through a relation to an other—which is to say, it is a form of both resisting and claiming the other, declaring the boundary where the self diverges from and merges with the other. In that declaration of identity and identification, there is always loss, the loss of not-being the other and yet remaining dependent on that other for self-seeing, self-being. (*Unmarked* 13)

In denying narrative coherence to Fish's note-writing gesture, the production of *Memory Play* places the burden of meaning on the audience members themselves. What the body does and what it means do not perfectly correspond. Making meaning out of a gesture necessarily involves a merging of interpreter and interpreted, of self and other. Harryman, like Phelan, is interested in the relationship of representation to being, a relationship she investigates via a strategy she characterizes as "non/narrative" when performed in prose, and which we might modify as "non/representation" in theater. As in *Memory Play*'s play of "story/ conversation," the slash here indicates not an opposition but an imbrication of two modes.

Mimesis and Misrecognition in Mirror Play

Harryman's *Mirror Play* revolves around violence perpetrated by nations against other nations or against (its own or other) individuals. Divided into four acts, a prologue, and an epilogue (all appearing in reverse order) but without stage directions or speech prefixes, its performance differs widely from production to production. What remains consistent, however, is a web of political and social references—for example, media portrayals of Rachel Corrie, the American peace activist killed in 2003 defending a Palestinian house against US-built bulldozers operated by the Israeli Defense Forces; images from the second Gulf War of US soldiers raiding Iraqi tombs and Iraqis' own destruction of Iraqi cultural artifacts; and the 1968 campy intergalactic antiwar movie *Barbarella*, whose star, Jane Fonda, was transformed in the 1970s from sex symbol to despised antiwar activist and then again in the 1980s to aerobic video icon. *Mirror Play* portrays an America defined not by physical borders but by complex military, economic, cultural, and political relationships, playing through the ways in which these relationships are constructed and maintained.

The play is both radically textual and radically gestural, using paratactic gesture and language, as well as architectural space, not to reflect the interiority of the subject but rather to help constitute and figure it. In this sense, *Mirror Play* represents a broad shift in thinking from the concept of an individual subject, seen as a self-sufficient and independent whole, to the concept of the social subject, in which the social (exterior) is a necessary and mutable circumstance of subject constitution (interior). Throughout the play, "wholes"—words, characters, clothes, rooms—are revealed as mere resting points in the ongoing process of meaning making. What is simultaneously difficult and hopeful about this piece is that it dares to imagine a politics (or ethics) for those who are produced in and by narrative. *Mirror Play* does not simply reveal or reflect this condition of narrativity; it tries to think a way that we might be active within this condition rather than merely subject to it.

Fig. 6. Elana Elyce, Roham Sheikhani, and Mary Byrnes in *Mirror Play* by Carla Harryman, Susan Hilberry Gallery, 2008. Photo by Barrett Watten. (Courtesy of Carla Harryman.)

The play opens with a simple image of homey domesticity—clothes hanging on a line, blowing in the wind—portrayed entirely in language: "Flying. Clothes flying. Sleeves wrapping / around clouds, cinching them in, dragging / them" (49).[12] The empty clothes are both human products and human forms, registering simultaneously the presence and absence of human beings themselves. As the sleeves first "wrap" around clouds, then "cinch," and finally "drag" them, the clothes imply a kind of "domestic" violence, possibly a reference to the Clothesline Project—protesting against, and memorializing the victims of, a private kind of "domestic" violence against women. But it is also perhaps a reference to that which inspired the Clothesline Project—the AIDS Quilt, originally created to memorialize the victims of AIDS and to protest against their neglect by American society and history. As theater and performance critic Elinor Fuchs has pointed out, participant-created AIDS quilts, in their jumbling of Jews, Catholics, Muslims, and New Age Buddhists with sequins, flags, prayers, a measuring spoon, and much more, perform a postmodern breakdown of master narratives—in direct contrast to the hero memorials of "modern imperial politics" (195–96).[13]

In the Detroit production directed by Jim Cave,[14] no flying shirts were visually present on stage; rather, they were represented in spoken dialogue, as artifacts of language, drawing attention to the ways in which narrative has been inscribed on bodies even to the point of replacing them altogether (as one speaker says in *Mirror Play*, "Images are crowding. Crowding us out" [79]). If the shirts had been physically represented—staged—they might simply have performed an iconic function, but because they are described in language—a reference to a reference—the textuality of the representation creates not a destruction of visual representation but a recognition of the very condition of representation.

Despite the lack of a narrative through-line, the play achieves continuity both by returning again and again to key words and images and by taking as its central focus the investigation of the conditions of representation. Later cycling back to the image of clothing, for example, the play meditates on the perspective created by choosing some descriptors over others.

> ... This scheme
> Imagines clothing in terms of whole or
> complete entities: a shirt, a hat, a shoe, etc.
> So there is still much that it cannot describe.
> For instance, in the great outdoors, the
> clothes rot and decompose. Birds pull at
> their threads. The threads mingle with other
> things. The thread is no longer a discrete
> thing but part of a unit for which there is no
> name until the nest is complete. Then the
> unit is a nest. I wear a sleeve on my heart.
> Note this also. And other harmless events.
> (note)
> (note)
> *echo makes a note*
> (63–64)

To imagine clothing as a finished object rather than a composite of that which went into its making or as a decomposite used, part by part, in the making of other objects is, the text asserts, a "scheme" rather than an inevitability. If the object that is no-longer-a-shirt-and-not-yet-a-nest has no name, it becomes subjugated, merely a stage in the creation of an "actual" object and meaningless except in relation to the end product (recalling Puchner's definition of gesture).

From this cluster of lines, organized thematically around the impact of language usage on conceptual thinking (which is hardly "harmless"), the play suddenly shifts paratactically to a reordered cliché—"I wear a sleeve on my heart"—with no apparent relation to the previous lines. One way an audience member might approach this shift is simply to give in to the experience of abrupt change, with no attempt to impose meaning. Habituated interpretive practices are more likely, however, to coerce a meaningful connection. Is this line perhaps another example of language that privileges object over process? What is the relationship of the "I" to the objects (clothing, nest) that came before? And what do we make of the shift in tone from material objects such as shirts, hats, threads, and nests, to symbolic objects, such a heart and, now, sleeve (which can be worn on a heart only metaphorically)? A nest made out of threads is a home (a physical place), and home is where the heart is (a symbolic place). Emotional vulnerability (wearing one's heart on one's sleeve) is re- placed with emotional self-preservation (wearing a sleeve on one's heart). What was formerly outside (clothing) moves inward (to "I"). Here the work mimes its meaning through the generation of interpretive possibili- ties: any single understanding represents a "scheme," useful perhaps but certainly not inevitable.

But the lines quoted above also move beyond semantic frontiers toward the semiotic border between language and music inhabited by the word *note*. This single word suggests simultaneously a musical sound, differ- ent speech modes (command—"note this"—or description), and textual objects (a hierarchical category designator [i.e., footnote] or a casual piece of writing). Although in the quotation from *Mirror Play* "note" seems to exist as a kind of stage direction rather than as dialogue, in performances of the play, all of the language is performed aloud, either as dialogue or as spoken stage direction. But the use of parentheses on the page—an instan- tiation that cannot be precisely perrformed onstage—is a textual conven- tion indicating that the word *note* might be read as a placeholder (as in "I intend to insert a note here") or as a stage direction (as in "Play a musical note here"). In either case, the note functions as an (explanatory or musi- cal) "echo."

The play's textual performance on the page, then, is not identical to its performance onstage. The relationship of the text to stage is neither directive nor documentary, neither script nor recording. Reading the text and attending the performance produce experientially distinct plays that nevertheless constitute linked "work" exploring the relationship between textual language and embodied performance. The semantic overdetermination of "note" in the text, for example, is linked but not identical to the overdetermination of the voice, as speech and as instrument, in performance. Both the Detroit and San Francisco productions featured a jaw harp, which produces sound uncannily in between language and music.[15] Working with sound and music at the limits of language, these performances in part explored the ways in which sounds morph into and out of meaning. While audience members of *Mirror Play* would not necessarily have access to the script, the radical non/narrativity of the work requires them to consider the choices being made in the play's performance. The performance conjures the absent text, but that text may or may not be consulted to lend authorial certainty to any particular interpretation.

What is at stake here is an awareness of the multiple processes by which we make experience meaningful. When a speaker asserts at the beginning of Harryman's play that "the composition of the sky is a matter of knowledge" (49), for example, she suggests both that the sky's physical makeup (one sense of "composition") can be scientifically known but also that this knowledge is itself a matter of narrative construction (a second sense of "composition"). The goal is not to question the makeup of the sky but rather to suggest that what is known must also take into account *how* it is known. A few lines later the play suggests that "addicts" to knowledge "suffer atmosphere" (50), a line that is vocally elongated in performance— "atmosssphhhere"—to suggest both the vaporous air that surrounds a planet and, simultaneously, a fear of the *atmos*, or vaporosity, perhaps the vaporosity or lack of solidity of knowledge itself. In this case, vocalized performance vaporizes our certainty about the meaning of the line, and in doing so, it both mimes and produces its meaning.

* * *

In the psychological space of *Mirror Play*'s collectivity, all aspects of discourse are both positive and negative. The play alludes to the imbricated discourses of health, war, beauty, and pornography, for example, in its repeated references to "Barbarella," the title role in the soft porn sci-fi film that made the actress Jane Fonda famous. In the film, Barbarella is a representative of the Federation of Earth who is sent on a peace-seeking mission to rid the world of a weapon that could mean the end of humanity.

Making love not war across the galaxy, Barbarella made Fonda a favorite pinup among GIs (Perlstein 3).

Mirror Play's reference to "fa(r)ce and pornography" (70) certainly alludes to *Barbarella*, but it might just as aptly describe Fonda's 1980s reincarnation as the aerobic ideal of her wildly popular workout video series. Dressed in form-hugging fitness fashion, Fonda bent over and spread her legs in a model of arrested movement. But in the period between *Barbarella* and the height of her workout popularity, Fonda also became an antiwar activist, speaking out against the Vietnam War starting in 1970. Although she remained a sexual icon, Fonda's perceived betrayal of American troops transformed her into a target of overt, if symbolic, sexual violence. "At places where soldiers or former soldiers congregate," Rick Perlstein reported, "there'll be stickers of her likeness on the urinals; one is an invitation to symbolic rape: Fonda in her 1980s 'work-out' costume, her legs splayed, pudenda at the bulls-eye. Every night at lights-out midshipmen at the US Naval Academy cry out 'Goodnight, bitch!' in her honour" (3).

Disturbing though this report is, it is the discourse behind the violence that interests me here. Ironically, this "symbolic rape" is in part encouraged by the false mirror—the farce/face—of aerobicism misrecognized as athleticism. Johannes Birringer has argued that the image of the aerobic body is structured around a

> scene of instruction/mimicry that promotes an exercise of subjective and corporeal transformation while masking the ritualized submission of the body to serial, monotonous, and stationary motion. In her willful self-production of an actively new feminine body, the woman participant misrecognizes the mirror structure in this performative exchange, aligned as it is around persistent cultural/hierarchical oppositions between mobility/immobility, seeing/being seen, and so forth. She is drawn into a phantom interaction with the two-dimensional, depthless and absent body of the video image that simulates an actual relation between body model and "real" performance in "real" time. (215)

The aerobic body, always a feminized body, is immobilized and put on display. In contrast, the military body might be thought of as an athleticized body, masculinized, mobile, and—recalling Harryman's discussion of the athleticism of muscles acting without the assistance of the skeleton—

competitive and aggressive. The discursive oppositions promulgated by the aerobic-athletic dichotomy contribute to, among other things, both kinds of "domestic" violence suggested in the play's opening verbal image of flying clothes (violence against women and against discursively feminized homosexual men). Although *Mirror Play* alludes to physical acts of violence (as in the Hilberry performance when a hooded male figure claiming "Nobody wanted war" conjures images of torture associated both with American prisoners of war in Vietnam and with Iraqi prisoners at the American military prison Abu Ghraib), these are not the focus of *Mirror Play*. Rather, Harryman's attends, as I have done in this example of the soldiers' violence against Fonda, to the discourses that both materialize the body and enable violence—discourses that rely on a range of mis/recognitions. Employing not a poetics of memory as witness but rather a poetics of memory as performative, as productive of the relationships it purports to describe and attend, *Mirror Play* plays through and with the notion of national(ist) memory.

* * *

Exploring the psychological space of collectivity, *Mirror Play* offers a counter to mass cultural reliance on what Retallack deems "naïve realism" and its attendant call "for intellectual and imaginative resignation, a naturalization of normapathic desire" (5). Such realism is "normapathic" because it works by irresponsibly burying difference, contradiction, irrationality—an irresponsibility that, Retallack notes, "is never benign" (19). Harryman's work, in contrast, remains open to radical difference. It engages with processes of social learning by rethinking the production and dissemination of knowledge. The realism of Harryman's work lies not in a normative reenactment of past events but rather in its existence as a thought experiment through which the past and its connection to the present moment are reconfigured. It is characterized by the ability to hold contradictions in interplay and by a willingness to see the overlay of conflicting realities.

In *Mirror Play* Harryman turns this exploration toward social-spatial constructions with material consequences in the perpetuation of national violence. Architecture, like language, always has both a form and a social use.[16] Postmodern theorist Linda Hutcheon recalls that Ludwig Mies van der Rohe, the architect of the classically modernist Seagram Building in Manhattan, "allowed only white blinds on the plate glass windows and demanded that these be left in only one of three positions, open, shut, or half-way" (28)—the building's design quite literally controlling the personal lives that inhabited its space. Viewing tenants either as children to be guided or as subjects on whom to experiment, modernist architects, Hutcheon argues, positioned themselves apart from the buildings' interior communities. Postmodernist architecture returns to the idea of community, but now as a *decentralized* entity with practical needs. And memory is, Hutcheon argues, "central to this linking of the *past* with the *lived*" (29).

Mirror Play's mise-en-scène is conceptual: as a foyer that has been cut away from the house, it represents the threshold between public and private, into and out of which "any body" may pass. The "antechamber" is both room and passageway that comes "before" the house, in between the inside and outside. It is a room defined only in relation to other rooms, not as a place in itself (and in vocalized performance the word slides between *antechamber* and *antichamber*). But in *Mirror Play* the antechamber has been torn away from the house, destroying the relation that constitutes its identity. Here, then, the antechamber is not a room but a moment in the midst of transition from one object (foyer) to another, as yet unknown, resting point.

Harryman's approach to architecture is influenced in part by Denis Hollier's notion of "antiarchitecture" as a means of getting out from under the authoritarian hierarchies with which architecture is complicit, a condition that led Georges Bataille to deem architecture "society's authorized superego" (Hollier ix). Hollier conceptualizes "an architecture that would not inspire, as in Bataille, social good behavior, or would not produce, as in Foucault's disciplinary factory, madness or criminality in individuals" (x). Antiarchitecture is therefore an alternative that leads

> against the grain to some space before the constitution of the subject, before the institutionalization of subjectivity . . . [or that would] open up a space anterior to the division between madness and reason; rather than performing the subject it would perform spacing: a space from before the subject, from before meaning; the asubjective, asemantic space of unedifying architecture, and architecture that would not allow space for the time needed to become a subject. (x–xi)

Such antiarchitecture works as loss or dismantling of the meaning that is assumed to inhere in architectural structures—such as houses, prisons, and tombs, all of which are implicitly or explicitly referenced in *Mirror Play*.[17]

Mirror Play's foyer investigates, in part, the penetration of exterior social space into a subject's interiority. But as a space that has been torn away from the house, presumably in an act of violence, the foyer is also what Hollier labels an "asubjective" space—a space that defies interpretive coherence. In this way, *Mirror Play* enters into the discourse of space and place as they figure interiority/exteriority (*from* the position of the subject) and insiderness/outsiderness (*as* the position of the subject); this is in part a difference between being from/in a place and belonging to a place. In contrast to what Chaudhuri has described as modernist drama's recourse to "a vague, culturally determined symbology of the home, replete with all those powerful and empowering associations of space that are organized by the notion of belonging" (xii), *Mirror Play* is organized around a violated home that is also an opening—a condition that acknowledges both the very human desire to belong and the simultaneous violence and promise of belonging. Whereas modernism's drama of the home is built around what Chaudhuri has labeled "a *victimage of location* and a *heroism of departure*," which "structure the plot as well as the plays' accounts of subjectivity and identity" (xii emphasis original), *Mirror Play* articulates the question its unattached foyer invites: "Can the antechamber lose its meaning its / substance? Or is it always the same even / if every aspect of it contradicts its / defining characteristics?" (63).

Dispersive Performance and the Theater of Others

According to Jerzy Grotowski, whose efforts to rethink actors' training have influenced Harryman's own approach to performance, the defining feature of theater is the performer-audience relationship (15). But in the postmodern era, the audience is notoriously difficult to characterize. In *The Audience*, Herbert Blau discusses the peculiar notion of the postmodern audience, both collective and disparate, joined to one another through a shared experience interpreted in highly individualized ways. Like Harryman, Blau locates the efficacy of postmodernist theater in its challenge to the primacy of ocularcentric knowledge. To position understanding as seeing is, he argues, an ideology that ignores the audience's original auditory role.

Postmodern theater audiences are a product of "the vast seduction of the dispersive media" (14) and marked by division, or what Blau describes as "an 'original splitting'" that is "not the image of an original unity but the mysterious rupture of social identity in the moment of its emergence" (10). The postmodern audience is therefore not a certainty, not a community to be joined or a position to be occupied,[18] but rather an effect of performance itself: "The audience . . . is not so much a mere congregation of people as a body of thought and desire. It does not exist before the play but is *initiated* or *precipitated* by it; it is not an entity to begin with but a consciousness constructed. The audience is what *happens* when, performing the signs and passwords of a play, something postulates itself and unfolds in response" (25 emphasis original). Blau historicizes the concept of a "public" as a modernist notion that (mistakenly) conceptualizes the audience as uniform, understandable, and authorizing—that is, as something that can be figured out and won over. In contrast, postmodernist audiences are seen as indeterminate, with each member experiencing an individual response, an individual identification.

Blau dubs this theater the "theater of otherness" as an alternative to the more traditional notion of a theater of essence (94). This "otherness" does not constitute a counterpublic—it is not the disidentificatory community that, for example, José Muñoz discusses in his study of contemporary minoritarian performance. Rather it is an interpretive "community" marked, paradoxically, by discontinuity and dispersion. It is a community formed in spite of (or perhaps because of or prior to) the foreclosure of normative identification. But, while Blau argues that such theater is marked by an oscillation between eye and ear that creates distance *rather than* identification, I want to propose that in Harryman's theater this oscillation forms the basis for an ethics of responsibility *toward* the identifications we form. In this sense, we might think of Harryman's theater not as a theater of otherness but as a theater of others, others to whom we are, for better or worse, ethically bound—a theater in which, to borrow Harryman's language, "Me talking fuses to you" ("Property" 16).

If the space of performance is, as Harryman argues in "The Ear of the Poet," a provisional space in which ideas, narratives, and social constructions may be tested, then what's being tested in *Mirror Play* is perhaps not only our methods for making sense of a post-9/11 world but also the very idea that making "sense"—a particular cognitive ordering of experience—is the correct goal. If "making sense" is a narrative proposition, then, Harryman's work suggests, poetry might provide a different paradigm more suitable to the present world's complex interconnectivities.

Poetry might offer, as Retallack asserts, a cognitive alternative to imagining borders and the crossing of lines, allowing us instead to think in terms of fractal geometries and the "swerve," an unpredictable (form of) change that can defamiliarize, disorient, and even estrange by "radically altering geometries of attention," resulting in "an unsettling transfiguration of once-familiar terrain" (1). As interruption, digression, and the unexpected, the swerve is produced in and by hybridity, the vitality of which lies in its inventiveness, in its generativity. The swerve is not an abdication of responsibility, Retallack stresses, but rather the recognition that all events are overdetermined, unpredictable, subject to chance. Openness to the unexpected, to generativity, thus becomes a kind of ethics.

Placing such generativity at the heart of an ethics of nonnormative obligation takes seriously Geoffrey Galt Harpham's assertion that "ethics does not solve problems, it structures them" (404). The modernist hero narrative, related to the sense of a universal ethical imperative on which ethical discourse has traditionally been founded, has been denounced in the postmodern era as an "ideological vehicle and the legitimation of concrete structures of power and domination" (Jameson 114; qtd in Harpham 387). The paradox of a postmodernist ethics of nonnormative obligation, then, is that while it does not posit a hierarchy of interpretive values, it does rely on the categorical imperative of obligation itself. This imperative may, Harpham suggests, be at the center of Derrida's notion of deconstructionism itself, seeping into it in the form of the subject who is allowed to "'return' on the condition that it be transformed and modernized—no longer the self-identical, self-regulating subject of humanism, but rather a subject inmixed with otherness. This otherness, Derrida said, would consist not only of the obligation that all other people owe to other people, but also of the iron laws, the internal othernesses, which we, as speaking animals, harbor within our living consciousnesses" (Harpham 392).

The paradox of dispersive theater's nonnormative obligation embodies the contradiction Harpham locates in ethics itself—the contradiction between "How ought one to live?" and "What ought I to do?," the contradiction between the distanced laws of generalizable norms and an individual in an actual (and unique) situation (395). For Harpham the key to ethics is not only the obligation but the *choice* between different ethics (e.g., between mercy and retribution). Dispersive theater makes us attentive to these choices, makes us aware that there *are* choices. This is not to say that all choices are equal or equally compelling but rather that each choice "violates some law or other, and violates it precisely because it is 'ethical'" (396). Dispersive theater is ethical, then, not because it offers a moral order but because it reveals the conditions of choice, the conditions that inform and compel our choices. *Mirror Play* presents a very postmodern problematic: while the body is materialized through the very act of narrative (including discourse, gesture, and image), narrative is always an imperfect mirror—a necessary framing that inevitably obfuscates, a "view [that] blocks what's behind it" (Harryman "Animal" 33). This presents a particular obstacle to audience members, who are presented with a range of possibilities for mis/recognition, but it also presents a threat to bodies, for violence—in the form of war, rape, social neglect, and government policy—is justified through such mis/recognitions.

And yet it is the very vulnerability of bodies that leads to claims of "bodily integrity and self-determinism," which are, as Judith Butler has pointed out, "essential to so many political movements" (*Precarious Life* 25). "The body," Butler continues,

> implies mortality, vulnerability, agency: the skin and the flesh expose us to the gaze of others, but also to touch, and to violence, and bodies put us at risk of becoming the agency and instrument of all these as well. Although we struggle for rights over our own bodies, the very bodies for which we struggle are not quite ever only our own. The body has its invariably public dimension. Constituted as a social phenomenon in the public sphere, my body is and is not mine. Given over from the start to the world of others, it bears their imprints, is formed within the crucible of social life; only later, and with some uncertainty, do I lay claim to my body as my own, if, in fact, I ever do. Indeed, if I deny that prior to the formation of my "will," my body related me to others whom I did not choose to have in proximity to myself, if I build a notion of "autonomy" on the basis of the denial of this sphere of a primary and unwilled physical proximity with others, then am I denying the social conditions of my embodiment in the name of autonomy? (26)

Here Butler helps us understand the vulnerability of the body in the public realm, a vulnerability of both its physicality and its identity. This mentally and physically projected "external" body inevitably figures one's internal subjectivity as well. And yet in figuring this subjectivity as autonomous,

Butler argues, we do violence to those others on whose denial that autonomy is based. "I" is not the measure, Harryman argues, but the "interference" ("Acker" 36). But it is necessary interference.

The woman who, in Harryman's account of the Iraqi pin performance,
interpreted the wearing of the pin as the admission of a secret understood,
at least subconsciously, that she was both actor and acted upon. Taking
Harryman's pin as the revelation of a guilty secret was perhaps a conditioned response—the only way she could make sense of the performance
within a political context characterized by a nationalist narrative drive toward "mission accomplished." And yet, in responding with a secret of her
own, she demonstrated a deeply felt, if unexpected, empathy that operated
according to a set of interpretive conditions not determined by borders or
even by autonomy. She, too, felt the vulnerability of her body in public, and
she, too, suffered a social policing that ultimately figured her subjectivity.

Avoiding narratives of witness, of moral imperative, of political identity, the Iraqi pin performance was certainly not a call to action. But for
the woman who revealed her own secret, and certainly for Harryman as
well, it was a moment of unexpected connection. It is probably too much
to imagine this moment as a swerve away from terror, as a swerve toward hope, but it may perhaps remind us that there is far more to every
event than any story can express. Generosity toward the generativity of
imperfect mirrorings and unexpected identifications becomes a way of
opening ourselves up to other possibilities of connection beyond explanation, justification, and noncontradiction. Poets' theater may not result
in the dissolution of atmosphere or *atmos*-fear, but as it swerves between
them, Harryman's work suggests, it has the potential to encourage critical
discussion and collective interpretation in which no one is "right" but in
which difference proliferates.

CHAPTER SIX

Poets' Theater as Postdramatic Theater

Learning from Suzan-Lori Parks's
The America Play

While several contemporary poet-playwrights embrace the poets' theater mantle, others have taken the lessons learned from poets' theater to strike out in different directions. Both Baraka and the Living Theatre, for example, experimented with poets' theater before turning to nonverbal environmental, ritualist approaches (if, in Baraka's case, only momentarily). Poets' theater's explorations of language, texts, and discourse have also been absorbed into the contemporary theater forms known as *postdramatic* theater, Hans-Thies Lehmann's term for the self-reflexive and often non-hierarchical use of a range of theatrical signs, including the visual, aural, gestural, and textual. Postdramatic theater, like poets' theater, explores the audience-performer relationship, often through a text that has been decentered but not abandoned, and frequently undermines stable conventions of communication and hierarchies of social meaning-making.

While the previous chapters have demonstrated various ways in which theatrical strategies and notions of the participatory audience member developed across different instances of poets' theater, this final chapter heads in a new direction by considering a postdramatic inheritor of poets' theater, Suzan-Lori Parks's *The America Play*. I have chosen *The America Play* as my example of poets' theater's legacy in postdramatic theater not only because, like many instances of poets' theater, it casts into relief the conventions and assumptions of normative communicative practices and demonstrates a concern with language as praxis, but also because it demonstrates particularly well one of the key lessons of postwar poets' theater: that dramatic texts are not merely potential, projected, or impaginated performances but rather that language and performance collaboratively shape one another, both within and across media.

One of the problems of watching a narrative play, Gertrude Stein grumbled, was that it was hard to keep all the characters straight so "it [is] always necessary to keep one's finger in the list of characters for at least the whole first act" ("Plays" 254). Having one's finger on the program at the same time that one's eyes were on the stage created a syncopation and a feeling of nervousness that Stein disliked intensely, and, as chapter 1 discussed, the "landscape" play was her attempt to do away with this nervousness based on her assertion that a landscape "does not have to make acquaintance" (263). But having one's finger on the program and one's eyes on the stage is a surprisingly appropriate characterization of the audience activity demanded by *The America Play*: the theater program contains, after all, footnotes that comment on the dialogue and unfolding dramatic action, obliging audience members to shift back and forth uneasily between program and stage. For Parks, this syncopation works as an intentionally antiabsorptive strategy, but the footnotes are also deceptive. While on the surface they appear to help explain the events unfolding on the stage, it soon becomes clear that they are actually part of the performance, cycling performatively back into the play itself. As the semiotic distinction between text and paratext breaks down, representation as an act of framing takes center stage.

It may therefore come as no surprise that in a 1994 interview—the year *The America Play* was published and had its premiere at Yale Repertory Theatre—Parks counted William Faulkner as her favorite writer, above Samuel Beckett and Adrienne Kennedy (Drukman 72). While *The America Play* had already been produced in workshop at the Dallas Theatre Center and Arena Stage in Washington, D.C. in 1993, the influential Yale Repertory Theatre in the early 1990s was a different sort of proving ground. Distinguished director Stan Wojewodski, Jr. had taken over as artistic director in 1991 and was leading the theater in a new direction. Whereas Lloyd Richards, Yale Rep's artistic director from 1979 to 1991, had nurtured artistically precise, well-made plays by such playwrights as August Wilson and Athol Fugard, Wojewodski championed the linguistically and structurally innovative poets' theater of Eric Overmyer, Len Jenkin, Mac Wellman, and Maria Irene Fornes. Parks's own *Death of the Last Black Man in the Whole Entire World* had been produced at the Yale Repertory Theatre in 1992, and producing another play by the relative newcomer to theater was a significant statement on her work's relationship to the direction of American theater in the late twentieth century.

In interviews that recount her own development as a playwright, Parks stresses that she initially wrote fiction but was urged toward playwriting by James Baldwin because of the dramatic way she read her stories aloud in his creative writing class at Mount Holyoke (Jiggetts 309). And when she first arrived in New York, she attended poetry readings rather than theater productions (Savran 146). Indeed, each of Parks's plays written and produced prior to 1997, including *Betting on the Dust Commander* (1987), *Imperceptible Mutabilities in the Third Kingdom* (1989), *The Death of the Last Black Man in the Whole Entire World* (1992), *The America Play* (1994), and *Venus* (1996), exhibit a writerly attention to language more commonly associated with poetry and experimental fiction, leading theater critic Edwin Wilson to label Parks "a poet and word-musician." Wilson is not alone in his characterization. Liz Diamond, who has directed multiple productions of *Imperceptible Mutabilities*, *The Last Black Man*, and *The America Play*, has called Parks a "truly brilliant poet" (Backalenick 34). This is not casual praise. At the Yale School of Drama, Diamond regularly taught master of fine arts classes that included plays by such writers as Tristan Tzara, Adrienne Kennedy, and Mac Wellman, and yet it is Parks whom Diamond credits with teaching her about "the nature of poetry and poetic meaning" (Drukman 59).

Some critics have read the unusual, poetic page layout of Parks's early plays via the textual conventions of dramatic scripts and stage directions. In her analysis of *Venus*, Elizabeth Dyrud Lyman, for example, argues, "The arrangement of elements on each page is carefully crafted for effect. In a scene from 'The Whirlwind Tour,' for instance . . . Parks's simulation of stage space with the positioning of the Negro Resurrectionist on one side and the Mother-Showman and Venus on the other, sets up a temporal as well as a spatial separation" (92). Such a reading makes sense from the perspective of the stage and implies an attempt to bring the stage into the space of the page. But as Parks herself acknowledges, she was more interested in poetry and radical modernism than in theater and plays, and she wrote plays even before she was fully familiar with the conventions of writing for the stage. In fact, the spatial arrangement that Lyman points to seems more descriptive of a textual design, with the "primary" text on one side and "marginalia" on the other—an arrangement that recalls, for example, James Joyce's experimental novel *Finnegans Wake* and Langston Hughes's collection of performance poetry *Ask Your Mama*. My point is not to raise a chicken-or-egg question but rather to point to the ways stage and page mutually inform one another in Parks's work.

Employing generativity in the service of a critique of the way American racial history has been written and reinforced, *The America Play* relies in part on the multivocality of language to challenge institutionalized histories, and it uses poetic strategies to mobilize audiences to question received meanings and generate new interpretive possibilities. Going beyond deconstructive critique, such theater requires creative engagement with language in general (as material reality, as tool of communication) and with particular social forms and practices of meaning making (textuality, history, performance). Engaging *The America Play* as simultaneously performance, poetry, and history underscores not only the play's creative use of textual conventions but also its sly recognition of the performativity of all texts.

While some of the earliest examples of emerging poets' theater discussed in the preceding chapters employed an inwardly focused metatheatricality, the theatricality at the heart of fully realized poets' theater seeks to produce engaged and aware audience members who are awakened by the performance's multivocality to their role as producers of meaning, in some sense subject to but also not entirely bound by the tools and conventions they employ. Likewise, postdramatic theater, Malgorzata Sugiera has argued, serves as "a means of inducing the audience to watch themselves as subjects which perceive, acquire knowledge and partly create the objects of their own cognition" (26). Part of what poets' theater encourages audience members to perceive are the different ways in which they are initiated into subjecthood, a perception that can encourage an act of critical recognition of that initiation into subjectivity.

Certainly one of the goals of *The America Play* is to awaken audience members to their own power as users and producers of meaning. And, while Parks has never labeled her own work poets' theater, she is an artistic inheritor of many of the artists and strategies discussed in this book's preceding chapters. Her early work undermines generic divisions, eschews narrative, denaturalizes character, relies on the poeticity of language for some of its performance effects, and explores the tensions in conventions of representation and reception. *The America Play* shines a spotlight on the authority of textual conventions in particular, using poets' theater's examination of the performative production of meaning to explore the boundary between texts and performances. Undermining the distinction between drama as "genre" and drama as "medium" (Jackson *Professing* 65), *The America Play* asks us to consider the rhetoric both of textuality and of performance as different ways of knowing. Moreover, it defamiliarizes our typical emotional responses to already circulating narratives, revealing us as active participants in the shaping of these meanings—and of history, more specifically.

Riffing on the History (Play)

The America Play, described by one critic as an articulation of "how popular history derives from repetition and 'hearsay' . . . and consists of what people want to believe" (Foster 30), invites a collaborative approach to the interpretation of history. In the first act, or "Lincoln Act," a black man whose physical resemblance to Abraham Lincoln has been remarked on by others all his life has built an historical theme park (an "exact replica," the text explains, of an amusement park back east known as "the Great Hole of History"). This man, known throughout the play only as "the Foundling Father" (in the authorial stage directions) or "the Lesser Known" (in the dialogue spoken by other characters), earns his living by playing victim for paying customers who wish to reenact Lincoln's murder at a theatrical production of *Our American Cousin*, a role he repeats again and again and yet always slightly differently to meet the desires of the various "Booths" who have come to play-assassinate him. As a play that stages a historical moment that occurred during a theatrical performance that was in part about the specific cultural identity of America, *The America Play* layers competing references together in a complex interrogation of "America." The second act, entitled "The Hall of Wonders," takes place at the now abandoned theme park site, apparently several years later, after the Foundling Father has died. Lucy and Brazil, his wife and son, have come seeking his remains. They are employed in the funeral business, as diggers and paid mourners, just as the Foundling Father was himself a digger who dug the exact replica of the Great Hole of History when he went out west (think frontier). At the play's end, Lucy and Brazil have excavated the Lesser Known's personal effects and decide to use them to stage their own historical attraction, the House of Wonders.

Parks's "Great Hole of History" has been interpreted metaphorically as "the whole of history, the absence from that whole of African American history . . . the wound in Lincoln's head, and a vagina" (Foster 28). Soyica Diggs Colbert identifies it with two other historical holes: "the hole the bullet bored in President Abraham Lincoln's head and the one resulting from the trans-Atlantic slave trade that the Middle Passage symbolizes" (2). And Jeanette R. Malkin calls it the "absence from which power emerges" (4). As a site that is both the hole on which the whole depends and a replica of a replica, the theme park built as an "exact replica of the Great Hole of History" is a rearticulation in a chain of absences whose power is created in the filling in of gaps in the historical record, as well as in the act of abstraction itself. The exact replica of the Great Hole is a mimetic rearticulation of that absence and that power, but it is also a performative reenactment that produces the effect of material reality in the form of history. Or, perhaps more accurately, *a* history, for, as W. B. Worthen has argued, "In the Great Hole of History, or its replica, words and things aspire to the condition of history, a history that—as citation—can only be rhetorical, devised in and by its performance" ("Citing" 7).

Many critics have explored and expanded on Parks's "rep and rev" (or repetition and revision) approach to history, which weds representational aesthetics to real effects. Kevin J. Wetmore Jr. sums it up succinctly as "Do it again; do it differently" (xvii). Harry J. Elam Jr. and Alice Rayner see rep and rev as a way of "animat[ing] the past in the reality of the performative present" (179), and Una Chaudhuri frames it as "the recognition that history, because it exists as language, is always subject to revision" (264). As the Lesser Known reenacts and embellishes the historical record, history itself is revealed as a performative act. But the Lesser Known's son, Brazil, might also be seen as a repetition of his father with a difference as he digs for his father's remains, performs the mourning wails his father has taught him, and retells the tales he's heard from his mother. "Brazil's own re-memberies of his own childhood are inscribed on his body and memories," remarks Christine Woodworth, "and [are] ever-present in his dialogues with his mother" (143). Troublingly, she notes, "Brazil seems trapped in the act of digging, thus illustrating the legacy left by his father as well as the impossibility of disrupting the familial and historical cycles" (ibid.).

The relationship between (historical) text and (theatrical) performance is at the heart of the play, and the Lesser Known re-creates the Lincoln assassination with some flourishes of his own. A stovepipe hat would never have been worn inside the theater, he notes, for example, but it is nevertheless "good for business" because "people dont [*sic*] like their Lincoln hatless" (168). The false blonde beard goes over less well, but the Lesser Known nevertheless finds occasion for such personal flair, which riffs on but does not precisely reenact the historical record. As performative reenactments with a difference, such riffs, note Elam and Rayner, "parallel the exclusions and losses between recorded history and lived experience" (179). We might think of a riff as a replaying that weds the original (in the sense of first or earliest) with something original (in the sense of new and unique). This replaying is, therefore, neither a copy nor, strictly, a fresh creation but rather a form of generative mimesis in which, as noted in other instances of poets' theater, the creation of something new in the act of imitation reveals the coercive nature of received truths. Rebecca Schneider explains the relationship between Parks's writing and jazz music in this way: "In jazz, one cannot accurately say that a tune is *misplayed* by the riff. So too history is not *mistold* via the riff by which Parks retells it. In fact, playing in difference might be one way to *get those notes right*" (65 emphasis original). The theatrical recreation of generative mimesis, like the jazz riff, can "get something both wrong and right simultaneously" (Schneider 66). This sense that Parks's riffs get it wrong and right simultaneously—and may in fact get it wrong *in order to* get it right—echoes Colbert's more pointed claim that Parks's riffs, and theatrical riffs more generally, can work reparatively, as theatrical acts of redress that symbolically refigure the social and political order. In *The America Play* such reparations are enacted via the remaking of history.

The America Play is therefore not a history play in the traditional sense of the term but a work of postdramatic poets' theater. The play's meaning is produced largely through its simultaneous use and thematization of performance as a means of unmastering and remembering historical knowledge. Creating experiences that are simultaneously real and representational, the play relies not on facts but on strategies and produces not knowledge but practice. It asks us to think along *with* it, not just about it. And then to think beyond it. Colbert has argued that we might think of the play as modeling "practices of reading more generally" because each reading, like each theatrical performance, creates its own individual, as well as shared, experience. While I concur, I also want to add that such an understanding figures not the passive reception of the absorbed audience member or reader but the active, committed involvement of poets' theater's participatory audience.

The Co-Performative Theater Program

Of course, contemporary theater employs multiple strategies for engaging and mobilizing audience members that go beyond the performance itself, including talkbacks and lobby exhibits. But perhaps the chief tool beyond the play itself for engaging and orienting audiences—and certainly the most ubiquitous—is the theater program, handed out to audience members only minutes before the curtains rise. Theater programs traditionally serve a wide range of practical functions. Contractually required by the Actors Equity Association (AEA), they create publicity for the entire production team and indicate actor substitutions or other changes to a publicized performance. For theaters and producers, programs create revenue by providing advertising space. And audience members often save them as souvenirs of an evening spent at the theater—a function most clearly evidenced in the abundant archives of souvenir theater programs across the country.[1]

Most histories of the contemporary theater program format trace it back to Frank Strauss, the Ohio ad man who first came up with the idea of transforming the handbill or theater poster into a multipage space for advertising—the now familiar *Playbill* format (see, e.g., Mandell). The magazine design also allowed for more pages devoted to production photographs and supplementary materials. But the theater program's explanatory function likely developed out of an earlier use of expanded, supplementary titles and promotional descriptions designed to lure broader audiences into attendance. Mid-nineteenth-century theater posters, for example, included not only title and location but also illustrations, brief characterizations, and, often, the promise of engrossing spectacle (and Parks's frequent allusions to circuses, amusements, and sideshows link her plays explicitly to this particular style of theatrical spectacle).[2]

Contemporary programs not constrained by the copyrighted *Playbill* format often include a greater range of notes and images that not only give specific information about the current production but also serve interpretive, interrogative, and even coperformative roles, a function that dramaturg D. J. Hopkins describes as a Barthesian "counter-text" that "presents an alternative site of authority in performance, an alternative center of gravity that exerts influence over the trajectory of a production process" (2). The aim of the coperformative theater program, Hopkins suggests, is "to invite the audience to participate in the counter-textual practice at work in the production" (15), a goal that extends Hopkins's own notion of "hybrid authorship" even beyond the cocreative work of the dramaturg with "playwright, director, designers, actors" to a collaboration with audience members as well. As a methodological field positioned within a range of cultural discourses, the countertext is independent, productive, collaborative, audacious, excessive, and performative. Geoffrey Proehl's writing on the dramaturgical sensibility revises Hopkins's notion of the dramaturgical countertext by noting that it does not actually function "counter to the work," although it is "an act of creation" (69), and he extends the idea of dramaturgical productivity to allow for audiences themselves engaging, poets' theater–like, in cocreative acts with the play (which we might think of as a kind of riffing on the play).

The America Play's ideal audience, and poets' theater's audiences in general, might therefore be characterized as having a dramaturgical sensibility. Despite their differences, both Hopkins and Proehl portray dramaturgy as an approach that resembles the participatory, collaborative audience practices created as an effect of poets' theater. For Hopkins and Proehl, dramaturgy is a creative activity that embraces a position of unknowingness, that treats the unanswerable question as a productive act that directly collaborates with the play. As Savran has suggested, Parks's plays, "like the plays of [Adrienne] Kennedy or [Gertrude] Stein, . . . demand that directors and readers conspire with the playwright as active producers of meaning. For they construct stable and fixed meanings but set the self in dialogue with itself, offering contradictory possibilities for meaning. They, in short, stage (double) consciousness" (140). Parks concurs that others must take an active role in relation to her plays: "I'll put in something like, 'He's in the big hole which is an exact replica of the Great Hole of History.' I want to see what the director says. And the director's going to say, 'It's a museum, it's a black hole, it's a fishbowl.' That is magical to me" (147). What Parks appears to be aiming for here is a tension between "production" and "reception" enacted in part by the possibility of multiple identifications—multiple identifications that are enacted by various coproducers of the play's meaning, including directors, dramaturgs, designers, performers, and audience members themselves. This tension can be understood in Savran's terms as a kind of "(double) consciousness"—a double consciousness that was promoted and extended by the Yale Rep production's theater program.

Consider the two-page image at its center: a derringer pistol aimed at the back of Abraham Lincoln's head, shown in profile (fig. 7). The image is reproduced from the book *Twenty Days*, one of the most popular books on the Lincoln assassination and a key source of material for both Parks's play and the program that accompanied it. Published in 1965 as "a narrative in text and pictures" of Lincoln's murder and the following twenty days that led up to his burial in Springfield, Illinois, the book's foreword calls it both an "arrangement" and a "record" compiled by the daughter and grandson of a collector of Lincoln memorabilia "who devoted a life-time to amassing the greatest collection in existence of photographs of Lincoln, his times, and his contemporaries" (Catton n.p.)—which, not coincidentally, is rather like Lucy and Brazil, wife and son of the Lesser Known, gathering the effects of the Lincoln impersonator for use in their own amusement park. As a historical rendering, *Twenty Days* works in part as an attempt to uncover the facts in a morass of competing witness accounts. But it also acknowledges the practical and even philosophical challenges in constructing a single historical narrative, an acknowledgment that *The America Play* takes as its starting point.

The caption that accompanies the Lincoln-and-derringer image in *Twenty Days* informs us that "the actual derringer pistol that killed Lincoln is used here with this tilted profile of the President to show the exact angle and the extremely close range at which he was hit" (Kunhardt and Kunhardt 39). In the program for the Yale Rep production, the same image is entitled "Lincoln Assassination" and is accompanied by a caption, attributed to John Wilkes Booth, that reads, "What a glorious opportunity there is for a man to immortalize himself by killing Lincoln" (n.p). The differences between these two presentations of the image are revealing. First, the caption in *Twenty Days* positions the image, spread across two oversized pages, as an authoritative depiction. But what is meant to be ascertained from the flat, two-dimensional re-creation of the angle of the gun, which necessarily misses a whole other dimension of the gun's angle? What "truth" can we learn from this "re-creation," especially when the book's foreword argues:

> Of necessity, history is selective. When it deals with an event like this it assembles the pertinent accounts and discards the irrelevant, carefully separates the probably true from the obviously false, pieces stray bits of testimony together, and presents us at last with a coherent story. This is the way history has to be, and if it were not told that way it would be unendurably confusing. Yet we may miss something when we read it that way, and what we miss can be important—the dreadful incoherence which the affair had at the time for the people who were involved in it. History's most compelling moments are not always as orderly as the books make them seem; sometimes they are in the highest degree disorderly, so bewildering that even people who lived through them may have only a shadowy idea of what they themselves saw. There is a confusion

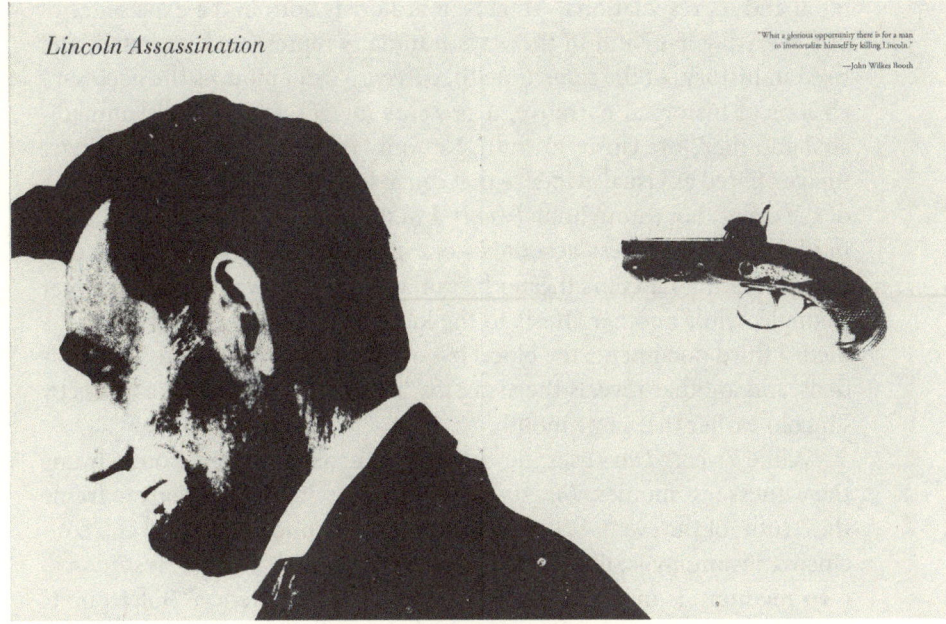

Lincoln Assassination

"What a glorious opportunity there is for a man to immortalize himself by killing Lincoln."

—John Wilkes Booth

Fig. 7. Image of Lincoln and derringer pistol from the Yale Repertory Theatre program for *The America Play*, Billy Rose Theatre Division, New York Public Library for the Performing Arts, Astor, Lenox, and Tilden Foundations. (Courtesy of the Yale Repertory Theatre and the Meserve Kunhardt Foundation.)

of tongues, which may indeed be a deep problem for the historian but which was after all part of the reality at the time. It is no wonder that history's tragedies give birth to myths and legends. Sometimes it seems marvelous that the real truth ever does take shape. (n.p.)

The argument with which *Twenty Days* opens, then, is that the creation of history is a performative endeavor and in the formation of a coherent historical narrative something is always left out—and what is left out is the "confusion of tongues," the multiplicity, contradiction, and indeterminacy that direct experience of an event and the resulting testimony produce.

As that which "responds to the crisis of truth by exceeding the facts," testimony, educational theorist Megan M. Boler suggests, is both a discursive practice and an enactment that refutes the transparency of language and knowledge (166). The crisis to which testimony responds is both material and representational—that is, it is a crisis both in the experience of our everyday lives and in the ways trauma is represented, narrated, and fixed in history. At the same time that *Twenty Days* mourns the necessary elisions of historical narrative, it presents images as essentially unmediated and therefore closer to truth. Not only is the Lincoln-and-derringer image offered as visual evidence that can at least partially reenact the truth of the event, but throughout *Twenty Days* images are used to clarify facts muddled in eyewitness accounts—one photo verifies the existence of a flag decorating Lincoln's theater box on the night he was assassinated, for example, while another attests to the location of the apartment where he died; a third documents the blood left on the bedclothes by a dying president, and another reveals the assassins' attendance at a public address by Lincoln earlier that same month.

While *Twenty Days* uses the "truth" of Lincoln's assassination to frame the witness testimonies, *The America Play* uses witness testimony to frame the "truth" of the event. Whereas truth is understood as univocal and conclusive, testimony is, like poetry, polysemous and dynamic. "Testimony's own medium 'is in process,' and has no self-transparency," Boler points out, and it "contains the energy and life force that cannot be captured as content or conclusions" (167). In recycling the Lincoln-and-derringer image performatively, the Yale Rep program dismantles its claim to precision, transparency, and factuality and recasts it as John Wilkes Booth's ultimate performance. In linking Lincoln's assassination not to presumably objective "facts" but rather to speech acts of Booth, who was both a theater actor in his own right and the brother of the acclaimed Shakespearian actor Edwin Booth, the program frames this moment in our nation's history as a performative, even theatrical, event. Meanwhile, in the play's onstage performance, the Lesser Known's multiple re-creations of the moment of Lincoln's assassination belie the historical value of a single, flat pictorial layout. The image, as well as the historical account of Lincoln's assassination, the play suggests, are always already mediated.

Several critics have read Parks's use of a Lincoln impersonator as a kind of deconstructive signifying on American cultural myths. In an especially cogent argument that links theatrical impersonation with "passing," Colbert argues that "the Foundling Father's faking elucidates how the theater exemplifies a 'real' that constantly slips and destabilizes bodies and thus race, which renders blackness a dubious guarantor of the real" (3). Yale Rep's program notes recommend a slightly more conventional notion of racial performance with an excerpt from John Wideman's "The Black

Writer and the Magic of the Word," an essay that promotes signifying as a means both of deconstructing the pretensions of "proper" English and of creating a black speech community. Within this context, Parks's use of the "Foundling Father" and the "w/hole" of history work deconstructively to reveal the absence of African American history upon which (white) American (textual) history is founded. The black writer must become "bilingual," Wideman argues, able to move easily between the textuality of the professional American writer and the oral poetics of African American culture.

At issue in this notion of a deconstructive signifying is the discrepancy between codes of literacy and codes of orality, but Parks transforms this from an either-or to a both-and proposition, suggesting that African American writing must reincorporate the testimonial "confusion of tongues," or multivocality, intentionally selected out of historical narratives such as *Twenty Days*. In doing so, it does not move back and forth between languages so much as speak multiple languages simultaneously—an assertion explicitly performed in the program notes by an image-sound-text (see fig. 8).

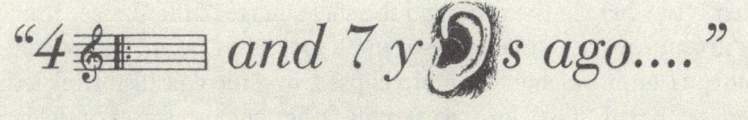

Fig. 8. "Four score and seven years ago" rebus from the Yale Repertory Theatre program for *The America Play*, Billy Rose Theatre Division, New York Public Library for the Performing Arts, Astor, Lenox, and Tilden Foundations. (Courtesy of the Yale Repertory Theatre.)

The images in this formulation do double representational duty, poetically and conceptually suggesting both the production and reception of sound and textually conjuring the words "score" and "ear," which complete the famous opening of Lincoln's Gettysburg Address. But in the absence of the actual words themselves, the Gettysburg quotation is available only aurally, as a subvocalization or imagined vocalization that occurs in the act of interpreting the images poetically. It is only in mobilizing eyes, voice, images, and text collaboratively that meaning can emerge, but this meaning is founded on absence as it oscillates between Lincoln's historical text and Parks's performative citation and between images that suggest sounds, sounds that suggest words, and words that suggest absent texts.

One of the ways in which this image-sound-text works is by poetically riffing on, or conjuring but not precisely reproducing, the opening line of the Gettysburg Address and, simultaneously, defamiliarizing that text and our emotional responses to it. Such defamiliarization creates the conditions under which we can, as Boler puts it, "excavate [our] structures of feeling" (172) rather than merely respond emotionally—rather like Lucy and Brazil have excavated and reemployed the Lesser Known's personal effects in a performance of their own. Against this background, we might expand on our initial deconstructive interpretation of "Foundling Father," a designation that appears in the character list but is never spoken as part of the play's dialogue. While it might be possible to read "Foundling Father" as a creative kind of stage direction (though it's unclear how such a direction would be performed), this understanding relies on a conventional notion of a script for the stage, putting the play text in the service of performance and the theatrical image. From the vantage point of poetry, we might view Parks's imagistic "Foundling Father, As Abraham Lincoln" differently, as the deconstruction of the transparency of the image, demonstrating the ways in which the page refigures both the historical image of Lincoln as revered American forefather (or "faux-father" elsewhere in the play) and the stage image of the "Lesser Known," an African American man dressed up to look like Lincoln whose cultural history is both indebted to and eclipsed by Lincoln's historical legacy. Likewise, Brazil "looks for traces of his father but also traces of the larger arc of history," Woodworth notes. "By knowing more of his father, he is better able to determine his own place in the world" (143). In the program notes, themes of legacy and parentage emerge in a collection of texts and images, cinching together Charles Olson's "abt the dead he sd . . . ," Robert Creeley's "A Variation," Wallace Stevens's "The Irish Cliffs of Moher," and Gertrude Stein's "The Gradual Making of *The Making of Americans*" with images of African Americans that suggest the play's main characters. In one photo, a man in white dress shirt and vest, with a pocket watch chain dangling across his chest, looks sideways at the camera. In the other, a woman and boy pose in formal attire, the woman looking past the viewer while the boy looks directly at the camera. Beside these images, the poetry selections explicitly thematize and interrogate notions of cultural and familial inheritance, extending them beyond the simple unidirectional passing on of histories and characteristics to consider the ways in which later generations refigure previous ones (Creeley), the struggle to come to terms with one's inheritance (Olson), and the impossibility of identifying origins (Stevens). In addition to these thematic connections, the excerpts function hermeneutically, tuning audience members' ears for the playful, poetic language of the play and imbricating production and reception. Together these texts and images alongside the play itself raise questions of parentage and inheritance, not only within biological relationships but across the histories of nations and races.

In the play's onstage performance, the imbrication of production and reception emerges most dramatically in the Lesser Known's Lincoln impersonation. Both *The America Play* and Parks's later award-winning *Topdog/ Underdog* summon the tension between the popular reception of Abraham Lincoln as the Great Emancipator and his more contested reputation among African Americans.[3] Basing their livelihoods on historical myth and hearsay, Parks's Lincoln impersonators are themselves on shaky ground. But Parks's Lincoln impersonators are also African American, and the defamiliarization that occurs through this casting is pointed.[4] We might say in Boler's terms that it reveals the "semiotics" of our emotional response to Lincoln as a white national hero martyred for his opposition to Confederate secession and celebrated today as the man who put an end to the institution of slavery (157). But such a sense of the "Great Man," Foster points out, comes "at the expense of all the ordinary people, the lesser knowns, of history, especially African Americans, who are deprived of a place in their own story" (32).

In using visual, gestural, and poetic means to defamiliarize the national hero narrative, the play encourages what Boler terms "testimonial reading." In testimonial reading, she theorizes, the reader or audience member

> must attend to herself as much as to the other—not in terms of "fears for one's own vulnerabilities," but rather in terms of the affective obstacles that prevent the reader's acute attention to the power relations guiding her response and judgments. For example, to experience a surge of irritation at the text allows the reader to examine potential analyses: does she dismiss the text out of irritation? Might irritation, for example, indicate the reader's desire to avoid confronting the articulated pain? (169)

Replacing Lincoln with a black "reiteration" invites a range of emotional responses from audience members, from amusement to irritation. It also undermines the racial relations on which the narrative of the white national hero is founded, crookedly alluding to the histories that are silenced by this white hero narrative at the center of African American history.

As the inheritor of both of his parents, Brazil struggles to express the significance of his inheritance in the terms that have been handed down to him. When Brazil unearths a medal for "fakin," he cries "This is his! This is his!!," correcting it to "This could be his!" only after Lucy reminds him to "Keep it tuh scale" (186). Admonishing Brazil to keep his stories "tuh scale," Lucy expresses her desire "tuh know the real thing from thuh echo. Thuh truth from thuh hearsay," a desire which, she notes, distinguishes her from the Lesser Known (185, 175). While there's no way of knowing whether or not the medal really was the Lesser Known's (a hole in history), the point also seems to be that it doesn't matter if it was really his as long as we believe it was his (the imaginative production of history that transforms a hole into a whole). As Foster writes, "The final arbiter of 'the history of History,' *The America Play* . . . suggests, is what its consumers want to see and believe and focus on. Major historical events and minor details are jumbled together in the popular imagination and actions that can be visually represented take precedence over intellectual or economic developments or other large-scale movements that can be less easily or less entertainingly recounted" (31). Authenticity, in this formulation, is not inherent but performative. Thus, *fakin'* functions as a key word for theatrical performance but also for a wide range of performative re-creations— including the production of history. As she continually tries to shut down Brazil's imaginative engagement with material objects, Lucy performs the role of the academic historian. When Brazil unearths "Mr. Washingtons" wooden teeth, he imagines them biting, and Lucy once again urges him to "Keep it tuh scale." Though the stories that Brazil speaks are testimonies and stories he's heard from his own mother, they come out of his mouth in altered form. Lucy's repeated reminders to stay to scale suggest that the past cannot come back to life but can only be imitated or reconstructed via narrative that must adhere to a standard of truthfulness—measured, significantly, by what is already "known" because it has already been told. In contrast to this standard of truthfulness, the play's poetic multivocality is conjured as political promise.

The America Play performs this tension between the truthfulness of testimony and that of history through its use of footnotes, a device that Parks returns to again and again, in different ways, in several of her plays, including not only *The America Play* but also *The Death of the Last Black Man*, *Imperceptible Mutabilities in the Third Kingdom*, and *Venus*. As other critics have noted, Parks's use of footnotes parodies conventions of academic historical documentation (Bullock and Foster), but printed within the program, as they were for the Yale Rep production of *The America Play*, and juxtaposed with a range of other types of text, the footnotes register as a textual-historiographic attempt to organize the testimonial confusion into a coherent narrative with truth value—an attempt, that is, to tie testimony's excess back to some sort of "scale."

Because *Twenty Days* serves as the source of most of *The America Play*'s footnotes (though Parks doesn't cite this source), the appearance of the footnotes within the production program performs a kind of disassemblage of the historical text into a "confusion of tongues." Consider especially *The America Play*'s most heavily footnoted passage, delivered in the Lesser Known's opening monologue (Parks's footnotes follow the passage).

It would be helpful to our story if when the Great Man died in death he were to meet the Lesser Known. It would be helpful to our story if, say, the Lesser Known were summoned to Big Town by the Great Mans wife: "*Emergency* oh, *Emergency*, please put the Great Man in the ground"[1] (they say the great Mans wife was given to hysterics: one young son dead other sickly: even the Great Man couldnt save them: a war on then off and surrendered to: "Play Dixie I always like that song"[2]: the brother against the brother: a new nation all conceived and ready to be hatched: the Great Man takes to guffawing guffawing at thin jokes in bad plays: "You sockdologizing old man-trap!"[3] haw haw haw because he wants so very badly to laugh at something and one moment guffawing and the next moment the Great Man is gunned down. In his rocker. "Useless Useless."[4] And there were bills to pay.) "*Emergency* oh, *Emergency*, please put the Great Man in the ground."

[1]Possibly the words of Mary Todd Lincoln after the death of her husband.

[2]At the end of the Civil War, President Lincoln told his troops to play "Dixie," the song of the South, in tribute to the Confederacy.

[3]A very funny line from the play *Our American Cousin*. As the audience roared with laughter, Booth entered Lincoln's box and shot him dead.

[4]The last words of President Lincoln's assassin, John Wilkes Booth. (160)

In the Lesser Known's version, history is a collection of testimony, misrepresentations, conjecture, hearsay, sympathy, critique, and trivial observations—all sewn together, paratactically, with gaps. As the Lesser Known reperforms the act of collection that structures *Twenty Days'* historical account, it is the gaps and silences that speak most loudly. Joseph Roach has argued that *The America Play* reveals the ways in which those belonging to "a history of events" come to represent those belonging to a history of everyday life, "imposing on them the effigies of which national memory is fabricated and honored while taking from them the stories without which they will tumble unmarked and unmourned into the Great Hole" (314). The Lesser Known is a collector, above all, of stories. As he tries to weave them all together, the resulting narrative comes out disjointed and "holey." The footnotes published in the program appear to smooth over the gaps, but they end up emphasizing them instead. The gaps function like the silences that Roach experiences as an indication of "the losses that must remain unnameable as a condition of their passage to its yet unplumbed depths," and they also work as a moment of performative memorialization (315).

Testimony attests here to its own excess as discursive practice and functions as a refutation of the transparency of "truth." The Lesser Known is a collector, an accumulator of information and bits of hearsay, rather than a historian who orders the collection and smooths over the gaps with narrative. The heavy use of footnotes becomes itself an exaggerated historiographic performance, an increasingly anxious attempt to ground and authenticate the narrative even as the gaps render it incomplete, suspect, holey. As the language and voices of others invade the Lesser Known's account via quotations attributed to Mary Todd Lincoln, Abraham Lincoln, *Our American Cousin*, and John Wilkes Booth, the story reverts to a confusion of tongues.

The anxiety that pervades this passage is, notably, a textual anxiety, identified not with the dialogue of the Lesser Known but rather with the footnotes that seek to control these testimonies from the margins. The text is defensive even as the performance is not. But if the Lesser Known is not anxious, it is because he has no authority to lose—he can speak merely from the sideshow and archaeological site, reciting only the stories that have been handed down to him and that others are willing to accept. Both the use of footnotes and Lucy's insistence on keeping things to scale reflect an obsessive interest in facts that can act as one of the "listening defenses" that prevents bearing witness (Dori Laub qtd in Boler 169). Indeed, the conflict of the second act of *The America Play* is built largely around the struggle between these two notions of "truth." The Yale Rep production's program notes do not merely gloss this idea but take it one step further, reworking "factual" presentation as speech acts and placing the entire play within a context of material and poetic language that contests truth's self-transparency. Meanwhile, the play's use of footnotes call the conventions of historiography and textual authority specifically into question, while at the same time the lack of full dramatic characterization prevents the audience's emotional identification and empathy. Cathexis is stymied. The program notes may offer a way to help "figure out" the play, but what is encountered there is not explanation but engagement.

As a social practice, textual annotation signifies both exclusion and inclusion. While annotation testifies to one's alienation from a text, and in this sense is "always . . . a response to a prior culture from which one believes oneself (and consequently, nearly everyone else) distanced," as Ralph Hanna asserts, it also signifies the text's importance to a critical community "of which the annotator is the designated representative" (178). Annotation therefore always points back to issues of community and institutional power. Within the receptive community created by the Yale Rep production, power oscillates among multiple nodes—the on-stage performance, the audience, and the footnotes. This oscillation is also figured within the play itself. As the "I" of the Foundling Father speaks directly to the audience about himself in the third person as the "Lesser Known," he places himself as both inside and outside "our story" and the narrative community of the theater audience. The paired "I" of the Foundling Father and "he" of the Lesser Known indicate the doubling of subject and object that constitutes the DuBoisian double consciousness, a double consciousness performatively experienced by audience members as they follow the play through its oscillating constructions of narrative subject and object and engage with the play's multivocal language. The Foundling Father's reference to himself as "I" only when talking about costuming suggests an alienated subjectivity, constituted by the act of impersonation. And when the Foundling Father dressed in a yellow beard remarks, "The sun on his fair hair looked like the sun itself," the aural generativity that joins illumination (sun) and reiteration (son) is attributed, via footnote, to "'The Sun,' a composition by the Foundling Father, unpublished" (168). As the only instance in the play, outside the character list, in which the Foundling Father is named for the theater audience, this reference to textual authorship momentarily transforms the Foundling Father into an object of the play text, and of the audience's act of looking/reading, before cycling him back into the play text as an authorizing figure, and therefore a shaper of audience perspective. And it is in this same moment that the performance of the Foundling Father onstage, now wearing the yellow beard, merges with the narrative of a historical past as we "pretend for a moment that our beloved Mr. Lincoln was a blonde. . . . the Great *Blonde Man*" (168).

No moment in the play better demonstrates the page-stage chiasmus than this one. Just as *The America Play*'s stage performance evokes strangeness (a black Lincoln, a blonde beard?) so, too, do its program notes (a footnoted reference to a fictional work written by one of the play's characters?). These defamiliarizing techniques work directly to prevent "insight" that could lead to catharsis and what Boler calls a "voyeuristic sense of closure" (169).

And yet while textual conventions are often aimed at the individual—and their variations, pluralities, and so on are often legible only in the solitary act of reading—theatrical performance is a public form. So what does it mean to combine these two elements? Parks has stated that her play is about the act of writing (Savran 161), but, as these examples demonstrate, she means specifically the writing of history. If history is public, but reading is private, what is the relation between the public and private here? On the page, footnotes are an invitation to digression and detour, but they are not a command, and readers approach footnotes idiosyncratically. Footnotes may be read individually where they are inserted, they may be read as a group once the reader reaches the bottom of the page, they may be briefly skimmed, or they may be ignored altogether. In the theater, footnotes embedded in the program notes are unlikely to be read during the performance. Instead, they may be read briefly before the performance along with the other notes, but they are most likely to be considered after the performance, when an audience member looks back at the theater program as a way of processing what he or she has experienced. But of course this, too, is a conditioned response to theater, a product of the historical development of the divided theater space in which the hushed audience watches attentively and passively from darkened seats, waiting for emotional release and escape.

Postdramatic Poets' Theater at the Disciplinary Threshold

The program notes for *The America Play* go far beyond the listing of credits, biographies, and explanatory comments. Recycling poems, images, historical documents, and elements of the play text itself, the program is a model enactment of historical deconstruction, poetic generativity, and creative engagement—an enactment that responds to, collaborates with, and extends Parks's own dramaturgical strategies. If, as Boler asserts, "emotions are a site of social control" (xvii), then these various framing devices can serve as a challenge to the model of empathetic identification and a critique from within the institutional structures of arts and humanities education. They draw our attention to acts of framing that influence our beliefs, values, and priorities. And they turn our actions to art as a form of knowledge production and moral/ethical evaluation in the service of cultural norms, not as a way to tear art down but a way to consider what art does, as well as what it can do. "[E]motions"—including trust in the authority and knowability of the historical record—"shape the selectivity of our cognitive and ethical attention and vision," Boler asserts (xviii). But how?

In *The America Play*, Brazil and Lucy act as paid mourners, a profession marked by the publication and consumption of private expression. Lucy and Brazil get paid to perform what we normally think of as the expression of deeply personal feelings. Their job descriptions reveal the cultural tracking of emotions into acceptable contexts. Crying and other expressions of emotion, including "wild" or briefly uncontrolled emotions, are acceptable and even desirable within the context of a funeral. Releasing and relieving these emotions allow us to go on with our lives rationally. Limiting these emotions to specific contexts prevents them from infecting our everyday lives. The Lesser Known's reenactments of Lincoln's assassination similarly drain that event of emotional trauma. His paying customers (consumers, again) are interested in the "factuality" of historical details or in the reenactment's entertainment value, not in the emotional horror of the traumatic event in its original context.

Such careful selection of which emotions to express, notice, and attend to, in which contexts, and for which purposes is what Boler describes as "inscribed habits of inattention" (16). Such inattention, she ventures, is socially determined via processes of "becoming civilized" and "obtaining language" (17)—both of which processes, I want to stress, involve habits of reading. Indeed, an important though all too brief component of Boler's theorization of testimonial reading addresses the shift from testimony as a face-to-face relation to understanding testimonial *reading* as a relation between the reader and the text. *The America Play* layers the conventions of reading and theater in order to demonstrate the shortcomings of both.

As we become critically aware of the codes, we are also able to engage actively with them ourselves in sustained acts of excavation and performative reproduction.

Lincoln's place in history is secured in part by his assassination. Like Lucy and Brazil's paid mourning, our nationalist mourning of Lincoln controls the emotional impact of a traumatic event by channeling emotional expression into a specific, contained context that gives meaning to the emotion. It is not, notably, the confusion of emotions of witness testimony or the jumble of images, artifacts, and emotions that constitutes the collector's cache or Brazil's out-of-scale attachments but the considered, ordered, and proper emotional expression sanctioned by cultural norms, textual conventions, and history.

History has made "sense" out of Lincoln's assassination in part by making a hero out of Lincoln and a villain out of Booth, but the actual historical events involve many more than two actors—they also involve, in some sense, the complicity of a vast majority of the nation. And this history didn't end (in more subtle ways, it has not ended) with the defeat of the Confederacy and the end of legal slavery. Testimony avoids the passive empathy produced by the excision of emotional expression and obsessive attention to facts through a historicization of events and the emotions they produce. The poetic, multivocal program-performance collaborations of the Yale Rep's production of *The America Play* both point the way toward the history of Lincoln's assassination—while at the same time pointing out that this history is itself merely one representation of truth—and historicize our contemporary emotional response to the assassination by cycling our attention back to the acts of framing that cultivate cultural norms of expression. And in doing so, this inheritor of poets' theater just may arouse the dramaturg in each of us.

Epilogue

Poets' Theater in the Twenty-First Century

The purpose of this book has been to examine the emergence and development of poets' theater within the larger history of twentieth- and early-twenty-first-century American theater and culture. But this isn't only a work of theater history, and there is a wide range of poets' theater currently on offer across the United States. I therefore end with a very brief look around from the present moment—a look that can only capture a glimpse of the variety of poets' theater that continues to stretch across the country and the range of styles, influences, interests, goals, and approaches that this work encompasses.

In recent years, poets' theater's particular co-performative combinations of text and body have gained new interest alongside a larger explosion in spoken word and poetry performance that includes the rise of poetry slams, the spread of hip-hop theater, and a range of intermedia performances. There have also been a number of revivals of historical poets' theater, including a production of Frank O'Hara's *Try! Try!* by the Howl! Arts Project in New York in 2009 and a reading of the play, featuring Judith Malina, at the City University of New York Graduate Center in 2013, a performance of Amiri Baraka's *Home on the Range* at the Festival of Poets Theater in Chicago in 2015, and a staged reading of Mary Manning Howe's *Passages from Finnegans Wake* by the Here Comes Everybody Players in Boston in 2016. Meanwhile, artists such as Carla Harryman (as I discuss in chapter 5) continue to expand the boundaries of poets' theater today. In fact, in the twenty-first century poets' theater has proliferated not only in play anthologies but on stages across the United States, with new groups continuing to emerge, poets' theater festivals now taking place annually in both San Francisco and Chicago, and individual playwrights producing a range of poets' theater nationwide.

Rodrigo Toscano's Collapsible Poetics Theater

One of the most celebrated poets' theater practitioners in recent years is the poet and activist Rodrigo Toscano, who founded the Collapsible Poetics Theater and is a descendant of West Coast poets' theater. Toscano's work utilizes the global cultural discourses of media, technology, and finance to explore the constant negotiations between codes and bodies. The voices that speak in Toscano's theater do not function as naturalized expressers of character but are, rather, "dispersed among systems that produce information, validate consensus, and secure identity" (Davidson "Introduction" 608). Collapsible Poetics Theater might be thought of as a portable theater of assemblage. That is, the performances are assembled by volunteers—whether poets, experienced actors, or amateurs—within twenty-four to seventy-two hours, and they take place wherever space can be found, in traditional theater and galleries or in makeshift spaces or in the street. Scripts can serve as blueprints for the assemblage, sometimes complete with diagrams. Many are Steinian in their lack of attention to staging requirements. The types of plays Toscano writes range from dramatic dialogues and poetic plays to polyvocal works for multiple readers, radio plays for voices, and "body movement poems."

Toscano is an activist who has worked at the Labor Institute in Manhattan, and his poets' theater, informed by Bay Area Language writing, focuses on the relationship between bodies, language, capitalism, and consumer culture, as well as on art itself. "Balm to Bilk," for example, begins as light wordplay between two speakers

> balm?
>   balm . . . *and* buggin.
> buggin already, uh?
>   buggin.
> And 'buggin's'
> 'balm' too?
>   barely blurted,
>   but true.
> razzle!
>   (Toscano "Balm" 27)

before developing into a discussion of the relationship between poetry and aesthetics. "[P]oetry for the movement? this shit?," asks the second speaker. ". . . where are the imbedded social demands / in this stuff?" (31). But as multivocal, poetic language passes back and forth between the speakers, the play demonstrates with subtle humor the power of language structures to produce identities and subject positions. In the radio poetic play "Eco-Strato-Static," one voice instructs a second on how to enlist the help of one's fellow citizens in trying to move a big blue ball over a wall of flames. Put on a "happy-pappy face," advises the first, and pretend to be selling "an innovative product" (Toscano "Eco-Strato-Static" 60). Sure enough, this works, but the crowd soon loses interest and the voice must find new ways to bring it back, first with dancing, then with promises of a prize, and with random acts of interest until finally the crowd forms into groups and subgroups of support. From one of these groups emerges a spokesperson who asks the voice if it has "some sort of license, or degree, or some kind of certificate, for this kind of work" (69). The tone is light, but the implications are cutting: organized into an impersonal system of global capitalism, people lose their personal connections, as well as their generosity.

Treating theater as a politically charged arena for testing social relations, Toscano's plays juxtapose dialects, social codes, and institutional discourses into polyvocal performances that Michael Davidson has described as "cosmopoetics" ("Introduction" 608). While the merging of poetry, dance, and theater into short absurdist scenes and bodily movements is often humorous, Toscano's blend of Brecht and Artaud is also politically charged, aimed, as Alec Schumacher writes, at "showing how dominant modalities of thought are the result of linguistic constructions and how these modes can be unraveled by their inherent contradictions" (221). Toscano's poets' theater explores the ways in which both global cultural discourses and conventions of language produce and organize social relations and identities.

Kevin Killian and the San Francisco Poets Theater Festival

Both Toscano's and Harryman's work have been among the dozens of plays and performance pieces featured at San Francisco's annual Poets Theater Festival, founded in 2001 by writer Kevin Killian and Small Press Traffic. The Bay Area's history of performance poetry, and its identity as a home

to both Beat writers and Language poets, has lent the festival both reputation and ample talent, but it is largely the labor and creativity of emerging poets interested in exploring new forms that has kept it active. Killian
identifies the festival with what he calls the "second wave of poets' theater"
in the Bay Area—following the San Francisco Poets Theater of the 1980s,
which itself was preceded by the performance poetics of Beat and other
Bay Area writers in the 1950s and 1960s. Stepping into what he saw as a
"vacuum" left behind by the dissolution of the first San Francisco Poets
Theater, Killian worked to revitalize but also reenvision the energy of the
original group. The festival quickly became a venue where poets could try
out other media, test new works, and experiment conceptually in a supportive and playful atmosphere.

Killian's own work is often associated with New Narrative writing,
which is both a response to and a development from Language writing. Employing poetic strategies in prose narrative, it is self-consciously
metatextual, aware of its own constructedness and motivations, "body-
positive," personal, sexual, and gossipy. New Narrative writing, like works
of poets' theater, creates a dialogue with audience members in an attempt
to enlist them in the process of meaning production, and Killian has written more than forty works of poets' theater.

In addition to being a playwright, Killian serves as organizer, actor,
and emcee at the San Francisco Poets Theater. (He is also coeditor of the
impressive *Kenning Anthology of Poets Theater, 1945–1985*.) Like the Poets' Theatre in Cambridge in the 1950s, the San Francisco Poets Theater
Festival encourages the development of new works. In addition, it sometimes stages "historical" pieces, as well as "neobenshi" performances—
films projected onto a screen with live actors performing new or revised
dialogue in front of it. Productions are staffed by a collaborative group of
poet-playwrights who also serve as designers, directors, and performers.
The tone is intentionally amateurish, with minimal props and scenic design and actors holding their scripts in their hands during performance.

The Chicago Festival of Poets Theater

A second poets' theater festival is held annually in Chicago—the Festival
of Poets Theater, founded in 2015 by Patrick Durgin of Kenning Editions
and Devin King of Green Integer Press. Featuring work influenced by
performance art, conceptual art, intermedia, and the historical avant-

garde, the Chicago festival, like its counterpart in San Francisco, is both ambitious and capacious in its offerings. The second year of the festival, for example, featured work by Killian, readings and talks, a screening of a film version of the Living Theatre's 1964 production of *The Brig*, and a staging of Harryman's poet's opera *Gardener of Stars*, which employed singing, piano, electronic music, concertina, and saxophone alongside spoken performance.

Although there are overlaps across the San Francisco and Chicago festivals in terms of featured plays and playwrights, the Chicago Festival of Poets Theater is especially dedicated to exploring the margins of theatrical practice across a range of artistic media. The multiday festival, held each December, frequently incorporates "new media" performance, installation, music, dance, sculpture, and other art forms alongside poets' theater—not because theater has been exhausted, as its organizers explain, but rather to reevaluate the presumed "unassimilability" into theater of writers and artists producing poets' theater and poetic scripts from the borders of the art world (see https://festivalofpoetstheater.com/).

Boston's Sleeping Weazel and Adara Meyers

Boston-based Sleeping Weazel, led by artistic director Charlotte Mee-han and managing director Adara Meyers, is known for its curation of shows that bring together avant-garde theater and history, the visual arts, dance, and activism, and poets' theater can often be found among its offerings and approaches. A special production in celebration of Black History Month 2014, for example, joined a talk by Debra Britt, founder of the National Black Doll Museum; Obie-winning playwright Ed Bullins's *The Man Who Dug Fish*, about a black man's comedic revenge against the white economic institutions that discriminate against him; and the world premiere of *The Purple Flower*, a poetic play by Harlem Renaissance writer Marita Bonner, in a shadow puppet production. Bonner's play, anthologized in Bay-Cheng and Cole's *Poets at Play*, is an exemplary modernist poetic allegory that mixes poetry and prose and incorporates elements of both expressionism and surrealism to imaginatively engage the conflict between black and white America. While the play itself is often characterized as a "closet drama" because of the difficulty in staging it, the Sleeping Weazel production as a whole combined poetry, reclaimed history, social critique, and an examination of the political power of social discourse.

Sleeping Weazel has also produced multiple plays by founding member Adara Meyers, whose work descends from Beckett and Brecht, as well as from Artaud, employing poetic leaps of logic, conceptual theater, and stylized movement. In her play *Birds*, for example, Meyers combines absurdism with a critique of both academic and political discourse and broad physical humor. The play revolves around Toby, an activist, citizen-scientist, and romantic concerned about the fate of pigeons and the environment. When he enrolls at the American Institute of Stress, he is faced with students and a faculty demagogue who are less concerned with truth than with reputation and competition. As this summary should make clear, Meyers does not eschew narrative; rather, she combines it with poetic strategies in order to explore the ways in which narrative can be both unifying and limiting. As with other poets' theater, what's important here is not the subtlety or even the humanity of characterization but rather the ways in which language, discourse, and ideology fracture and polarize our world. Meyers considers "text in itself to be a kind of performance," and she suggests that a playwright can be a kind of performer via text (Meyers 319). In composing work that incorporates poetic language, movement, and music through a joining that brings text and body together without privileging either, she finds parallels between the poet-playwright and the movement-based artist in the sense that each relies on "bodily, visceral impulses" (ibid.).

Conclusion

While poets' theater may have long been absent from the critical record, it is clearly very much alive in theaters and festivals across the United States. Some of its strategies have been absorbed into so-called antitextual theater and, later, into postdramatic theater, even as a new generation of groups, festivals, and practitioners have claimed the mantle of "poets' theater" for their own purposes. This twenty-first-century poets' theater is actively responding to a new historical moment, engaging in different (and sometimes not so different) cultural critiques, and employing the techniques and strategies of an ever-evolving theater. This book is just one pathway through a vast array of people and practices that have shaped twentieth- and twenty-first-century American theater in subtle and not so subtle ways, and I look forward to other mappings of poets' theater joining this one. The story of poets' theater does not end here.

Notes

Introduction

1. In addition to the Tony, *The Cocktail Party* earned a New York Drama Critics Circle award for Best Foreign Play in 1949–50. *The Lady's Not for Burning* won a New York Drama Critics Circle award for Best Foreign Play in 1950–51, and Fry's *Venus Observed* won the same award in 1951–52.

2. Later, in the 1980s Victor Turner and Richard Schechner further developed the notion of performance as enactment via their work on social drama and ritual, which bridged the fields of theater and anthropology.

3. While poets' theater was not simply a US phenomenon, the proliferation of US poets' theaters at midcentury arose in part as a result of the particular interart collaborations fostered by artists' collectives and communities such as Black Mountain and the New York School. English playwrights were also busy casting off the mustiness of Victorian verse drama and the elitism of intellectual theater by such figures as Eliot and Fry, but the development of verse drama in postwar England was also shaped by the centralization and institutionalization of a national theater in that country. For a discussion of the development of verse drama within the particular social and aesthetic conditions of twentieth-century England, see Morra.

4. Punctuation of the term *poets' theater* varies. Here Killian and Brazil use the unpunctuated *poets theater*, which is common among West Coast practitioners.

5. *Three Travellers* was performed by the New York Poets Theatre in 1964 on a bill with Frank O'Hara's *Love's Labor, An Eclogue* and Diane Di Prima's *Murder Cake.*

6. See, for example, John Tytell's account of a reading by Frank O'Hara and Gregory Corso hosted by the Living Theatre, where the atmosphere of drinking and jeering displayed "a kind of raw, disreputable energy," an energy that Tytell observes became a hallmark of the Living Theatre (153).

7. See Daniel Kane's *All Poets Welcome* for an examination of the Lower East Side poetic community in the 1960s.

8. As W. B. Worthen remarks, "Olson's attention to the objective nature of the drama [through discussions of Pound's translation of *The Trojan Women* and T. S. Eliot's plays] amplifies and specifies the work of projective poetry as a theory of writing and performance" (*Print* 118). Notably, Olson's yoking of poetry and performance enters into

practice most seamlessly not in the theater but in the contemporary poetry reading, and Worthen limits his own chapter-long study of the relationship of theater to poetry to this "principal form of performed poetry," sidestepping the matter of poets' theater (101).

9. Bay-Cheng and Cole accept Worthen's distinctions, but they retain the term *poetic drama* for what Worthen distinguished as "poetic theater." I use the term *poetic theater* here to signal its proximity to postwar poets' theater.

Chapter One

1. For a discussion of Stein's influence on the twentieth-century American avant-garde, see Bay-Cheng, especially chapter 6.

2. See, for example, Dubnick and Steiner.

3. *The Making of Americans* was begun in 1903 (as dated by Leon Katz based on examinations of Stein's unpublished notebooks) but not published until 1925.

4. For detailed discussions of the structure of *The Making of Americans*, see Meyer, especially xviii–xxxii, and Malcolm "Someone" and *Two Lives*.

5. Although Marjorie Perloff would probably disagree with my reading of "Chicken" (see her review of Steiner) because, as she argues of Stein's portraits "Matisse" and "Chair," "the title serves less as referent than as a signal that begins a particular train of thought: the portrait intentionally becomes an anti-portrait" (348), Stein's use of titles is precisely what distinguishes her portraiture from other, similarly movement-oriented writing such as *Four Saints in Three Acts*. Furthermore, the fact that Stein went to the trouble of selecting titles suggestive of both figural and still-life portraiture suggests that she wanted to create some connection, however idiosyncratic, between her portrait and the object indexed by the title.

6. I retain throughout this chapter Stein's original spelling of Therese. All page references are to *Four Saints in Three Acts* as published in *Gertrude Stein, Writings 1903–1932*.

7. For a detailed comparison of Stein's verbal portrait of Thomson and Thomson's musical portrait of Stein, see Walden, chapter 1.

8. Bérard's portrait of Stein had also been previously used as the frontispiece for selections from Stein's *The Making of Americans* that had been translated into French by Hugnet and Thomson, further strengthening the affinities between the novel, portraiture, and *Four Saints*.

9. There are two versions of the original *Dix Portraits*. The "artists' book" refers to the first hundred copies, which included Stein's verbal portraits, as well as the visual portraits of their subjects. An additional four hundred copies of the book were published with Stein's verbal portraits alone. For more on *Dix Portraits*, see Latimer.

10. For a more detailed examination of these portraits, as well as of other aspects of the souvenir program that go beyond my discussion here, including the photos of the artistic contributors and cast members, in relation to racial dynamics and narratives of modernist cultural production, see Latimer.

11. For online audio of the original May 25, 1947, radio broadcast on which the Thomson recording was based, see http://www.kpfahistory.info/music/4_saints.html

12. For the story of this relationship, see Barbara Will's *Unlikely Collaborations* and Janet Malcolm's *Two Lives*. See also Alan Riding's *And the Show Went On*.

Chapter Two

1. Audio recordings of this premiere production are available on Harvard University's Woodberry Poetry Room website, https://library.harvard.edu/poetry/listeningbooth/poets/ohara.html

2. All references to *Everyman* are taken from an audio recording of the 1951 premiere performance, available on Harvard University's Woodberry Poetry Room website, https://library.harvard.edu/poetry/listeningbooth/poets/ohara.html

3. Textual citations of *The Apparition* refer to the published version of the play in Eberhart's *Collected Verse Plays*. My discussion of the performance (which differs somewhat, as indicated, from the published version) refers to an audio recording of the 1951 premiere available on Harvard University's Woodberry Poetry Room website, https://library.harvard.edu/poetry/listeningbooth/poets/ohara.html

4. *Try! Try!* might also be considered the first play produced by the San Francisco Poets Theater, when Steve Benson, Carla Harryman, Nick Robinson, and Eileen Corder staged it at the Grand Piano coffee shop on Haight Street in 1979 (Cole et al. 277).

5. A substantially different version of *Try! Try!*, which dispenses with the Noh frame, was presented by the Artists' Theatre in February 1953, directed by Herbert Machiz. "In the earlier version, the characters' two-dimensionality enables them to function simultaneously as soap opera characters and as characters in a contemporary poetic play," Philip Auslander notes, but "in the later version, they are simply stereotypes" (60). Both versions are published in O'Hara's *Amorous Nightmares of Delay: Selected Plays*. My quotations are taken from an audio recording of the 1951 premiere performance, which is slightly different from the published script, available on Harvard University's Woodberry Poetry Room website, https://library.harvard.edu/poetry/listeningbooth/poets/ohara.html

6. Wilder's outburst, recounted by Nora Sayre and others, has entered the realm of lore, but a recording of the event was discovered in 2014 on an uncatalogued sound reel. For a measured discussion of Wilder's response as well as a link to the recording, see Roffman.

7. All citations of Lyon Phelps's *Three Words in No Time* are taken from the unpublished play manuscript, folder 527, Poets' Theatre Collection. An audio recording of the 1951 premiere performance is available on Harvard University's Woodberry Poetry Room website, https://library.harvard.edu/poetry/listeningbooth/poets/ohara.html

8. In an earlier draft, Lang's protagonist was named Max rather than Jack. This name change further invites comparisons with O'Hara's play.

9. Accounts notes in the Poets' Theatre archive indicate that the production closed with a loss of 472 dollars. But the bills continued to come in, and Lurie's memoir places the figure much higher, recalling that the show "contracted a debt of fifteen hundred dollars which nearly wrecked the organization" (14).

10. An unsigned letter from the Poets' Theatre to MacLeish dated June 8, 1953 (folder 519, Poets' Theatre Collection), states that the group came out of the previous season "comfortably in the black. Our community support has never been stronger, thanks to last year's productions of *Fire Exit*, and, primarily, *Agamemnon*, to say nothing of the Dylan Thomas reading of *Under Milk Wood*, which seems to have left everyone feeling very benign in regard to us." The letter goes on to note that the group was now seeking

to hire a full-time stage manager and was in a position to pay directors an honorarium, which would help it attract more professionals.

11. Howe's script was later adapted into a feature-length film of the same title by Mary Ellen Bute, which was named Best Debut of the Year at the Cannes Film Festival in 1965.

12. In his account of the Boston poetry scene from 1955 to 1960, Peter Davison writes that the Poets' Theatre awarded its first Rockefeller grants to "two of its earliest and dearest cronies: V. R. Lang, who went on a honeymoon for the autumn, and Frank O'Hara, who sat around Harvard Square saloons from January to June chatting emphatically about movies" (29). Lurie indicates, however, that the fellowship began only after Lang returned from her honeymoon (66).

13. The following year the grant was again mired in controversy, this time over the similarities between grant recipient W. S. Merwin's play *Favour Island* and the novel *Boone Island*, published by Kenneth Roberts in 1956. After research and consultation with legal counsel, the board eventually accepted the script as original, and the play was produced in 1957.

14. A revival of the Poets' Theatre took place in 1986 and continued until 2004. It was revived once again in 2014, premiering with a commemorative and star-studded reading of Dylan Thomas's *Under Milk Wood*. According to its mission statement, this newest incarnation of the Poets' Theatre "aspires to elevate the poetic possibilities of the theatre" and strives to "illuminate the vast and beautiful diversity of the human experience" (the mission statement is available at https://www.poetstheatre.org/our-mission), —goals that perhaps align it more easily with poetic verse drama than with postwar poets' theater.

Chapter Three

1. See, for example, Bigsby 63–65, Martin, and Sell.

2. In her diary, Malina noted that while she had originally enrolled in the Dramatic Workshop to study acting, watching Piscator's work convinced her that she wanted to direct. But Piscator initially rejected her interest because he felt that, as a woman, she would soon get married and leave theater behind. He eventually relented, but when Malina completed her studies, she was sent an acting rather than a directing diploma and had to have it exchanged. See her entry for June 17, 1947 (*Diaries* 3).

3. Although Beck and Malina had planned to launch their theater much earlier, in 1948, with a production of Noh plays translated by Ezra Pound in a basement space on Wooster Street, that plan was ultimately abandoned due to difficulties with preparing the space and finding performers (see Tytell 47).

4. The original interview is in Rosten, 41.

5. For a detailed description of the production, as well as a discussion of its political strategies, see Durham 74–84.

6. Picasso usually wrote in Spanish, but this play was written in French. This quotation is taken from the English-language published version of the play, entitled *Desire Caught by the Tail*, translated by Sir Roland Penrose. The Living Theatre production used a different translation, by Herma Briffault, entitled *Desire Trapped by the Tail*. That translation is unpublished.

7. In his essay on Artaud, David Graver notes that it has been shown that spectators' heartbeats and breathing patterns adjust in order to be in harmony with stage rhythms (54).

8. Graver, for example, places Artaud in the context of other twentieth-century theater theorists and practitioners, such as the German expressionist Oskar Kokoschka, the Russian artist and theorist Wassily Kandinsky, the Russian director and producer Vsevolod Meyerhold, and the English director Edward Gordon Craig, who revolted against the subjugation of performance to dramatic literature by emphasizing the primacy of theatrical performance over the text.

9. For Malina's account of the arrest and detention, see her diary entry for August 1957 (*Diaries* 441–62). See also Tytell 133–37 and Martin 59–60.

10. According to Sell, the audience at *The Connection*, at least before word started filtering out, was largely working-class blacks and middle-class white and black jazz fans (75).

11. Some of the actors were also real heroin junkies, who admitted to actually shooting up in front of the audience.

12. To call something "deconstructive" implies, as Sell suggests, that its purpose is to "trouble" distinctions. Poets' theater is less interested in troubling distinctions— although this is certainly part of what it does—than in promoting a performative epistemology.

13. On its European tour, *Many Loves* was awarded the Grand Prix de Nations, as well as the Paris Theatre Critics Circle Award.

14. Beck's remarks resemble John Cage's claims that "due to Norman O. Brown's remark that syntax is the arrangement of the army, and Thoreau's that when he heard a sentence he heard feet marching, I became devoted to nonsyntactical 'demilitarized' language" ("Writing" 133).

Chapter Four

1. Werner Sollors explains that Baraka's "Black Communications Projects" were "all-Black affairs, attempts to reach Black audiences in order to make them more Black-conscious. These activities, although cultural in origin and scope, moved Baraka into more visibly political arenas, from Black Power conferences to Pan-African conferences" (179).

2. To put this figure into perspective, in 1949 off-Broadway theater houses were limited by the Actors' Equity Association to no more than three hundred seats, while Broadway theaters might have as many as a thousand or fifteen hundred (Aronson 107–9). Spirit House had only thirty to forty seats (Baraka "Amiri Baraka" 20).

3. The play shared a bill with theater pieces by Ed Bullins and Robert Macbeth, among others, and with speeches by H. Rap Brown, Marlon Brando, Mrs. Eldridge Cleaver, and Bobby Seals, as well as by Amiri Baraka (then known as LeRoi Jones) himself. The event was recorded by the National Broadcasting Company (NBC), the British Broadcasting Corporation (BBC), and the National Educational Television Network (NET). There is some discrepancy in the critical record over how much of *Home on the Range* was actually performed at the benefit. The title *Home on the Range* appears in the

list of performances, and several critics reading the historical record have therefore assumed the full scripted play was performed. But reviews of the night's performance (see Sullivan and Velde) refer only to a music and vocal performance. Those descriptions resemble the prologue that was used in the 1970 PASLA Players production of *Home on the Range*. It is therefore possible that the Black Panther benefit included only the prologue rather than the fully scripted play. I discuss this discrepancy in more detail below.

4. There are no productions of *Home on the Range* on record after 1970 until it was produced on December 4, 2015, at the Festival of Poets Theater in Chicago, directed by Avery R. Young. The play was reprinted for the first time in 1999 in Annemarie Bean's *A Sourcebook of African-American Performance*.

5. Baraka dropped "Imamu," as a "bourgeois" affectation, after his conversion to Third-World Marxism.

6. Although there is a cultural politics inherent in Umbra's emphasis on African American traditions, James Edward Smethurst notes that the first issue of Umbra's eponymous journal championed aesthetics over politics. Nevertheless, he argues that "radical politics . . . was central to the lives of many of the members" (148). In fact, the demise of Umbra is generally attributed to "ideological conflict [especially conflict between Marxism and black nationalism] and the relation of ideology to group action" (149).

7. In fact, Newark's transformation from a majority white to majority black city in the 1960s was astonishing. According to a 2002 Rutgers University publication, "In Newark, as a result of post-war suburban migration, the white population plummeted to approximately 158,000 in 1967 from 363,000 in 1950 and 266,000 in 1960. Correspondingly, the black population of Newark rose from 70,000 in 1950 to 125,000 in 1960 and an estimated 220,000 in 1967. By 1967, a majority of Newark residents (55%) were African-American" (Herman 11).

8. It is worth noting that BART/S and Spirit House represent perhaps the most revolutionary wing of the Black Theatre Movement (BTM) but by no means the only ones. Other BTM theaters include Harlem's New Lafayette Theatre, founded in 1967 and led by Robert Macbeth; the Negro Ensemble Company (NEC), founded in 1967; the National Black Theatre (NBT), founded by Barbara Ann Teer in 1968; and Woodie King Jr.'s New Federal Theatre, founded in 1970. The New Lafayette, which survived for six years, had the highest profile of any BTM theater, and it played a role in bringing Ed Bullins to national prominence when it hired him as an artist-in-residence, subsequently producing several of his plays. The NEC was the most adversarial to Black Arts and black nationalism, a position revealed by its location downtown at St. Mark's Playhouse, as well as by its use of the word *Negro* in its title. Tension between the NEC and the Black Arts Movement (BAM) eventually led Barbara Ann Teer to split from the NEC to form the NBT. Like BART/S and Spirit House, the NBT was a school and workshop as well as a performance group. It was also the longest-surviving New York company that had its foundations in the BAM and was a "pioneer of ritual black theater [and] became an integral part of the Harlem Black Arts loft scene that also included the Black Mind, the Last Poets' East Wind, the Studio Museum in Harlem, and, for a time, the New Lafayette Theatre" (Smethurst 104). Although, as Smethurst notes, the fact that the NBT produced no public performances before 1970 (indeed, its heyday was the mid-1970s to the mid-1980s) makes its impact difficult to judge, many Black artists cite it as an important training ground (105). Woodie King Jr.'s New Federal Theatre had a close relationship

with Black Arts but was itself a multiethnic, multiracial arts program that originally grew out of the publicly funded, antipoverty Mobilization for Youth and was more professionally oriented than most BAM institutions.

9. The original typescript for *Home on the Range*, with corrections in Baraka's handwriting, is held at the New York Public Library's Schomburg Center for Research in Black Culture.

10. *Schwarz* also translingually echoes the vocal component of the incantatory prologue described by *Commonweal* reviewer Paul Velde as assuming "a chanting quality: 'black, blackness, blackness, black'" (441).

11. "Lift Every Voice and Sing," popularly known as the Negro national anthem, was written by James Weldon Johnson in 1900 for presentation at a celebration in honor of Abraham Lincoln. It served as the official song of the NAACP from the 1920s through the 1960s.

12. Smethurst defines *cultural nationalism* as "an insider ideological stance (or a grouping of related stances) that casts a specific 'minority' group as a nation with a particular, if often disputed, national culture. Generally speaking, the cultural nationalist stance involves a concept of liberation and self-determination, whether in a separate republic, some sort of federated state, or some smaller community unit (say, Harlem, East Los Angeles, or the Central Ward of Newark). It also often entails some notion of the development or recovery of a true 'national' culture that is linked to an already existing folk or popular culture. In the case of African Americans, cultural nationalism also usually posited that the bedrock of black national culture was an African essence that needed to be rejoined, revitalized, or reconstructed" (17). *Revolutionary nationalism*, on the other hand, is defined by "an open engagement with Marxism (and generally Leninism), particularly with respect to political economy, Leninist notions of imperialism, and often Communist formulations of the 'national question'" (16).

13. Although "Oh Susanna" is usually thought of as a "folk" song, it was actually written by Stephen Foster and popularized on the minstrel circuit. Its original lyrics told the story of two black lovers trying to reunite after they had been separated, probably by slavery, but the song's theme of itinerancy appealed to American pioneers migrating westward, and soon the song "became the national anthem of westward expansion" (Lott 206).

14. Although Coltrane himself said he played "My Favorite Things" for its chord changes, what matters most here is not the reason for the choice but rather what he did with it.

15. The layout of the *Black Theatre* issue of *TDR* was a kind of argument in itself about the politics of theater. The issue was divided into two sections: "Black Revolutionary Theatre" and "Theatre of Black Experience." Larry Neal's "The Black Arts Movement" manifesto led off the issue; Baraka's *Home on the Range* and *The Police* were the final plays in the "Black Revolutionary Theatre" section. Bullins's own play *Clara's Ole Man* was included in "Theatre of Black Experience," although his "Short Statement on Street Theatre" was in "Black Revolutionary Theatre."

16. There is no doubt that Baraka's postapocalyptic black world is still highly patriarchal. Note, for example, that it is the male characters whose language usage matters most at the end of the play.

17. The only other dramatic play by Baraka to be produced at Spirit House was *Great Goodness of Life* in November 1967.

18. Bottoms describes the Chelsea as "always more self-consciously industry-oriented than its Village counterparts" and points out that founder Robert Kalfin actively sought financial backing and paid Equity wages. Noting that the Chelsea was given a fifteen-thousand-dollar NEA grant in 1967 (before it took up residence at the Brooklyn Academy of Music), "three times what [the NEA] gave either [established and influential off-off-Broadway theaters] La Mama or the Open Theatre in the same funding round," he concludes, "Clearly, the available grant money was heading in the direction of those whose aspirations were toward assimilation into the professional theater world" (271), of which the Chelsea was one.

19. That play was *Great Goodness of Life*. *A Black Quartet*, which also included Ben Caldwell's *Prayer Meeting*, Ron Milner's *The Warning—A Theme for Linda*, and Ed Bullins's *The Gentleman Caller*, was first produced at the Chelsea on April 25–26, 1969. As with most Chelsea productions, admission was free. The quartet was subsequently produced at Tambellini's Gate Theater on the Lower East Side, where it had a highly successful run of 111 performances, from July 30 to November 2, 1969.

20. *Home on the Range* was also the first of two one-act plays by Baraka (the second was *A Black Mass*) comprising *Roi*, produced in July 1970 in Los Angeles by the Performing Arts Society of Los Angeles (PASLA) and directed by Jita Hadi. The PASLA Players were nonprofessional actors from the local black community. See Jones for a review of that production.

Chapter Five

1. The website for the *Grand Piano*, the ten-volume "collective autobiography" written by ten Language poets, including Harryman,includes a partial list of Poets Theater plays, as well as links to some program, poster, and production images, http://www.thegrandpiano.org/poetstheater.html See also Silliman *Grand*.

2. Harryman finds in RoseLee Goldberg's *Performance Art*, for example, the implication that once performance has served its function as a testing ground that can release the art object from categorical or conventional constraints, the art object is reinstated and performance is retired.

3. *Third Man* was performed as part of the annual Poets Theatre festival, which is produced by Small Press Traffic each January and/or February.

4. For play texts, see *Hills* 9 (1983). For criticism and commentary on the Poets Theater and related theater, see Kennedy and Tuma, *Mantis* 3 (2002), and *Poetics Journal* 5 (May 1985).

5. Reptile seems to be recognizing here what Erving Goffman has termed "disclosive compensation," the theatrical convention of giving the audience what it needs, and *only* what it needs, in order to construct and maintain the dramatic fiction. See Goffman *Frame* 142.

6. See Vickery chapter 7 for an excellent discussion of, especially, the genderedness of theory in Language writing.

7. While I appreciate Bernstein's notion of "aurality," the collection in which this

quotation appears, *Close Listening*, relies on an overly flexible notion of "performance." When Bernstein describes poetry readings as "anti-performative"—meaning, he notes, "anti-expressivist"—he is pointing to the poet's rhetorical strategy rather than to the event's ontological status. Yet this equation of performativity with expressivity seems to reinforce the notion of performance as presence that Bernstein is attempting to counter with this anthology. Peter Middleton's use of performativity later in the anthology is much more in line with Judith Butler's notion of constitutive acts. Middleton argues that poetry readings perform "the affirmation or transgression of foundational social structures" in their formation of an audience into an intersubjective network (265). Nick Piombino's discussion of "aural ellipsis" seems to use "performance" in the sense of live oral delivery, although it also opens the door for consideration of the object/subject formation that might more strictly be considered "performative." Furthermore, while the anthology overall makes a good case for taking readings seriously in themselves rather than as mere supplements to texts, it tends to perpetuate the opposition of speech and writing. For challenges to that oppositionality, see the essays in Morris's *Sound States*.

8.   Bourdieu argues that "depositories of deferred thoughts . . . can be triggered off at a distance in space and time by the simple effect of re-placing the body in an overall posture which *recalls* the associated thoughts and feelings, in one of the inductive states of the body which, as actors know, give rise to states of mind" (69).

9.   This is because the syntaxes of gesture and speech are different. Speech builds up its meaning out of independently meaningful parts. Gesture, on the other hand, becomes meaningful only in the aggregate. Speech is spread out, and each part can be analyzed separately, but a gesture is "synthetic," compressing its semantic components (actor, action, path) into one symbol: "Thus, when gesture and speech combine, they bring into one meaning system two distinct semiotic architectures. Each modality, because of its unique semiotic properties, can go beyond the meaning possibilities of the other" (McNeill and Duncan 144).

10.   This production of *Memory Play* was directed by Catharine Sullivan, produced by the Renaissance Society, and performed at Experimental Station, Chicago, on March 7, 2008.

11.   Cognitive psychology supports this view. Cognitive psychologists David McNeill and Susan D. Duncan have developed the concept of the "growth point" (GP), originated by McNeill, as an analytical framework for the combination of "imagery and linguistic categorical content" that insists on an understanding of both gesture and speech as "material carriers of thinking" (144, 155). In this view, speech and gesture are not "the packaged communicative outputs of a separate internal production process but rather . . . the joint embodiments of that process itself" (155). Speech-gesture combinations do not simply reflect already formed similarities, then, but contribute to the establishment a correspondence between the two and are therefore productive of thought. Furthermore, McNeill and Duncan argue, GPs "are a way of cognitively existing, of cognitively being, at the moment of speaking. By performing the gesture, the core idea is brought into concrete existence and becomes part of the speaker's own existence at that moment" (156). In this view, gesture is not an expression of being but rather constitutive of being, and in this sense we can consider gesture performative. It is also significant that, although a GP is highly synchronous, "strongly resist[ing] forces trying to divide it" (145), this synchrony "is disrupted . . . if speech and gesture are drained of meaning through

repetition; i.e., such that GPs may be circumvented in their production" (145). See also McNeill.

12. The play has been performed in San Francisco, Chicago, Detroit, Tubingen, and Paris. Each production uses a different version of the script (in some cases bilingual). Some performances have used a full cast (Detroit, Chicago), while others have consisted only of Harryman herself reading the text to live musical accompaniment by John Raskin (San Francisco). All of these versions, however, are derived from the full-length English text entitled *Mirror Play* included in Harryman's collection *Sue in Berlin*, 49–88.

13. Notably, the AIDS quilt grew out of a simple, non-narrative performance as San Francisco marchers carried placards with the names of men lost to AIDS. It was only with the durable AIDS Memorial Quilt that individual micronarratives began to be incorporated in the form of images, quotations, and other forms of characterization.

14. This production was performed at the Susanne Hilberry Gallery in the Detroit suburb of Ferndale on August 14, 2007.

15. In both productions, the jaw harp was played by John Raskin, who also composed all the music. Harryman comments, "Initially, I had conceived of *Mirror Play* as a polyvocal piece for one performer: I liked the idea of one performer working with multiple voices within the conceptual antechamber space. However, that one immediately turned into two as I felt that an instrumental voice needed to be an aspect of the speaking voice. I started working with Jon Raskin, developing the piece for spoken voice (mine) and jaw harps. Now the poly-vocality is being extended to many voices and more instruments" (Hinton n.p.).

16. See Hutcheon 27–36 for a brief discussion of postmodernism's foundations in architecture.

17. Hollier notes that there have been "endless arguments over whether the origin of architecture was the house, the temple, or the tomb, etc. For Bataille it was the prison" (ix).

18. In contrast, Harry J. Elam Jr. argues that social protest theater, such as the Black Nationalist performances discussed in chapter 4, attracts audience members who, by means of their shared values, beliefs, and politics, do in fact constitute a community (See Elam *Taking*.) Certainly the Black Nationalist audiences discussed in chapter 4 were encouraged to envision themselves in this way.

Chapter Six

1. In fact, AEA contracts make distinct mention of cast lists, programs, and souvenir programs, indicating the particular significance of the theater program's souvenir function.

2. Enrica Jemma Glickman's discussion of Celestina Paladini's successful use of expanded titles to reach a broader cross section of the public offers an even earlier, related example of theater posters' emerging explanatory function. See Glickman 71.

3. "In the popular historical imagination," Verna Foster notes, "the Emancipation of the Slaves is ascribed to Abraham Lincoln and mixed up with the Gettysburg Address and Lincoln's death" (32).

4. In the Yale Rep production, both the Lesser Known and the customer-assassins are played by African American actors, though this is not explicitly indicated in Parks's notes. Such casting is, however, widely assumed. Casting a white actor would, of course, produce a very different dramaturgical effect.

Bibliography

Accounts letter, *Fire Exit*, printed material, Folder 403, Poets' Theatre Collection, Houghton Library, Harvard University.

Ackerman, Alan, and Martin Puchner. *Against Theatre: Creative Destructions on the Modernist Stage*. New York: Palgrave Macmillan, 2007.

Adorno, Theodor W. *Aesthetic Theory*. Minneapolis: University of Minnesota Press, 1997.

Allen, Donald. *The New American Poetry, 1945–1960*. Berkeley: University of California Press, 1960.

Amory, Hugh. Letter to Bradley Phillips, October 15, 1956, Folder 92, V. R. Lang Papers (MS Am 1951), Houghton Library, Harvard University.

Aronson, Arnold. "American Theatre in Context: 1945–Present." *The Cambridge History of American Theatre*. Vol. 3. Ed. Don B. Wilmeth and Christopher Bigsby. Cambridge: Cambridge University Press, 2000. 87–162.

Artaud, Antonin. "An Affective Athleticism." *The Theater and Its Double*. Trans. Mary Caroline Richards. New York: Grove, 1958. 133-141.

Artaud, Antonin. "Metaphysics and the Mise en Scène." *The Theater and Its Double*. Trans. Mary Caroline Richards. New York: Grove, 1958. 33-47.

Artaud, Antonin. "Oriental and Occidental Theater." *The Theater and Its Double*. Trans. Mary Caroline Richards. New York: Grove, 1958. 68-73.

Artaud, Antonin. "The Theater and Culture." *The Theater and Its Double*. Trans. Mary Caroline Richards. New York: Grove, 1958. 7-13.

Ashbery, John. "Everyman." Poets' Theatre Reading with Frank O'Hara, Richard Eberhart, and Lyon Phelps (1951). Audio Recording. Woodberry Poetry Room, Harvard University. https://library.harvard.edu/poetry/listeningbooth/poets/ohara.html

Ashbery, John. *The Heroes*. *The Kenning Anthology of Poets Theater, 1945–1985*. Ed. Kevin Killian and David Brazil. Chicago: Kenning Editions, 2010. 35-51.

Atkinson, Brooks. "Avant-Garde 'Many Loves': Play by William Carlos Williams in Premiere; Judith Malina Is Seen in Four Roles." *New York Times*, January 14, 1959: 28.

Atkinson, Brooks. "'Tonight We Improvise': Avant-Garde Drama by Pirandello Here; Julian Beck Stages Play in Revival." *New York Times*, November 7, 1959: 27.

Auslander, Philip. *The New York School Poets as Playwrights: O'Hara, Ashbery, Koch, Schuyler, and the Visual Arts*. New York: Peter Lang, 1989.

Austin, J. L. *How to Do Things with Words*. 2nd ed. Cambridge, MA: Harvard University Press, 1975 [1962].

Backalenick, Irene. "A Director's Journey." *TheaterWeek*, March 15–21, 1993: 32, 33–35.

Banes, Sally. "Institutionalizing Avant-Garde Performance: A Hidden History of University Patronage in the United States." *Contours of the Theatrical Avant-Garde: Performance and Textuality*. Ed. James M. Harding. Ann Arbor: University of Michigan Press, 2000. 217–38.

Baraka, Amiri. *The Autobiography of LeRoi Jones/Amiri Baraka*. New York: Freundlich, 1984.

Baraka, Amiri. *Black Magic: Poetry, 1961–1967*. Indianapolis: Bobbs-Merrill, 1969.

Baraka, Amiri. *A Black Mass. Four Black Revolutionary Plays: All Praises to the Black Man*. Indianapolis: Bobbs-Merrill, 1969.

Baraka, Amiri. *Blues People: Negro Music in White America*. New York: Morrow, 1963.

Baraka, Amiri. "The Changing Same." *The LeRoi Jones/Amiri Baraka Reader*. Ed. William J. Harris. New York: Thunder Mouth, 1991. 186–209.

Baraka, Amiri. *The Dead Lecturer: Poems*. New York: Grove, 1964.

Baraka, Amiri. *Dutchman and The Slave: Two Plays*. New York: Harper Perennial, 2001.

Baraka, Amiri. *The System of Dante's Hell*. New York: Grove, 1966. 84–97.

Baraka, Amiri. "The Fire Must Be Permitted to Burn Full Up Black Aesthetic." *Raise, Race, Rays, Raze: Essays since 1965*. New York: Random House 1971. 117–23.

Baraka, Amiri. *Home: Social Essays*. New York: Akashic, 2009.

Baraka, Amiri. *Home on the Range. The Drama Review: TDR* 12.4 (Summer 1968): 106–11.

Baraka, Amiri. "Hunting Is Not Those Heads on the Wall." *Home: Social Essays*. New York: Akashic, 2009. 173–78.

Baraka, Amiri. "The Legacy of Malcolm X, and the Coming of the Black Nation." *The LeRoi Jones/Amiri Baraka Reader*. Ed. William J. Harris. New York: Thunder Mouth, 1991. 161–68.

Baraka, Amiri. *The LeRoi Jones/Amiri Baraka Reader*. Ed. William J. Harris. New York: Thunder Mouth, 1991.

Baraka, Amiri. *Madheart. Four Black Revolutionary Plays: All Praises to the Black Man*. Indianapolis: Bobbs-Merrill, 1969.

Baraka, Amiri. "Marvin Pancho Camillo (1937–1988)." *Eulogies*. New York: Marsilio, 1996. 103–7.

Baraka, Amiri. "The Myth of a 'Negro Literature.'" *Home: Social Essays*. New York: Akashic, 2009. 105–15.

Baraka, Amiri. "The Revolutionary Theatre." *Liberator*, July 1965: 4–6.

Baraka, Amiri. *Slave Ship. Crosswinds: An Anthology of Black Dramatists in the Diaspora*. Ed. William B. Branch. Bloomington: Indiana University Press, 1993.

Barish, Jonas. *The Antitheatrical Prejudice*. Berkeley: University of California Press, 1981.

Barthes, Roland. *S/Z: An Essay*. New York: Farrar, Strauss and Giroux, 1975.

Bay-Cheng, Sarah. *Mama Dada: Gertrude Stein's Avant-Garde Theater*. New York: Routledge, 2004.

Bay-Cheng, Sarah, and Barbara Cole, eds. *Poets at Play: An Anthology of Modernist Drama*. Selinsgrove: Susquehanna, PA: University Press, 2010.

Bean, Annemarie. *A Sourcebook of African-American Performance: Plays, People, Movements*. London: Routledge, 1999.

Bean, Heidi R., and Laura Hinton, eds. "Introduction." *Poet's Theater*. Special issue of *Postmodern Culture* 20.1 (September 2009): n.p.

Beck, Julian. "Feelings on the Theatre" (1960). Living Theatre Records, *T-Mss 1988–005, Billy Rose Theatre Division, New York Public Library for the Performing Arts, Box 54, Folder 1.

Beck, Julian. "Mister Beck without Reefer." *The Brig*. By Kenneth H. Brown. New York: Hill and Wang, 1965. v–vi.

Beck, Julian. "Storming the Barricades." *The Brig*. By Kenneth H. Brown. New York: Hill and Wang, 1965. 3–35.

Beck, Julian. "Three Meditations on Strategies." *The Life of the Theatre: The Relation of the Artist to the Struggle of the People*. San Francisco: City Lights, 1972. n.p.

Beck, Julian. Untitled lecture on avant-garde theater (1961). Living Theatre Records, *T-Mss 1988–005, Billy Rose Theatre Division, New York Public Library for the Performing Arts, Box 54, Folder 1.

Beck, Julian. "Why Avant-Garde?" (1959). Living Theatre Records, *T-Mss 1988–005, Billy Rose Theatre Division, New York Public Library for the Performing Arts, Box 18, Folder 11.

Belgrad, Daniel. *The Culture of Spontaneity: Improvisation and the Arts in Postwar America*. Chicago: University of Chicago Press, 1998.

Bendixen, Alfred, and Stephen Burt, eds. *The Cambridge History of American Poetry*. Cambridge: Cambridge University Press, 2014.

Benjamin, Walter. "The Work of Art in the Age of Its Technological Reproducibility (second version)." *The Work of Art in the Age of Its Technological Reproducibility, and Other Writings on Media*. Cambridge, MA: Harvard University Press, 2008. 19–55.

Benson, Steve. "Hooks and Conceit in *La Quotidienne*." *Jimmy & Lucy's House of "K"* 2 (August 1984): 21–24.

Benston, Kimberly W. *Baraka: The Renegade and the Mask*. New Haven, CT: Yale University Press, 1976.

Benston, Kimberly W. *Performing Blackness: Enactments of African-American Modernism*. New York: Routledge, 2000.

Bernheimer, Alan. "The Simulacrum of Narrative." *Poetics Journal* 5 (May 1985): 69–71.

Bernstein, Charles. "Introduction." *Close Listening: Poetry and the Performed Word*. Ed. Charles Bernstein. New York: Oxford University Press, 1998. 3-28.

Bigsby, C. W. E. *A Critical Introduction to Twentieth-Century American Drama*. Vol. 3: *Beyond Broadway*. Cambridge: Cambridge University Press, 1985.

Bigsby, C. W. E. *Modern American Drama, 1945–2000*. Cambridge: Cambridge University Press, 2000.

Biner, Pierre. *The Living Theatre*. New York: Horizons, 1972.

Birringer, Johannes. *Theatre, Theory, Postmodernism*. Bloomington: Indiana University Press, 1991.

Blau, Herbert. *The Audience*. Baltimore: Johns Hopkins University Press, 1990.

Boler, Megan M. *Feeling Power: Emotions and Education*. New York: Routledge, 1999.

Bottoms, Stephen J. *Playing Underground: A Critical History of the 1960s Off-Off-Broadway Movement*. Ann Arbor: University of Michigan Press, 2004.

Bourdieu, Pierre. *The Logic of Practice*. Stanford, CA: Stanford University Press, 1990.

Bowers, Jane Palatani. *"They Watch Me as They Watch This": Gertrude Stein's Metadrama*. Philadelphia: University of Pennsylvania Press, 1991.

Brewster, Ben, and Lea Jacobs. *Theatre to Cinema: Stage Pictorialism and the Early Feature Film*. Oxford: Oxford University Press, 1997.

Brown, John Russell, and Bernard Harris, eds. *American Theatre*. Stratford-upon-Avon Studies, no. 10. London: Edward Arnold, 1967.

Brown, Kenneth H. *The Brig*. New York: Hill and Wang, 1965.

Buechler, Steven M. *Social Movements in Advanced Capitalism*. Oxford: Oxford University Press, 2000.

Bullins, Ed. "The So-Called Western Avant-Garde Drama." *Liberator* 7.12 (December 1967): 16–17.

Bullock, Kurt. "Famous/Last Words: The Disruptive Rhetoric of Historico-Narrative 'Finality' in Suzan-Lori Parks's *The America Play*." *American Drama* 10.2 (2001): 69-87.

Butler, Judith. *Bodies That Matter*. New York: Routledge, 1993.

Butler, Judith. *Precarious Life: The Powers of Mourning and Violence*. London: Verso, 2004.

Cage, John. "Writing for the Second Time through *Finnegans Wake*." *Empty Words: Writings, '73–'78*. Middletown, CT: Wesleyan University Press, 1981. 133–76.

Calloway, Earl. "Theatre Wing." *Daily Defender*, May 2, 1968: 17.

Carlson, Marvin. *Speaking in Tongues: Language at Play in the Theatre*. Ann Arbor: University of Michigan Press, 2006.

Case, Sue-Ellen. "Performing Lesbian in the Space of Technology, Part I." *Theatre Journal* 47:1 (March 1995): 1–18.

Case, Sue-Ellen. "Performing Lesbian in the Space of Technology, Part II." *Theatre Journal* 47.3 (October 1995): 329–43.

Catton, Bruce. "Foreword." *Twenty Days: A Narrative in Text and Pictures of the Assassination of Abraham Lincoln and the Twenty Days and Nights That Followed; the Nation in Mourning, the Long Trip Home to Springfield*. By Dorothy Meserve Kunhardt and Philip B. Kunhardt. New York: Harper and Row, 1965. n.p.

Chansky, Dorothy. *Composing Ourselves: The Little Theatre Movement and the American Audience*. Carbondale: Southern Illinois University Press, 2004.

Chaudhuri, Una. *Staging Place: The Geography of Modern Drama*. Ann Arbor: University of Michigan Press, 1995.

Colbert, Soyica Diggs. *The African American Theatrical Body: Reception, Performance, and the Stage*. Cambridge: Cambridge University Press, 2011.

Cole, Norma, Carla Harryman, Mac McGinnes, Nick Robinson, and Leslie Scalapino. "Remarks on Poets' Theater: Poets and Players." *Mantis* 3 (2002): 276–97.

Conquergood, Dwight. "Performance Studies: Interventions and Radical Research." *TDR* 46.2 (Summer 2002): 145–56.

Crary, Jonathan. *Suspensions of Perception: Attention, Spectacle, and Modern Culture*. Cambridge, MA: MIT Press, 1999.

Crow, Thomas. *Modern Art in the Common Culture*. New Haven, CT: Yale University Press, 1998.

Davidson, Michael. "Framed by the Story." *Poetics Journal* 5 (May 1985): 76–80.

Davidson, Michael. "Introduction: American Poetry, 2000–2009." *Contemporary Literature* 52.4 (Winter 2011): 597–629.

Davis, Tracy. "Theatricality and Civil Society." *Theatricality*. Ed. Tracy Davis and Thomas Postlewait. Cambridge: Cambridge University Press, 2003. 127–55.

Davison, Peter. *The Fading Smile: Poets in Boston, from Robert Frost to Robert Lowell to Sylvia Plath, 1955–1960*. New York: Knopf, 1994.

Day, Jean. "Two Books by Carla Harryman." *Jimmy & Lucy's House of "K"* 6 (May 1986): 118–22.

DeKoven, Marianne. *A Different Language: Gertrude Stein's Experimental Writing*. Madison: University of Wisconsin Press, 1983.

Diamond, Elin. *Unmaking Mimesis: Essays on Feminism and Theater*. London: Routledge, 1997.

Dillon, Steven. *Wolf-Women and Phantom Ladies: Female Desire in 1940s US Culture*. Albany: State University of New York Press, 2015.

Di Prima, Diane. *Recollections of My Life as a Woman*. New York: Viking, 2001.

Drukman, Steven. "Suzan-Lori Parks and Liz Diamond: Doo-a-Diddly-Dit-Dit." *TDR* 39.3 (1995): 56–75.

Dubnick, Randa. *The Structure of Obscurity: Gertrude Stein, Language, and Cubism*. Urbana: University of Illinois Press, 1984.

DuBois, W. E. B. *The Souls of Black Folk*. New York: Penguin, 1996 [1903].

Durham, Leslie Atkins. *Staging Gertrude Stein: Absence, Culture, and the Landscape of American Alternative Theatre*. New York: Palgrave Macmillan, 2005.

Duval, Elaine Isolyn. "Theatre and the Double: Revolutionary Consciousness in Baraka and Artaud." Diss. University of Tennessee, Knoxville, 1988.

Eberhart, Richard. *The Apparition. Collected Verse Plays*. Chapel Hill: University of North Carolina Press, 1950. 43-56.

Eberhart, Richard. *The Apparition*. Audio Recording. Woodberry Poetry Room, Harvard University. https://library.harvard.edu/poetry/listeningbooth/poets/ohara.html

Eberhart, Richard. "Poets' Theatre II." *Center: A Magazine for the Performing Arts* 2.3 (1955): 19–21.

Economou, George. "Some Notes towards Finding a View of the New Oral Poetry." *boundary 2*, 3 (1985): 653–63.

Elam, Harry J., Jr. *Taking It to the Streets: The Social Protest Theater of Luis Valdez and Amiri Baraka*. Ann Arbor: University of Michigan Press, 1997.

Elam, Harry J., Jr. "The TDR Black Theatre Issue: Refiguring the Avant-Garde." *Not the Other Avant-Garde: The Transnational Foundations of Avant-Garde Performance*. Ed. James M. Harding and John Rouse. Ann Arbor: University of Michigan Press, 2006. 41–66.

Elam, Harry J., Jr., and Alice Rayner. "Echoes from the Black (W)hole: An Examination of *The America Play* by Suzan-Lori Parks." *Performing America: Cultural Nationalism in American Theatre*. Ed. Jeffrey D. Mason and J. Ellen Gainor. Ann Arbor: University of Michigan Press, 1999. 178–92.

Elisberg, Daniel. "The Playgoer: At Christ Church Parish House," *Harvard Crimson*, March 1, 1951.

Epstein, Andrew. *Beautiful Enemies: Friendship and Postwar American Poetry*. Oxford: Oxford University Press, 2006.

Epstein, Andrew. "'First Bunny Died': Frank O'Hara with, and after, Bunny Lang." *spoKe* 4 (2017): 227–37.

Eyerman, Ron, and Andrew Jamison. *Social Movements: A Cognitive Approach*. Cambridge: Polity, 1991.

Fazzino, Jimmy. "Amiri Baraka's Revolutionary Theatre: Black Power Politics, Avant-Garde Poetics." *Beat Drama: Playwrights and Performances of the "Howl" Generation*. Ed. Deborah R. Geis. London: Bloomsbury Methuen Drama, 2016. 83–96.

Fazzino, Jimmy. *World Beats: Beat Generation Writing and the World of U.S. Literature*. Hanover, NH: Dartmouth College Press, 2016.

Féral, Josette. "Foreword." *SubStance* 31.2–3 (2002): 3–13.

Fischer-Lichte, Erika. "The Avant-Garde and the Semiotics of the Antitextual Gesture." Trans. James Harding. *Contours of the Theatrical Avant-Garde: Performance and Textuality*. Ed. James M. Harding. Ann Arbor: University of Michigan Press, 2000. 79-95.

Foster, Verna. "Suzan-Lori Parks's Staging of the Lincoln Myth in *The America Play* and *Topdog/Underdog*." *Journal of American Drama and Theatre* 17.3 (2005): 24–35.

Fredman, Stephen. "San Francisco and the Beats." *The Cambridge History of American Poetry*. Ed. Alfred Bendixen and Stephen Burt. Cambridge: Cambridge University Press, 2015. 823–43.

Fried, Michael. "Art and Objecthood." *Art and Objecthood: Essays and Reviews*. Chicago: University of Chicago Press, 1998. 148–72.

Fuchs, Elinor. *The Death of Character: Perspectives on Theater after Modernism*. Bloomington: Indiana University Press, 1996.

Gelber, Jack. *The Connection*. New York: Grove, 1960.

Gillespie, John K. "L'Oeil Ecoute: The Impact of Traditional Japanese Theatre on Postwar Western Performance." *Modern Drama* 35.1 (Spring 1992): 137–48.

Glickman, Enrica Jemma. "Italian Dramatic Companies and the Peruvian Stage in the 1870s." *Latin American Theatre Review* 7.2 (Spring 1974): 69–80.

Goffman, Erving. *Frame Analysis: An Essay on the Organization of Experience*. Cambridge, MA: Harvard University Press, 1974.

Goffman, Erving. *The Presentation of Self in Everyday Life*. New York: Anchor, 1959.

Goldberg, RoseLee. *Performance Art: From Futurism to the Present*. New York: H. N. Abrams, 1988.

Golding, Alan. "The 'Community of Elements' in Wallace Stevens and Louis Zukofsky." *Wallace Stevens: The Poetics of Modernism*. Ed. Albert Gelpi. Cambridge: Cambridge University Press, 1985. 121–40.

Goodman, Paul. "Advance-Guard Writing, 1900–1950." *Kenyon Review* 8.3 (1951): 359–80.

Gottfried, Martin. "America's Most Exciting New Theater?" *New York Times,* February 21, 1971: D3.

Graver, David. "Antonin Artaud and the Authority of Text, Spectacle, and Performance." *Contours of the Theatrical Avant-Garde: Performance and Textuality*. Ed. James M. Harding. Ann Arbor: University of Michigan Press, 2000. 43–57.

Gray, Richard. *A History of American Poetry*. Malden, MA: Wiley Blackwell, 2015.

Greene, Alexis. "Theater Review: *The America Play* and *Freefall*." *Theater Week,* March 21–27, 1994: 33.

Grotowski, Jerzy. *Towards a Poor Theatre*. New York: Simon & Schuster, 1968.

Hanna, Ralph, III. "Annotation as Social Practice." *Annotation and Its Texts*. Ed. Stephen A. Barney. Oxford: Oxford University Press, 1991. 178–84.

Hansen, Miriam. "Early Cinema, Late Cinema: Permutations of the Public Sphere," *Screen* 34.3 (Autumn 1993): 197–210.

Harding, James M., ed. *Contours of the Theatrical Avant-Garde: Performance and Textuality*. Ann Arbor: University of Michigan Press, 2000.

Harding, James M. "Introduction." *Contours of the Theatrical Avant-Garde: Performance and Textuality*. Ed. James M. Harding. Ann Arbor: University of Michigan Press, 2000: 1–11.

Harpham, Geoffrey Galt. "Ethics." *Critical Terms for Literary Study*. Ed. Frank Lentricchia and Thomas McLaughlin. Chicago: University of Chicago Press, 1995. 387–405.

Harries, Martin. "Theater after Film, or Dismediation." *ELH* 83.2 (Summer 2016): 345–61.

Harris, William J. *The Poetry and Poetics of Amiri Baraka: The Jazz Aesthetic*. Columbia: University of Missouri Press, 1985.

Harryman, Carla. "Acker Un-Formed." *Lust for Life: On the Writing of Kathy Acker*. Ed. Amy Scholder, Carla Harryman, and Avital Ronell. London: Verso, 2006. 35–44.

Harryman, Carla. "Animal Instincts." *Animal Instincts: Prose, Plays, Essays*. Berkeley, CA: This, 1989. 33–43.

Harryman, Carla. *Animal Instincts: Prose, Plays, Essays*. Berkeley, CA: This, 1989.

Harryman, Carla. "The Ear of the Poet in the Mouth of the Performer." *How2* 2.1 (Spring 2003). http://www.asu.edu/pipercwcenter/how2journal/archive/online_archive/v2_1_2003/current/index.htm

Harryman, Carla. "La Quotidienne: An Atmospheric Play." *Animal Instincts: Prose, Plays, Essays*. Berkeley, CA: This, 1989. 81–89.

Harryman, Carla. *Memory Play*. Oakland, CA: O Books, 1994.

Harryman, Carla. *Mirror Play*. *Sue in Berlin*. Rouen: Presses universitaires de Rouen et du Havre, 2018. 49–88.

Harryman, Carla. "Property." *Animal Instincts: Prose, Plays, Essays*. Berkeley, CA: This, 1989. 15–26.

Harryman, Carla. "Site Sampling in 'Performing Objects Stationed in the Sub World.'" *Additional Apparitions*. Ed. David Kennedy and Keith Tuma. Sheffield: Cherry on the Top Press, 2002: 157–71.

Harryman, Carla. *There Is Nothing Better Than a Theory*. *Animal Instincts: Prose, Plays, Essays*. Berkeley, CA: This, 1989. 90–105.

Harryman, Carla. "Toy Boats." *Animal Instincts: Prose, Plays, Essays*. Berkeley, CA: This, 1989. 107–10.

Hatch, James. "Interview with Amiri Baraka (March 30, 1984)." *Artist and Influence*. Ed. Leo Hamalian and Judith Wilson. New York: Hatch Billops Collection, 1985. 1–23.

Heble, Ajay. "The Poetics of Jazz: From Symbolic to Semiotic." *Textual Practice* 2.1 (Spring 1988): 51–68.

Herman, Max. "Ethnic Succession and Urban Unrest in Newark and Detroit during the Summer of 1967." Cornwall Center for Metropolitan Studies, Rutgers University, July 2002. http://www.cornwall.rutgers.edu/pdf/Herman-July%202002-Report.pdf

Hinton, Laura. "To Write within Situations of Contradiction: An Introduction to the Cross-Genre Writings of Carla Harryman." *Postmodern Culture* 16.1 (September 2005): n.p.

Hitchcock, H. Wiley, and Charles Fussell. "Virgil Thomson's and Gertrude Stein's 'Four Saints in Three Acts.'" *Four Saints in Three Acts*. By Virgil Thomson and Gertrude Stein. Ed. H. Wiley Hitchcock and Charles Fussell. Middleton, WI: A-R Editions, 2008. xiii–lvi.

Hoffman, Tyler. *American Poetry in Performance: From Walt Whitman to Hip Hop*. Ann Arbor: University of Michigan Press, 2013.

Hollier, Denis. *Against Architecture: The Writings of Georges Bataille*. Cambridge, MA: MIT Press, 1989.

Hopkins, D. J. "Research, Counter-text, Performance: Reconsidering the (Textual) Authority of the Dramaturg." *Theatre Topics* 13.1 (March 2003): 1–17.

[Howe,] Mary Manning. *Passages from Finnegans Wake by James Joyce*. Cambridge, MA: Harvard University Press, 1955.

Howe, Mary Manning, Catharine Huntington, and William Hunt. Letter dated December 8, 1955. Miscellaneous Papers concerning season 1955–56, Folder 557, Poets' Theatre Collection, Houghton Library, Harvard University.

Hudson, Theodore R. "A Conversation between Imamu Amiri Baraka and Theodore R. Hudson." *Conversations with Amiri Baraka*. Ed. Charles Reilly. Jackson: University Press of Mississippi, 1994. 71–76.

Hughes, Elinor. "Poets' Theatre: *A Door Must Be Open or Shut, I Too Have Lived in Arcadia*." *Boston Herald*, October 27, 1954.

Hutcheon, Linda. *A Poetics of Postmodernism: History, Theory, Fiction*. New York: Routledge, 1988.

Huyssen, Andreas. *After the Great Divide: Modernism, Mass Culture, Postmodernism*. Bloomington: Indiana University Press, 1986.

Inglehart, Ronald. *Cultural Shift in Advanced Industrial Society*. Princeton, NJ: Princeton University Press, 1990.

Innes, Christopher. "Text/Pre-Text/Pretext: The Language of Avant-Garde Experiment." *Contours of the Theatrical Avant-Garde: Performance and Textuality*. Ed. James M. Harding. Ann Arbor: University of Michigan Press, 2000. 58–78.

Jackson, Richard. "The Operas of Gertrude Stein and Virgil Thomson." MA thesis, Tulane University, 1962.

Jackson, Shannon. *Professing Performance: Theatre in the Academy from Philology to Performativity*. Cambridge: Cambridge University Press, 2004.

Jacobs, Alan. "Introduction." *The Age of Anxiety*. By W. H. Auden. Princeton, NJ: Princeton University Press, 2011. xi–xlix.

Jameson, Frederic. *The Political Unconscious: Narrative as a Socially Symbolic Act*. Ithaca, NY: Cornell University Press, 1981.

Jannarone, Kimberly. *Artaud and His Doubles*. Ann Arbor: University of Michigan Press, 2010.

Janssen, Marian. *Not at All What One Is Used To: The Life and Times of Isabella Gardner*. Columbia: University of Missouri Press, 2010.

Jiggetts, Shelby. "Interview with Suzan-Lori Parks." *Callaloo* 19.2 (1996): 309–17.

Jones, Charles E. "*Roi*." *Soul Illustrated*, July 1970: 17–18.

Kane, Daniel. *All Poets Welcome: The Lower East Side Poetry Scene in the 1960s*. Berkeley: University of California Press, 2003.

Kennedy, David, and Keith Tuma, ed. *Additional Apparitions: Poetry, Performance, and Site-Specificity*. Sheffield: The Cherry on the Top Press, 2002.

Killian, Kevin, and David Brazil, eds. *The Kenning Anthology of Poets Theater, 1945–1985*. Chicago: Kenning Editions, 2010.

Kirby, Michael. "On Acting and Not-Acting." *The Art of Performance: A Critical Anthol-*

ogy. Ed. Gregory Battcock and Robert Nickas. New York: Dutton, 1984. Originally published in *The Drama Review: TDR* 16.1 (March 1972): 3–15.

Kostelanetz, Richard. *Old Poetries and the New*. Ann Arbor: University of Michigan Press, 1981.

Krasner, David. *A Companion to Twentieth-Century American Drama*. Malden, MA: Wiley-Blackwell, 2008.

Kunhardt, Dorothy Meserve, and Philip B. Kunhardt Jr. *Twenty Days: A Narrative in Text and Pictures of the Assassination of Abraham Lincoln and the Twenty Days and Nights That Followed; the Nation in Mourning, the Long Trip Home to Springfield*. New York: Harper and Row, 1965.

Lang, V. R. "At Battle's End: A Verse Drama in the Manner of the Noh." Typescript, Folder 3, V. R. Lang Papers (MS Am 1951), Houghton Library, Harvard University.

Lang, V. R. *At Battle's End. The Kenning Anthology of Poets Theater, 1945–1985*. Ed. Kevin Killian and David Brazil. Chicago: Kenning Editions, 2010. 52–59.

Lang, V. R. *Fire Exit. Poems and Plays*. New York: Random House, 1975. 151–252.

Lang, V. R. *I Too Have Lived in Arcadia. Poems and Plays*. New York: Random House, 1975. 253–97.

Latimer, Tirza True. *Eccentric Modernisms: Making Differences in the History of American Art*. Oakland: University of California Press, 2017.

Lehman, David. *The Last Avant-Garde: The Making of the New York School of Poets*. New York: Doubleday, 1998.

Lehmann, Hans-Thies. *Postdramatic Theatre*. Trans. Karen Jürs-Munby. New York: Routledge, 2006.

Lepidus, Lawrence. "Nothing Great about 'The America Play.'" *The Westsider*, March 17, 1994: 15.

Lott, Eric. *Love and Theft: Blackface Minstrelsy and the American Working Class*. Oxford: Oxford University Press, 1993.

Lurie, Alison. "V. R. Lang: A Memoir." *Poems and Plays*. By V. R. Lang. New York: Random House, 1975. 3–71.

Lyman, Elizabeth Dyrud. "The Page Refigured: The Verbal and Visual Language of Suzan-Lori Parks's Venus." *Performance Research* 7.1 (2002): 90–100.

Maccoby, Michael. "The Playgoer: *Fire Exit* at the Brattle." *Harvard Crimson*, December 2, 1952.

Machiz, Herbert. "Introduction." *Artists' Theatre: Four Plays*. Ed. Herbert Machiz. New York: Grove, 1960.

Mackey, Nathaniel. "Other: From Noun to Verb." *Representations* 39 (Summer 1992): 51–70.

Malcolm, Janet. "Someone Says Yes to It: Gertrude Stein, Alice B. Toklas, and 'The Making of Americans.'" *New Yorker*, June 13 and 20, 2005: 148–65.

Malcolm, Janet. *Two Lives: Gertrude and Alice*. New Haven, CT: Yale University Press, 2008.

Malina, Judith. *The Diaries of Judith Malina, 1947–1957*. New York: Grove, 1984.

Malina, Judith. "Directing *The Brig*." *The Brig*. By Kenneth H. Brown. New York: Hill and Wang, 1965. 83–107.

Malina, Judith. *The Piscator Notebook*. New York: Routledge, 2012.

Malkin, Jeanette R. *Memory-Theater and Postmodern Drama*. Ann Arbor: University of Michigan Press, 1999.

Mandell, Jonathan. "Theater: Theater's Memory Bank Expands." *New York Times*, August 25, 2002: A5.

Marranca, Bonnie. "Introduction: Presence of Mind." *Last Operas and Plays*. By Gertrude Stein. Ed. Carl Van Vechten. Baltimore: PAJ Books, 1995. vii–xxviii.

Marranca, Bonnie. *The Theatre of Images*. Baltimore: Johns Hopkins University Press, 1996.

Martin, Bradford D. *The Theater Is in the Streets: Politics and Performance in Sixties America*. Amherst: University of Massachusetts Press, 2004.

McCabe, Susan. "'Delight in Dislocation': The Cinematic Modernism of Stein, Chaplin, and Man Ray." *Modernism/Modernity* 8.3 (2001): 429–52.

McFarland, Thomas. "Synecdochic Structure in Blake's Marginalia." *European Romantic Review* 1.1 (1990): 75–90.

McNeill, David. *Hand and Mind: What Gestures Reveal about Thought*. Chicago: University of Chicago Press, 1992.

McNeill, David, and Susan D. Duncan. "Growth Points in Thinking-for-Speaking." *Language and Gesture*. Ed. David McNeill. Cambridge: Cambridge University Press, 2000. 141–61.

Mellow, James R. *Charmed Circle: Gertrude Stein & Company*. New York: Praeger, 1974.

Melzer, Annabelle Henkin. "The Dada Actor and Performance Theory." *The Art of Performance: A Critical Anthology*. Ed. Gregory Battcock and Robert Nickas. New York: Dutton, 1984. 37–55.

Meyer, Steven. "Introduction." *The Making of Americans*. By Gertrude Stein. Ed. William H. Gass. Normal, IL: Dalkey Archive, 1995. xiii–xxxvi.

Meyers, Adara. "A Dialogue on Plays in Boston (with Allison Vanouse)." *spoKe* 4 (2017): 318-321.

Middleton, Peter. "The Contemporary Poetry Reading." *Close Listening: Poetry and the Performed Word*. Ed. Charles Bernstein. New York: Oxford University Press, 1998. 262–99.

Mode, Becky. "America, the Hideous." *Our Town*, March 24, 1994: 18.

Morra, Irene. *Verse Drama in England, 1900–2015: Art, Modernity, and the National Stage*. London: Bloomsbury, 2016.

Morris, Adalaide, ed. *Sound States: Innovative Poetics and Acoustical Technologies*. Chapel Hill: University of North Carolina Press, 1997.

Moten, Fred. *In the Break: The Aesthetics of the Black Radical Tradition*. Minneapolis: University of Minnesota Press, 2003.

Munk, Erika. "Only Connect: The Living Theatre and Its Audiences." *Restaging the Sixties: Radical Theaters and Their Legacies*. Ed. James M. Harding and Cindy Rosenthal. Ann Arbor: University of Michigan Press, 2006. 33–55.

Muñoz, José. *Disidentifications: Queers of Color and the Performance of Politics*. Minneapolis: University of Minnesota Press, 1999.

Murray, Rolland. "How the Conjure-Man Gets Busy: Cultural Nationalism, Masculinity, and Performativity." *Yale Journal of Criticism* 18.2 (2005): 299-321.

Neal, Larry. "The Black Arts Movement." *The Drama Review: TDR* 12.4 (Summer 1968): 29–39.

Nelson, Cary, ed. *The Oxford Handbook of Modern and Contemporary American Poetry*. Oxford: Oxford University Press, 2012.

Nordell, Rod. "*Fire Exit* by Poets' Theatre." *Christian Science Monitor*, December 2, 1952: 10.

Nussbaum, Martha. *Poetic Justice.* Boston: Beacon, 1995.

O'Hara, Frank. "Personism: A Manifesto." *The Collected Poems of Frank O'Hara.* Ed. Donald Allen. Berkeley: University of California Press, 1995 [1961]. 498.

O'Hara, Frank. *Try! Try!* Poets' Theatre Reading with John Ashbery, Richard Eberhart, and Lyon Phelps (1951). Audio Recording. Woodberry Poetry Room, Harvard University. https://library.harvard.edu/poetry/listeningbooth/poets/ohara.html.

O'Hara, Frank. *Amorous Nightmares of Delay: Selected Plays.* Baltimore: PAJ Books, 1997.

Olson, Charles. "Projective Verse." *The New American Poetry, 1945-1960.* Ed. Donald Allen. Berkeley: University of California Press, 1960. 386-397.

Omi, Michael, and Howard Winant. *Racial Formation in the United States from the 1960s to the 1980s.* New York: Routledge, 1986.

"Papp Grant Tops U.S. Arts Awards." *New York Times,* September 15, 1971: 38.

Parks, Suzan-Lori. *The America Play. The America Play and Other Works.* New York: Theatre Communications Group, 1994. 157-99.

Parks, Suzan-Lori. "From Elements of Style." *The America Play and Other Works.* New York: Theatre Communications Group, 1994. 6-18.

Pearce, Michele. "Alien Nation: An Interview with the Playwright." *American Theatre* 11.3 (March 1994): 26.

Perelman, Bob. *The Marginalization of Poetry: Language Writing and Literary History.* Princeton, NJ: Princeton University Press, 1996.

Perloff, Marjorie. "Review: *Exact Resemblance to Exact Resemblance: The Literary Portraiture of Gertrude Stein, the Arts Betrayed.*" *Yearbook of English Studies* 11 (1981): 347-49.

Perlstein, Rick. "Operation Barbarella." *London Review of Books* 27.22 (2005): 3.

Phelan, Peggy. *Mourning Sex: Performing Public Memories.* New York: Routledge, 1997.

Phelan, Peggy. *Unmarked: The Politics of Performance.* New York: Routledge, 1996 [1993].

Phelps, Lyon. "The Objectives of the Poets' Theatre" (1951). Typescript, Folder 542, Poets' Theatre Collection, Houghton Library, Harvard University.

Phelps, Lyon. "Three Words in No Time." Audio Recording. Woodberry Poetry Room, Harvard University. https://library.harvard.edu/poetry/listeningbooth/poets/ohara.html

Phelps, Lyon. "Three Words in No Time." Unpublished script, folder 527, Poets' Theatre Collection, Houghton Library, Harvard University.

Phelps, Lyon, Mary Manning, and Jack Rogers. Discussion concerning the History of the Poets' Theatre, 1958 typescript, carbon transcript, Folder 567, Poets' Theatre Collection, Houghton Library, Harvard University.

Picasso, Pablo. *Desire Caught by the Tail.* Trans. Roland Penrose. London: Calder and Boyars, 1945.

Pirandello, Luigi. *Tonight We Improvise.* Trans. J. Douglas Campbell and Leonard G. Sbrocchi. Ottawa: Canadian Society for Italian Studies, 1987.

Poets' Theatre. Executive Committee, Meeting Minutes from September 25, 1952, Folder 8, Poets' Theatre Collection, Houghton Library, Harvard University.

Poets' Theatre. Meeting Minutes from September 7, 1954, Folder 9, Poets' Theatre Collection, Houghton Library, Harvard University.

Poets' Theatre Collection. Poets' Theatre (Cambridge, Mass.) Records, 1936-1989 (MS Thr 833), Harvard Theatre Collection, Houghton Library, Harvard University.

Proehl, Geoffrey S. *Toward a Dramaturgical Sensibility*. Madison, NJ: Fairleigh Dickinson University Press, 2008.

Puchner, Martin. *Stage Fright: Modernism, Anti-theatricality, and Drama*. Baltimore: Johns Hopkins University Press, 2002.

Quartermain, Peter. "Sound Reading." *Close Listening: Poetry and the Performed Word*. Ed. Charles Bernstein. New York: Oxford University Press, 1998. 217–31.

Quasha, George. "DiaLogos: Between the Written and the Oral in Contemporary Poetry." *New Literary History* 8.3 (Spring 1977): 485-506.

Rancière, Jacques. *The Emancipated Spectator*. London: Verso, 2009.

Rasula, Jed. "Understanding the Sound of Not Understanding." *Close Listening: Poetry and the Performed Word*. Ed. Charles Bernstein. New York: Oxford University Press, 1998. 233–61.

Retallack, Joan. *The Poethical Wager*. Berkeley: University of California Press, 2003.

Richardson, Mark. "New York Is Killing Me: Albert Ayler's Life and Death in the Jazz Capital." *Pitchfork*, April 28, 2016. https://pitchfork.com/features/from-the-pitchfork-review/9857-new-york-is-killing-me-albert-aylers-life-and-death-in-the-jazz-capital/.

Riding, Alan. *And the Show Went On: Cultural Life in Nazi-Occupied Paris*. New York: Vintage, 2010.

Roach, Joseph. "The Great Hole of History: Liturgical Silence in Beckett, Osofisan, and Parks." *South Atlantic Quarterly* 100.1 (Winter 2001): 307-17.

Robinson, Kit. "Raising 'Collateral.'" *Poetics Journal* 5 (May 1985): 123-26.

Robinson, Marc. *The Other American Drama*. New York: Cambridge University Press, 1994.

Roffman, Karin. "Thornton's Lost Rant: On Wilder's Poets' Theatre Outburst." Woodberry Poetry Room, Harvard University. https://woodberrypoetryroom.com/?p=129.

Román, David. *Acts of Intervention: Performance, Gay Culture, and AIDS*. Bloomington: Indiana University Press, 1998.

Rosenthal, Cindy. "The Living Theatre: Historical Overview." *Restaging the Sixties: Radical Theaters and Their Legacies*. Ed. James M. Harding and Cindy Rosenthal. Ann Arbor: University of Michigan Press, 2006. 27–31.

Rosten, Bevya. "The Fractured State: Gertrude Stein's Influence on American Avant-Garde Directing as Seen in Four Productions of *Dr. Faustus Lights the Lights*." Ph. D. diss City University of New York, 1998.

Rowell, Charles Henry. "'Words Don't Go There': An Interview with Fred Moten." *Callaloo* 27.4 (2004): 954–66.

Ryan, Betsy Alayne. *Gertrude Stein's Theatre of the Absolute*. Ann Arbor, MI: UMI Research Press, 1984.

Salaam, Kalamu ya. "Amiri Baraka Analyzes How He Writes." Interview. *African American Review* 37.2-3 (Summer–Fall 2003): 211–36.

Salvato, Nick. *Uncloseting Drama: American Modernism and Queer Performance*. New Haven, CT: Yale University Press, 2010.

Samuels, Lisa. "Eight Justifications for Canonizing Lyn Hejinian's *My Life*." *Modern Language Studies* 27.2 (Spring 1997): 103–19.

Savran, David. "Suzan-Lori Parks." Interview. *The Playwright's Voice: American Dramatists on Memory, Writing, and the Politics of Culture*. New York: Theatre Communications Group, 1999. 139–64.

Sayre, Nora. "The Poets' Theatre: A Memoir of the Fifties." *Grand Street* 3.3 (Spring 1984): 92–105.

Sayre, Nora. *Previous Convictions: A Journey through the 1950s.* New Brunswick, NJ: Rutgers University Press, 1995.

Schechner, Richard. "White on Black." *The Drama Review: TDR* 12.4 (Summer 1968): 25–27.

Schechner, Richard. *Between Theater and Anthropology.* Philadelphia: University of Pennsylvania Press, 1985.

Schneider, Rebecca. *Performing Remains: Art and War in Times of Theatrical Reenactment.* New York: Routledge, 2011.

Schoenberg, Robert J. "*I Too Have Lived in Arcadia* at the Poets' Theatre." *Harvard Crimson,* October 28, 1954.

Schumacher, Alec. "Collapsible Poetics Theater: Considerations on Body, Language, and Labor." Review. *Latin American Theatre Review* 45.1 (Fall 2011): 220–22.

Selenick, Laurence. "Text and Violence: Performance Practices of the Modernist Avant-Garde." *Contours of the Theatrical Avant-Garde: Performance and Textuality.* Ed. James M. Harding. Ann Arbor: University of Michigan Press, 2000. 15–42.

Sell, Mike. *Avant-Garde Performance and the Limits of Criticism.* Ann Arbor: University of Michigan Press, 2005.

Shannon, Sandra G. "Amiri Baraka on Directing." *Black American Literature Forum* 21.4 (Winter 1987): 425–33.

Shannon, Sandra G. "Evolution or Revolution in Black Theater: A Look at the Cultural Nationalist Agenda in Select Plays by Amiri Baraka." *African American Review* 37.2–3 (Summer–Fall 2003): 281–98.

Silliman, Ron, Carla Harryman, Lyn Hejinian, Steve Benson, Bob Perelman, and Barrett Watten. "Aesthetic Tendency and the Politics of Poetry: A Manifesto." *Social Text* 19/20 (Autumn 1988): 261-275.

Silliman, Ron, Bob Perelman, Barrett Watten, Steve Benson, Carla Harryman, Tom Mandel, Kit Robinson, Lyn Hejinian, Rae Armantrout, and Ted Pearson. *The Grand Piano: An Experiment in Collective Autobiography.* Part I-X. Detroit: Mode A, 2006-10.

Simpson, Megan. *Poetic Epistemologies: Gender and Knowing in Women's Language-Oriented Writing.* Albany: State University of New York Press, 2000.

"'Slave Ship' Closed Again by 14 Actors." *New York Times,* January 25, 1970: 70.

Smethurst, James Edward. *The Black Arts Movement: Literary Nationalism in the 1960s and 1970s.* Chapel Hill: University of North Carolina Press, 2005.

Smith, Susan Harris. *American Drama: The Bastard Art.* Cambridge: Cambridge University Press, 1997.

Sollors, Werner. *Amiri Baraka/LeRoi Jones: The Quest for a "Populist Modernism."* New York: Columbia University Press, 1978.

Solomon, Alisa. "Four Scenes of Theatrical Anarcho-Pacifism: A Living Legacy." *Restaging the Sixties: Radical Theaters and Their Legacies.* Ed. James M. Harding and Cindy Rosenthal. Ann Arbor: University of Michigan Press, 2006. 56–74.

Somers-Willett, Susan B. A. *The Cultural Politics of Slam Poetry: Race, Identity, and the Performance of Popular Verse in America.* Ann Arbor: University of Michigan Press, 2009.

Sontag, Susan. "Happenings: An Art of Radical Juxtaposition." *Against Interpretation and Other Essays*. New York: Farrar, Straus and Giroux, 1966. 263–74.

Stein, Gertrude. "Composition as Explanation." *A Stein Reader*. Ed. Ulla E. Dydo. Evanston, IL: Northwestern University Press, 1993. 493–503.

Stein, Gertrude. *Doctor Faustus Lights the Lights*. *Writings, 1932-1946*. Ed. Catharine R. Stimpson and Harriet Chessman. New York: Library of America, 1998. 575-607.

Stein, Gertrude. *Four Saints in Three Acts*. *Writings, 1903–1932*. Ed. Catharine R. Stimpson and Harriet Chessman. New York: Library of America, 1998. 608–50.

Stein, Gertrude. "The Gradual Making of *The Making of Americans*." *Writings, 1932–1946*. Ed. Catharine R. Stimpson and Harriet Chessman. New York: Library of America, 1998. 270–86.

Stein, Gertrude. *Ladies' Voices*. *Geography and Plays*. Madison: University of Wisconsin Press, 1993. 203–4.

Stein, Gertrude. *The Making of Americans*. Normal, IL: Dalkey Archive, 1995.

Stein, Gertrude. "Plays." *Writings, 1932–1946*. Ed. Catharine R. Stimpson and Harriet Chessman. New York: Library of America, 1998. 244–69.

Stein, Gertrude. "Portraits and Repetition." *Writings, 1932–1946*. Ed. Catharine R. Stimpson and Harriet Chessman. New York: Library of America, 1998. 287–312.

Stein, Gertrude. *Tender Buttons*. *Writings, 1903–1932*. Ed. Catharine R. Stimpson and Harriet Chessman. New York: Library of America, 1998. 313–55.

Stein, Gertrude. "What Are Master-Pieces and Why Are There So Few of Them?" *Writings, 1932–1946*. Ed. Catharine R. Stimpson and Harriet Chessman. New York: Library of America, 1998. 355–63.

Steiner, Wendy. *Exact Resemblance to Exact Resemblance: The Literary Portraiture of Gertrude Stein*. New Haven, CT: Yale University Press, 1978.

Stevens, Wallace. "Of Modern Poetry." *The Palm at the End of the Mind: Selected Poems and a Play by Wallace Stevens*. Ed. Holly Stevens. New York: Vintage, 1972. 175.

Stevens, Wallace. *Three Travellers Watch a Sunrise*. *Opus Posthumous: Poems, Plays, Prose*. Ed. Samuel French Morse. New York: Knopf, 1957. 127–43.

Stewart, Garrett. *Reading Voices: Literature and the Phonotext*. Berkeley: University of California Press, 1990.

Stroffolino, Chris. "Carla Harryman." *Dictionary of Literary Biography*. Ed. Joseph Conte. American Poets since World War II, sixth series, vol. 193. Buffalo: State University of New York Press, 1998. 171–79.

Sugiera, Malgorzata. "Beyond Drama: Writing for Postdramatic Theatre." *Theatre Research International* 29.1 (March 2004): 16–28.

Sullivan, Dan. "Black Panther Benefit Is Held in East Village: 3 Theater Troupes Perform; LeRoi Jones Speaks." *New York Times*, May 21, 1968: 42.

"A Talk with Liz Diamond on Suzan-Lori Parks." *Yale News* 2.3 (January 1994): 1.

Tallmer, Jeffrey. Review of *Many Loves* by William Carlos Williams. *Village Voice*, January 21, 1959: 9.

Taylor, Markland. "The America Play." Review. *Variety*, January 31, 1994: 70.

"Theater for Poets Will Use East End." *New York Times*, January 9, 1965: 15.

Thomas, Lorenzo. "The Shadow World: New York's Umbra Workshop and Origins of the Black Arts Movement." *Callaloo* 1.4 (1978): 53–72.

Thome, Joel, cond. *Four Saints in Three Acts*. By Virgil Thomson (composer) and Gertrude Stein (librettist). Orchestra of Our Time. Nonesuch Records, 1982. 79035.

Thomson, Virgil, cond. *Four Saints in Three Acts*, abridged by the composer. By Virgil Thomson (composer) and Gertrude Stein (librettist). Reissue of 78 rpm recording. 1948. RCA Victor Gold Seal CD 09026-68163-2.

Thomson, Virgil. *Virgil Thomson*. New York: Penguin, 1985.

Toscano, Rodrigo. "Balm to Bilk." *Collapsible Poetics Theater*. Albany, NY: Fence Books, 2008. 27-34.

Toscano, Rodrigo. "Eco-Strato-Static." *Collapsible Poetics Theater*. Albany, NY: Fence Books, 2008.

Turner, Victor. *From Ritual to Theatre: The Human Seriousness of Play*. Baltimore: PAJ Books, 1982.

Tytell, John. *The Living Theatre: Art, Exile, and Outrage*. New York: Grove, 1995.

Van Deburg, William L. *New Day in Babylon: The Black Power Movement and American Culture, 1965–1975*. Chicago: University of Chicago Press, 1992.

Vanden Heuvel, Michael. *Performing Drama/Dramatizing Performance: Alternative Theater and the Dramatic Text*. Ann Arbor: University of Michigan Press, 1993.

Velde, Paul. "Pursued by the Furies." *Commonweal*, June 28, 1968: 440–41.

Vickery, Ann. *Leaving Lines of Gender: A Feminist Genealogy of Language Writing*. Hanover, NH: Wesleyan University Press, 2000.

Walden, Joshua S. *Musical Portraits: The Composition of Identity in Contemporary and Experimental Music*. New York: Oxford University Press, 2018.

Walker, Julia A. *Expressionism and Modernism in the American Theatre: Bodies, Voices, Words*. Cambridge: Cambridge University Press, 2005.

Walker, Julia A. "Why Performance? Why Now? Textuality and the Rearticulation of Human Presence." *Yale Journal of Criticism* 16.1 (2003): 149–75.

Warner, Michael. *Publics and Counterpublics*. Brooklyn: Zone, 2002.

Warrick, John. "*The Blacks* and Its Impact on African American Theatre in the United States." *Jean Genet: Performance and Politics*. Ed. Clare Finbergh, Carl Lavery, and Maria Shevsova. New York: Palgrave, 2006. 131–42.

Watson, Steven. *Prepare for Saints: Gertrude Stein, Virgil Thomson, and the Mainstreaming of American Modernism*. Berkeley: University of California Press, 1995.

Watts, Jerry Gafio. *Amiri Baraka: The Politics and Art of a Black Intellectual*. New York: New York University Press, 2001.

Wayde, Willis. Correspondence with Harvard University Press, Folder 171, Poets' Theatre Collection, Houghton Library, Harvard University.

Wetmore, Kevin J., Jr. "Introduction: Perceptible Mutabilities; the Many Plays of Suzan-Lori Parks/The Many Suzan-Lori Parks of Plays." *Suzan-Lori Parks: A Casebook*. Ed. Kevin J. Wetmore Jr. and Alycia Smith-Howard. New York: Routledge, 2007. xvii-xix.

Wheeler, Lesley. *Voicing American Poetry: Sound and Performance from the 1920s to the Present*. Ithaca, NY: Cornell University Press, 2008.

Wideman, John. "The Black Writer and the Magic of the Word." *New York Times Book Review*, January 24, 1988: 28–29.

Will, Barbara. "The Strange Politics of Gertrude Stein." *Humanities* 33.2 (March–April

2012). https://www.neh.gov/humanities/2012/marchapril/feature/the-strange-politics-gertrude-stein

Will, Barbara. *Unlikely Collaborations: Gertrude Stein, Bernard Faÿ, and the Vichy Dilemma*. New York: Columbia University Press, 2013.

Williams, William Carlos. *Many Loves. Many Loves and Other Plays: The Collected Plays of William Carlos Williams*. Norfolk, CT: New Directions, 1961. 1–104.

Wilmeth, Don B., and Christopher Bigsby, eds. *The Cambridge History of American Theatre*. Vol. 1-3. Cambridge: Cambridge University Press, 1998-2000.

Wilson, Edwin. Review of *The America Play. Wall Street Journal*, January 26, 1994: A12.

Woodard, Komozi. *A Nation within a Nation: Amiri Baraka (LeRoi Jones) and Black Power Politics*. Chapel Hill: University of North Carolina Press, 1999.

Woodworth, Christine. "Parks and the Traumas of Childhood." *Suzan-Lori Parks: Essays on the Plays and Other Works*. Ed. Philip C. Kolin. Jefferson, NC: McFarland, 2010. 140–55.

Worth, Katherine J. "The Poets in American Theatre." *American Theatre*. Ed. John Russell Brown and Bernard Harris. Stratford-upon-Avon Studies, no. 10. London: Edward Arnold, 1967. 102–7.

Worthen, W. B. "Citing History: Textuality and Performativity in the Plays of Suzan-Lori Parks." *Essays in Theatre/Etudes Théâtrales* 18.1 (1999): 3–22.

Worthen, W. B. "Drama, Performativity, and Performance." *PMLA* 113.5 (1998): 1093–1107.

Worthen, W. B. *Modern Drama and the Rhetoric of Theater*. Berkeley: University of California Press, 1992.

Worthen, W. B. *Print and the Poetics of Modern Drama*. Cambridge: Cambridge University Press, 2005.

Index

Note: Page numbers in italics indicate figures

4'33" (composition, Cage), 18

abstract expressionism, 20, 87, 88, 94, 114–15
"abt the dead he sd . . ." (Olson), 198
action painting, 5–6, 20, 61, 88, 97, 104
Actors Equity Association (AEA), 192, 217n2, 222n1
actors playing themselves, 105, 112, 120, 121
"Advance-Guard Writing, 1900–1950" (essay, Goodman), 15
"Aesthetic Tendency and the Politics of Poetry: A Manifesto" (essay, Benson, Harryman, Hejinian, Perelman, Silliman, Watten), 164
African Americans
  The America Play and, 189, 197–99, 223n4
  Black Arts Movement (BAM), 153, 218n8
  Black Arts Repertory Theatre/School (BART/S), 125, 126, 127, 142, 218n8
  Black Community Development and Defense Organization, 124–25
  A Black Mass and, 131
  Black Panthers, 123, 150–51, 152, 153, 154, 217–18n3

Black Power, 124, 129, 144, 154, 217n1
  The Blacks and, 137–38
  Black Theatre Movement (BTM), 218n8
  casting of, 41, 137–38, 151–52, 198, 223n4
  cultural history and traditions, 124, 125, 127, 137, 141–42, 146, 218n6
  cultural nationalism and, 140, 155, 219n12
  Dutchman and, 131
  Home on the Range and, 27–28, 122–24, 127, 137–40, 149, 152–55
  multivocality and, 197
  Newark, New Jersey population statistics, 218n7
  Umbra Poets' Workshop and, 218n6
  See also black nationalism
Agamemnon (Alfred), 76, 215n10
Age of Anxiety, The (Auden), 98
agitprop, *Home on the Range* as, 123, 147, 149, 154
AIDS Quilt, 173, 222n13
Albee, Edward, 126
Alfred, William, 68, 76, 215n10
Allen, Donald, 17, 18, 71, 87
American Theatre for Poets, Inc. *See* New York Poets Theatre

241